Politics, Values, and Public Policy

Other Titles of Interest

Rhetoric and Reality: Presidential Commissions and the Making of Public Policy, Terrence R. Tutchings

National Planning in the United States: An Annotated Bibliography, David E. Wilson

The National Planning Idea in U.S. Public Policy: Five Alternative Approaches, David E. Wilson

Valuing Life: Public Policy Dilemmas, edited by Steven E. Rhoads

Science, Politics, and Controversy: Civilian Nuclear Power in the United States, 1946–1974, Steven L. Del Sesto

Judgment and Decision in Public Policy Formation, edited by Kenneth R. Hammond

A Westview Special Study

Politics, Values, and Public Policy:
The Problem of Methodology
Frank Fischer

Addressed to the growing concern about values in public policy, this study develops a political method for policy evaluation. It is designed to move evaluation beyond its current emphasis on efficient achievement of policy goals by extending it to include a political assessment of the goals themselves. Raising fundamental problems associated with the traditional fact-value dichotomy, Dr. Fischer points to the methodological integration of empirical and normative data as a major methodological barrier to a relevant political method for policy questions. Although he does not purport to resolve the disputes long surrounding the fact-value separation, he does offer an alternative avenue for bypassing the epistemological impasse. Constructed around insights drawn from Habermas's communications theory and practical discourse derived from Toulmin and Taylor, the alternative incorporates elements from political theory, the philosophy of science, policy analysis and organizational behavior. The methodology, presented as a logic of empirical and normative policy questions, is illustrated by applications to specific policy issues.

Frank Fischer is assistant professor of political science and administrative studies at Rutgers University in Newark. He has also taught at New York University and the State University of New York and has gained a wide range of practical experience as a public policy analyst.

Politics, Values, and Public Policy: The Problem of Methodology

Frank Fischer

Westview Press / Boulder, Colorado

A Westview Special Study

Published in 1980 in the United States of America by
Westview Press, Inc.
5500 Central Avenue
Boulder, Colorado 80301
Frederick A. Praeger, Publisher

Second printing, 1982.

Library of Congress Cataloging in Publication Data
Fischer, Frank, 1942–
    Politics, values, and public policy.
    (A Westview special study)
    Bibliography: p.
    1. Policy sciences—Methodology. I. Title.
H61.F54   361.6'1'018   80-16248
ISBN 0-89158-799-3

Printed and bound in the United States of America

Contents

Tables

Preface

This book is addressed to the growing concern about the role of values in public policy evaluation. In the political and social sciences, few subjects have been discussed more extensively than the question of the relation of facts to values in social investigation. Even though the prolonged debate about facts and values remains inconclusive, mainstream social scientists continue to adhere to a methodological separation of facts and values and to the principle of value neutrality. Inherited from positivism, this position asserts that values rest fundamentally on personal preference or conviction and, therefore, are beyond the reach of rational scientific assessment. For the policy sciences, these assumptions have established the epistemological groundwork for an empirical orientation that emphasizes technical analyses of the efficiency of program goals. The choice of which goals and values to pursue is understood to be beyond rational assessment.

However, in recent years both political theorists and policy analysts have increasingly questioned the wisdom of adhering to these behavioral science principles. Although the evaluation of public policy has developed into a small industry, early enthusiasm about the use of evaluation findings has in many quarters turned to skepticism. As one analyst summed it up, everyone supports policy evaluation in principle, but few have much hope that its conclusions will be utilized in real-world policymaking. The limitations of a policy science dominated by the criteria of efficiency emerge dramatically when confronted by our domestic social crises. Significantly, a growing number of writers attribute the political failures that policy evaluation has encountered to its narrow instrumental focus. Most of our social crises involve more than matters of inefficient programs: first and foremost, they involve basic value conflicts. In this respect, we have developed a policy science aimed at the relatively less important aspects of our social problems and have in turn developed no method for assessing the more fundamental questions that underlie them.

Such questions have renewed methodological exploration in the political and policy sciences. Some policy writers have begun to recognize the necessity of studying the normative political dimensions of policy evaluation and decision making. Beyond the emphasis on efficiency, these theorists understand the need to include the political assessment of policy goals. For them, a major barrier to a social science that can contribute to policy questions is the methodological integration of empirical and normative analyses. This requires the development of a political methodology addressed to the analytical tasks of policy evaluation.

In this study, I have attempted to offer a practical solution to this methodological problem. Although the study does not purport to resolve the metaethical disputes long surrounding the fact-value dichotomy, it does suggest an alternative approach for bypassing basic epistemological problems at the level of practical deliberation. Political theorists have for some time discussed the construction of a critical evaluation method, but few have said much about what it might look like in public policy evaluation. I have attempted to open a preliminary discussion in this direction.

My alternative is constructed around insights drawn from Jürgen Habermas's communications model of practical discourse, Stephen Toulmin's informal logic of normative reason, and Paul Taylor's logic of evaluation. Through a synthesis of key aspects of the works of these theorists, I have presented a methodological framework for political evaluation that is designed to serve as the basis for a critical political method. As a suggestive beginning, this framework organizes key questions from both the empirical and normative traditions in the fact-value controversy. Toward this end, the methodologically diverse contributions of evaluation research, phenomenological sociology, the behavioral systems perspective, and political philosophy are integrated as specific phases of a full evaluation. For policy evaluation, the relationships among these perspectives provide the methodological basis for developing a logic of questions designed to facilitate the probe of policy judgments. In this regard, I have sought to translate the epistemological requirements of these relationships into practical guidelines for policy deliberation and to link them to emerging lines of investigation in the policy sciences, especially the forensic or communications model of policy argumentation.

Although social scientists interested in policy evaluation constitute the primary audience of this study, it should be clear that much of the discussion is concerned with problems that fall between philosophy and social science and between theory and practice. As such, the study is bound to be received with a certain amount of consternation, especially by some analysts in particular methodological camps. It is inevitable that a study as interdisciplinary as this one will confront a number of general communication barriers. At times, the communication gap between political philosophers, phenomenologists, political scientists, and policy analysts is quite difficult to bridge. Even basic definitions, as well as general perspectives or outlooks, are sometimes controversial. More specifically, some analysts will find the treatment of particular issues inadequate, some political philosophers will complain that important epistemological issues require more attention, and some political scientists will find the work too theoretical. Where such criticisms are valid, it is hoped that writers in future studies will help clarify these problems.

Responsibility for what follows rests, of course, upon the author. Nonetheless, a number of people have been very helpful along the way. To Walter Weisskopf, who first introduced me to many of the traditions that inspired my interest in this study, I owe a fundamental intellectual debt. Also, I am much indebted to Alan Mandell for his careful reading of the manuscript. In numerous discussions, his suggestions and criticisms have helped me clarify many of the ideas presented in the book. In addition, I wish to thank Bertell Ollman, Richard Flathman,

Roy Sparrow, Gordon Adams, Craig Wanner, Stephen Bronner, Ted Norton, Carmen Sirianni, Lynne Rienner, Jeanne Remington, Leslie Burger, and Debra Balducci. I am indebted to them for valuable academic and editorial advice. Finally, I wish to acknowledge my deeper and more personal gratitude to Riecelle Schecter for patience and understanding, as both friend and editorial assistant.

Frank Fischer
Rutgers University

1
Introduction:
The Problem of Methodology

The main evidence that a methodology is worn out comes when progress within it no longer deals with main issues.
—Alfred N. Whitehead[1]

In recent years social scientists have emphasized the study of public policy and the development of a methodology for policy analysis.[2] Policy analysis has grown up under the influence of the positivistic methodology of the behavioral sciences and constitutes a collection of approaches that rely on the scientific method and its techniques: cost-benefit analysis, survey research, mathematical simulation models, experimental design, input-output studies, multiple regression, and systems analysis. By adapting highly developed scientific techniques to policy studies, the field of policy analysis has established itself as a rigorous, applied social science in a relatively short period of time.[3] Over the developmental period, however, the methodology of behavioral science has itself come under criticism. There has been growing dissatisfaction in the social and political sciences over the use of scientific methods in the study of normative political and social phenomena. From the outset, some theorists complained about the application of positivistic methodology in the social sciences, and, more recently, many mainstream writers as well have begun to question some of behavioral science's basic methodological principles, particularly its separation of facts and values.[4] More recently, these questions have filtered into the policy analysis literature, where the normative dimension of political behavior is frequently a crucial issue.

The fact-value separation is based on positivism's adherence to the metaethical theory known as "value noncognitivism." According to this theory, value judgments are essentially emotional responses to life conditions. As subjective commitments, they contain no verifiable truth content. To qualify as objective knowledge, statements must be verifiable by formal scientific methods. Although important aspects of value statements can be investigated scientifically, particularly statements about the conditions that lead to adoption of specific values or statements about consequences that result from the acceptance of value positions, there is no way of scientifically establishing the categorical truth of a value judgment. Thus, in the final analysis, value judgments must fall beyond the reach of rational methods that are defined as the formal rules and procedures of science. Even though in practice there are various degrees of adherence to the "fact-value dichotomy," at the methodological level the debate remains a dominant governing principle in the behavioral sciences. To be judged as proper, all research must—at least officially—pay its respects to the principle.

The practice of public policy analysis often appears to be far removed from such basic epistemological questions. In reality, however, the problem is nowhere more urgently important. Public policies are essentially political agreements designed for the practical world of social action where facts and values are inextricably interwoven. Policy science, as an applied discipline designed to empirically analyze value-laden policy issues, thus uniquely straddles the fact-value problem. Given the value-laden character of public policy, it is difficult methodologically in policy science to separate facts and values without distorting the basic purposes. Although many policy writers have tried to avoid conflict with the fact-value separation (sometimes by merely ignoring it) an increasing number believe that major difficulties encountered by the development of policy science are inherently linked to this underlying principle governing the methodological treatment of values.

There have been attempts to deal with the normative dimensions of public policy; in fact, the number of essays on the subject is beginning to grow steadily. Within policy science, however, few writers have been willing to completely divorce themselves from the grip of positivism and the fact-value dichotomy. In general, this bias has restricted attempts to deal with values in policy analysis to an overly simplistic concept of value clarification. While there can be no disagreement about the importance of clarifying value orientations, the positivistic approach leads to misleading assumptions about the nature of values and the role of normative discourse. Under positivism and its modern-day variants, values tend to emerge as external to or detached from specific social or material conditions rather than as inherently tied to the particular life understandings that gave rise to them. Normative relationships are generally treated as formal, static, noncomplex relationships rather than changeable, multidimensional, dialectical processes. Normative analysis is limited to the methods of formal logic and verification, ruling out the informal discursive processes that mediate the construction of social reality.

In large part, positivism's insistence that value judgments be submitted to the formal methods of scientific verification is the source of the problem. Preoccupation with establishing the theoretical and scientific validity of value noncognitivism has led positivists to either reject or ignore the study of normative discourse in everyday life. Since fundamental values, in this view, are ultimately arbitrary and irrational, everyday normative discourse must necessarily rest on irrational foundations. Such discourse, therefore, cannot have truth content in the formal sense of the term. As subjectively based discourse grounded in a particular social context, normative knowledge must be relegated to an epistemological limbo—*if* one accepts noncognitivist premises. However, even if it proves true that fundamental values cannot be established by the formal methods of science, noncognitivism fosters a distorted understanding of the basic nature and process of normative discourse. In actual substantive terms, it does not follow that normative discourse proceeds without recourse to rational methods. This viewpoint does not deny that normative deliberation ultimately rests on fundamental values or argue that these values can in fact be proven scientifically; rather, it recognizes the complexity of normative discourse. Not all levels of normative discourse are designed to fulfill the same purposes, nor are they governed by the same epistemological requirements.

Some contemporary schools of thought in epistemology and ethics, particularly variants of ordinary-language philosophy, indicate several aspects of normative discourse that facilitate rational discussion of practical value judgments. First, actors in everyday life seldom confront the lofty intellectual task of justifying fundamental values. In fact, most deliberation about practical affairs is conducted below the level of fundamental values and carried out within a general social consensus about high-level values. Second, within this framework, the task of the policymaker is to choose between competing policy alternatives designed to facilitate the achievement of accepted ideals. The process by which the policymaker arrives at these choices will not conform to the canons of scientific rationality but is nonetheless an identifiable process with rational elements. In fact, it is the possibility of such normative decision making that provides the basis for the construction of society. Positivists have overlooked the rational elements that establish the framework for such deliberation; as a result, they have failed to adequately explore the normative inferential methods employed in policy augmentation. From the perspective of policy analysis, it is possible to argue that positivism has thrown the proverbial baby out with the bath.

This has placed the social and policy sciences in an unfortunate all-or-nothing dilemma with respect to normative inquiry. While noncognitivism may confront important problems that arise in ethical inquiry, misinterpretation or overextension of the fact-value separation has impeded the development of useful methods for improving rational judgment in practical deliberation. This study does not purport to resolve the metaethical disputes that have long surrounded value noncognitivism, but it does attempt to present the problem in a new and different light.

The development of an alternative political methodology for the evaluation of policy decisions requires an exploration of the wealth of material that in recent years has begun to appear in the philosophy of social science and related fields. Much of this work has developed as part of an assault on the traditional, positivistic conception of the physical or natural sciences. By the 1950s and 1960s, a significant group of physical scientists had begun to question the adequacy of positivistic explanations of scientific method. Since then, growing numbers of social scientists and philosophers have begun to trace the implications of this methodological rethinking for a social science constructed on traditional scientific methodology. Particularly important in the philosophy of the social sciences have been the contributions of phenomenological sociology, ordinary-language analysis, and the revitalization of the speculative methods of political philosophy. My purpose is to show that a synthesis of elements drawn from these disciplines can supply an alternative foundation for a political methodology for policy evaluation by organizing the competing metanormative approaches into a unified methodological system. Compared to the positivistic approach, the policy methodology derived from this logical foundation is better suited to the policy questions analysts confront and more consistent with the procedures analysts already employ in practice.

The Policy Literature

It is not difficult to locate the problem of methodology in policy literature. Generally, analysts agree that the purpose of public policy analysis is to intelligently consider the decision-making problems of governmental organizations. The decisions of public organizations, like all organizations, can be divided into two fundamental categories: instrumental and integrative.[5] The instrumental decision is concerned with efficient achievement of organizational goals. It relates primarily to empirical questions about provision and delivery of services and, as such, is the principal concern of economics. The integrative decision is more the subject of political science and sociology and is aimed at the normative political problem of "conflict maintenance." The objective of the integrative decision is to hold the organization together so that it can solve its instrumental problems. Although the two types of decisions are separated for analytical purposes, in the real world they are usually closely interwoven.[6]

Effective policy decisions result from considering both of these problems in the deliberative process. Even though governmental decisions are ultimately decided by political bargaining between participants, policymakers can turn to policy analysts for analytical assistance in both instrumental and integrative phases of the decision processes. In the analytical language of decision making, March and Simon have labeled these two methodological phases "problem solving" and "persuasion."[7] Problem solving is directed at the instrumental decision. In this phase, participants assume they share relevant criteria and goals and attempt to determine a course of action through collective investigation of the problem. This involves gathering empirical data and proposing and assessing alternatives until all concerned feel content with the scope of the inquiry. If the participants discover that they do not share the same criteria and goals, decision making shifts to the second analytical phase, persuasion. In this phase, the task is to examine and test the discordant beliefs and values producing the discrepant criteria and goals. Emphasizing the beliefs and values of the participants instead of the empirical aspects of the problem, the policy analyst proceeds by searching for more general criteria shared by the disputants that enhance the possibility of reconciling conflicting views. To be useful to the decision maker, the policy analyst should be able to provide information in both of these analytical phases.

Although the policy literature acknowledges these two analytical phases of decision making, emphasis on the fact-value separation in the behavioral sciences has channeled most of the attention and energy of policy writers into the instrumental problem-solving aspect of evaluation. Although scientific policy techniques lend themselves to the problem of instrumental efficiency, they are not suited to dealing with the subjective problems that characterize political persuasion. Questions of which problem or action is relevant or which standard or criteria ought to be employed in a decision cannot be answered by scientific analysis. The implications of this methodological impasse are reflected in the policy literature. Not only is there a dearth of studies about the normative political aspects of public policy, but, in addition, the political dimension itself is at times denigrated. All too often in the policy literature, politics has been described in negative terms such as "pressures and expedient adjustments," or "haphazard acts—unresponsive to a planned analysis of the needs of efficient decision design."[8] These characterizations clearly capture an attitude reflecting the primacy of scientific policy methods over substantive political problems: If politics doesn't fit into the methodological scheme, then politics is the problem.

Failure to deal with the normative political dimensions of policy analysis is also reflected in governmental affairs. The limitations of a policy science dominated by efficiency were demonstrated dramatically in the late 1960s and early 1970s: In response to the domestic crises of the period, the federal government and some states initiated a number of reform measures that emphasized policy evaluation. Spurred by the federal adoption of program budgeting and a vast amount of Great Society legislation carrying policy evaluation requirements, policy analysis developed into a small industry, both inside and outside the universities. However, early enthusiasm about the utilization of policy evaluation gave way to much pessimism in a surprisingly short period of time. James Schlesinger, in front of a congressional subcommittee examining the uses of policy analysis in defense budgeting, conceded that everyone is, in principle, in favor of policy evaluation but few are hopeful that its conclusions will be utilized in real-world policymaking processes.[9] Much of the political failure encountered by policy evaluation can be attributed to its narrow emphasis on the technical evaluation of means. The crises of the late 1960s were more than a problem of inefficient programs; first and foremost, they represented basic conflicts in social values.

Increasingly it has become apparent that a significant part of the problem confronting policy evaluation is attributable to the failure of policy methodologists to directly confront the task of political evaluation. Writers like Alice Rivlin have expressed doubt as to whether giving the highest priority in policy analysis to instrumental techniques such as cost-benefit is the most effective approach:

> Politicians and decision makers are unlikely to pay attention to them. They and their constituents have strong, intuitive ideas about the relative importance of health, education, and social well-being, that

are not likely to be shaken by cost-benefit estimates. The ratios are unlikely to sway the choice of a congressman between a reading program and a cancer program. . . . Both cancer research and literary programs have public benefits, but it is not obvious how to value them. . . . Some people put a high subjective value on living in a literate society, and some do not. . . . Any decision requires weighing individual preferences against each other; while estimating dollar values may clarify the problem, only the political process can resolve it.[10]

The problem is more than a matter of policies that fail to achieve acceptance. The lack of attention to the political dimensions of policy analysis contributes significantly to the use of evaluation as an ideological tool. A number of writers have shown that the primary use of cost-benefit and systems-analysis techniques has been to justify policy decisions based on previously established political predilections. Ida Hoos, for instance, has contended that analytical policy studies are generally "shrouded from critical review," cited "when they bolster a particular ideological position, sealed when they are likely to embarrass persons in power."[11] Fred Kramer has illustrated this idea by showing that policy analysis is frequently utilized as the rationale for eliminating Office of Economic Opportunity programs for minorities but seldom for politically supported defense spending that fails to meet specifications.[12]

By the late 1960s, social scientists were generating one instru-mental analysis after another in a society that was beginning to come apart at the political seams.[13] The political dissent and violence that characterized the period were translated into epis-temological dispute in disciplines such as political science and sociology. The failure to deal with the political dimensions of public policy assumed a central position in intellectual debate. Reflecting the tensions in the society as a whole, the social sciences themselves began to separate at the seams.

Most policy analysts have not considered the immediate relevance of epistemology to their own concerns, but normative political theorists have been quick to renew their attack on the fact-value separation, the barrier to an epistemologically adequate methodology. These theorists have asserted the political scientist's responsibility to confront values and political evaluation in policy analysis. As two leading writers stated:

> Why should students and members of the public care to know about politics? Surely one reason, among others, is that they find the moral, ethical, evaluative problems raised by political choice puzzling and would like to think more clearly about the differences between good policies and bad ones.[14]

According to these writers, this is what the astute student of politics and policy is requesting when he or she demands "relevance" in political science—"relevance to the urgently puzzling problems of political evaluation."[15]

Within policy science, concern for these issues has been expressed by some theorists who see a need for the exploration and development of "political feasibility" studies. Many leading policy writers have become much more aware that attention must be paid to the political dimensions of policy decision making, especially recognition of diverse political values, recruitment of political support, and accommodation of contradictory goals and objectives. Arnold Meltsner, for example, argued that the researcher's focus on the political dimensions of policy "will be the lever by which the analyst achieves some measure of usefulness and success."[16]

These concerns raise the question of how a particular policy relates to the distribution of social and political values in the society. An analyst intent upon ascertaining the political acceptability or feasibility of a policy must determine whether it generates support for the particular institution that proposes it. Yehezkel Dror has emphasized "the need for evaluation of the probability that a policy will be sufficiently acceptable to the various secondary political decision-makers, executors, interest groups and publics whose participation or acquiescence is needed for it to be translated into political action."[17] Methodologically, the question is one of how qualitative political norms and values relate to quantitative program performance data—the fact-value question again. In many respects, it is the technical embodiment of the epistemological problem. Meltsner noted the lack of a convenient methodology and suggested the need to "provoke discussion and to encourage others to develop a political method for policy analysis."[18] The principal test of such a methodology would necessarily rest on its ability to integrate facts and values and empirical and normative judgments. The search for such a political method poses a fundamental challenge to a scientific policy methodology designed to enforce a separation of facts and values.

Many policy writers, especially those working within the scientific tradition, do not fully appreciate the significance of the challenge. The concern of this tradition is to work normative variables into the structure of analytical policy models. Since normative variables rest upon subjective commitments that seldom lend themselves to quantification, integration is usually attempted through indirect proxy variables designed to estimate normative characteristics. Scientific policy writers are generally willing to concede the shortcomings of their approach, but, rather than accept underlying epistemological problems, they point to operational difficulties associated with normative variables such as research design problems, inadequate data, or lack of rigor. Their recommended solution is to adhere to the scientific ideal, supplementing it with other less rigorous approaches such as the development of political judgment and conjecture. Admittedly less than perfect, these approaches are advanced as interim measures for use during the developmental period of policy science. What is particularly interesting about these interim solutions is their remarkable similarity to intuitive methods employed outside the scientific tradition.

The Approach

A small but growing number of writers have begun to adopt a different orientation. Drawing on the newer, nonpositivistic approaches in the philosophy of science, they argue that the difficulty in establishing a nonpositivistic methodology of policy evaluation can be traced to the fact-value problem itself. For example, Martin Rein in the policy sciences and Richard Bernstein in the philosophy of the social sciences maintain that the methodological integration of facts and values is a major barrier to a social science that can contribute to policy questions.[19]

From this perspective, the problem is not one of finding an interim procedure but rather a matter of rethinking one of the most vexing questions that confronts the social sciences.[20] To do this, it is necessary to turn to insights drawn from normative methods such as political philosophy and phenomenology, which up to this point have been ruled unacceptable by leading political and policy methodologists.

This study follows the general lead of Rein and others searching for an alternative to the positivist model. The specific approach adopted is largely inspired by the pathbreaking contributions of Jürgen Habermas.[21] In particular, it draws on insights derived from Habermas's revitalization of practical discourse as an epistemological category and his communications model of society. As metatheory, Habermas has offered an epistemological base for a critical theory of society by combining practical discourse with a theory of communicative competence. Although much remains to be worked out, as a programmatic beginning Habermas's approach establishes an alternative epistemological method that is a major advance.[22] With the guidance of this theoretical contribution, my analysis is able to synthesize a number of seemingly divergent methodological approaches from the literatures of political science, phenomenological sociology, political philosophy, ordinary-language analysis, and the policy sciences. Its underlying purpose is to provide a synthesis of empirical and normative perspectives that forms the basis of a multimethodological approach capable of aiming both political theory and policy practice in a productive new direction.

Practical discourse, as an area of epistemological inquiry, is concerned with establishing knowledge about "what ought to be done" rather than descriptive knowledge about "what is the case." Epistemological exploration of practical reason stresses normative discourse's autonomous rules of rational judgment and seeks to explicate the interaction between facts and values in practical deliberations. Amidst the prolonged and inconclusive fact-value debate, it suggests the possibility of avoiding— if not resolving—a number of pitfalls traditionally associated with normative inference. Moreover, it directly addresses the fact-value problem in the social and policy sciences. From a methodological point of view, the key dimension that remains to be resolved is the elaboration of rules and procedures for mediating between empirical and normative judgments in practical argumentation. What are the methodological rules for accomplishing this?

The groundwork for such rules can be found in the works of Stephen Toulmin, Kurt Baier, and Paul Taylor. As analytical philosophers, these writers have been concerned with the explication of the language and rules governing the "informal logic" of practical inquiry. Toulmin and Baier have focused on the development of the epistemological foundations of an informal logic while Taylor has offered a metanormative analysis of the informal logic of evaluation. Taylor's logic of evaluation presents a system of rules and questions that can be adapted to a communications model of practical argumentation.[23]

Justification for the adoption of the methodological framework is based on its ability to address two sets of problems. First, it addresses directly the metanormative problems involved in relating empirical and normative judgments. As a framework for inquiry, it organizes the methodological questions and metanormative implications of the basic competing methodological traditions that bear on the fact-value polemic in the contemporary social sciences: evaluation research, phenomenological sociology, the behavioral systems perspective, and political philosophy.

Second, by securing practical reason as the logical foundation for a political methodology, the approach facilitates the development of a framework of policy questions. This study initiates the development of a methodological framework for normative judgment in fact-value policy disputes. Derived from the inferential rules of practical thought, such a framework is essentially a logic of questions that directs the probing and testing required to achieve clarification, agreement, and consensus. As a methodology of practical judgment, it permits the policy analyst to organize relevant factual assertions and recommended political norms in a formal decision framework designed to facilitate logical conclusions. The questions are examined in the context of specific policy studies and shown to relate directly to the actual questions that arise in policy research and argumentation.

In the process, this alternative framework is linked with two separate but interrelated lines of investigation developing within the policy sciences. The first one is a forensic communications model of policy argumentation. Struggling with the normative dimension of policy, writers such as C. W. Churchman and Duncan MacRae have introduced a practical approach to policy debate that in a number of ways resembles Habermas's theoretical communications model.[24] These writers, however, remain fundamentally within the positivistic fact-value tradition. An approach based on practical reason is shown to advance this policy model in two ways: It raises normative inquiry to full methodological partnership with the empirical side of policy evaluation, and it offers an epistemological basis for developing a normative methodology that can be utilized to adjudicate fact-value policy disputes. This relates to a second line of investigation in the policy sciences advanced by Ralph Hambrick and several others.[25] These writers have focused on the development of logical rules and questions for probing policy arguments. Their approaches, however, are basically trained on the empirical dimensions of policy inquiry. Practical reason extends the investigation of policy arguments into the normative dimensions as well.[26]

The following chapters unravel the development of my project. Each chapter is designed to build on the preceding chapter; for this reason, they should be read in sequence. Chapter 2 presents the reemergence of the fact-value debate in the contemporary social sciences and traces it to normative problems in policy science. The chapter also discusses methodological positions in the polemic, principally post-behavioral policy analysis in political science, phenomenological sociology, and political philosophy, and shows that the key aspects of this polemic bear directly on the methodological problem of values in the policy sciences, particularly the concern with political feasibility. Finally, the chapter indicates a growing awareness of the need for alternative approaches to the fact-value problem and explores some of the most innovative approaches to appear within the policy sciences: the communication models of Churchman, MacRae, and others. The works of these theorists represent an important step in the development of an alternative but do not provide a methodological framework for normative judgment.

Chapter 3 presents the basic metanormative problems that stand in the path of rational value judgments, particularly as they relate to the concept of a "political" evaluation. Practical discourse is shown to offer a solution to the key problem presented by scientific value theory. In particular, the "informal" approach to practical reason of Toulmin, Baier, and Taylor is suggested as a method well suited for the questions that arise in policy evaluation.

Chapters 4 and 5 present Taylor's logic of evaluation and relate its analytical phases to the methodological issues in political evaluation. Each of the four phases of the logic is examined in terms of its relationship to methodological problems and questions that arise in policy evaluation. Taylor's logic is shown to organize the empirical and metaethical contributions of the methodologies that bear on the fact-value polemic in the social sciences (evaluation research, phenomenological sociology, the behavioral systems perspective, and political philosophy). Each methodology is illustrated to pose questions that appear in actual policy research. Finally, the framework is shown to converge upon methodological requirements outlined by Habermas for the construction of a critical theory of politics and society.

Chapter 6 adapts the logic of political evaluation to the requirements of policy methodology. As a methodological foundation, this logic provides the basis for specific questions used in policy evaluation. Finally, a logic of policy questions is presented and discussed in the context of methodological issues.

Notes

1. Alfred N. Whitehead, cited by Barrington Moore, "Strategy in Social Science," in *Sociology on Trial,* ed. Maurice Stein and Arthur Vidich (Englewood Cliffs, N.J.: Prentice-Hall, 1963), p. 66.

2. Public policy is defined here as a guiding rule or course of action adopted and pursued by actors in dealing with a problem or matter of public concern. See James E. Anderson, *Public Policy-Making* (New York: Praeger Publishers, 1975); and David G. Gil, *Unravelling Social Policy* (Cambridge, Mass.: Schenkman, 1973).

3. For a detailed discussion of policy analysis, see Walter Williams, *Social Policy Research and Analysis* (New York: American Elsevier, 1971), pp. 12-13. Williams states that policy analysis describes a "policy-oriented approach, method and collection of techniques of synthesizing available information including the results of research: (a) to specify alternative policy and program choices and preferred alternatives in comparable, predicted qualitative and quantitative cost/benefit type terms as a format for decision making; (b) to assess organizational goals in terms of value inputs and to specify the requisite output criteria for organizational goals as a basis of goal determination and measurement of outcome performance; and (c) determine needed additional information in support of policy analysis as a guide for future decisions concerning analytical and research activities."

The term "evaluation research" specifically refers to the problem of determining by controlled experimentation, and its derivatives, the effectiveness of a particular program, that is, the extent to which the program achieves its intended effects. Although evaluation research and policy analysis address different aspects of the policy decision-making problem, they are complementary. In the ideal situation, the effectiveness of alternative policies would be determined by experimental evaluation research. Policy analysis, however, is designed to deal with the problem of limited information. In policy analysis, partial information available at the time of a decision is considered to be more important than complete information after the decision.

In the policy literature, there is some confusion associated with the use of the terms "policy analysis" and "evaluation." In part, this stems from the fact that all policy analysis is evaluative. The terms "policy analysis" and "policy evaluation" are used interchangeably in this study to refer to the skill discipline or profession concerned with the evaluation of policy alternatives. The term "evaluation research" is reserved for experimental program evaluation.

4. In this study, the term "methodology" is employed in the European sense. It is not used to designate a how-to quide to research but rather refers to the task of clarifying logical relationships between modes of inquiry, empirical and normative. See Anthony Giddens, *New Rules of Sociological Method* (New York: Basic Books, 1976). Concerned with the theory of inquiry, methodology remains closely related to epistemology—the theory of the nature of knowledge—and has often been identified with logic itself. Formal logics are derived from the explication of the implicit rules employed in the thought process that govern the making of consistent arguments, analysis, and deduction. Formal, or "reconstructed," logics serve in research as calculi for deriving valid statements or conclusions

within a set or system of definitions, operations, and axioms. For further discussion of methodology and logic in the social sciences, see Abraham Kaplan, *The Conduct of Inquiry: Methodology for Behavioral Science* (Scranton, Pa.: Chandler Publishing Co., 1964).

5. For a discussion of this distinction see Amitai Etzioni, *The Comparative Analysis of Complex Organizations* (New York: Free Press, 1961).

6. Banfield and Wilson have stated this point succinctly: "Since the two functions are performed at the same time by the same set of institutions, they are often concretely indistinguishable. A mayor who intervenes in a dispute about the location of a new public library manages a service at the same time that he settles a conflict, but he usually is thought of, and thinks of himself, as doing a single thing—'running the city government.' One function may at times be much more conspicuous than the other." See Edward C. Banfield and James Q. Wilson, *City Politics* (New York: Vintage Books, 1963), p. 18.

7. James G. March and Herbert A. Simon, *Organizations* (New York: John Wiley & Sons, 1958), pp. 129–131.

8. Melvin Anshen and David Novick, cited by Aaron Wildavsky, "The Political Economy of Efficiency," in *Planning Programming Budgeting,* ed. Fremont J. Lyden and Ernest G. Miller (Chicago: Markham, 1967), p. 394.

9. U.S., Congress, Senate, Subcommittee on National Security and International Operations, *Planning-Programming-Budgeting Hearings,* 91st Cong., 1st sess., 1969, p. 310.

10. Alice Rivlin, *Systematic Thinking for Social Action* (Washington, D.C.: Brookings Institution, 1971), p. 59.

11. Ida R. Hoos, "Systems Techniques for Managing Society: A Critique," *Public Administration Review* 32 (March–April 1972):158.

12. Fred Kramer, "Policy Analysis as Ideology," *Public Administration Review* 35 (September–October 1975):516.

13. In social science jargon, Robin Williams summed up the dilemma this way: "In the past, heavy emphasis in American policy has been upon the goal-attainment sector. . . . Conspicuously neglected have been . . . other . . . functional aspects of social systems—the integration of components and pattern maintenance. In our national drive to 'get things done,' we have generated vast internal social cleavages and frictions—dislocations and disintegrations. . . . the intense concentration upon political, military, technological, and economic attainments probably has severely strained the maintenance of some parts of the central systems of beliefs and value criteria." Robin M. Williams, Jr., "Individual and Group Values," *The Annals* 371 (May 1967):22.

14. Brian Barry and Douglas W. Rae, "Political Evaluation," in *The*

Handbook of Political Science, ed. Nelson W. Polsby and Fred D. Greenstein (Reading, Mass.: Addison-Wesley Publishing Co., 1975), 1:338–339.

15. Ibid., p. 339.

16. Arnold J. Meltsner, "Political Feasibility and Policy Analysis," *Public Administration Review* 32 (November–December 1972):859.

17. Yehezkel Dror, *Public Policymaking Reexamined* (San Francisco: Chandler Publishing Co., 1968), p. 35.

18. Arnold J. Meltsner, "Political Feasibility," p. 866.

19. Martin Rein, *Social Science and Public Policy* (New York: Penguin Books, 1976), p. 249; and Richard J. Bernstein, *The Restructuring of Social and Political Theory* (New York: Harcourt Brace Jovanovich, 1976). The reader is directed to Rein's book for an excellent statement of the fact-value problem as it confronts policy analysis; see especially Chapter 2, "The Fact-Value Dilemma."

20. Abraham Edel has stated, "When the intellectual history of contemporary social science comes to be written, one of its major themes will be the relation of social science to value." He suggested that "it will be a story of mutual isolation, affecting theory and practice, with losses to both the social sciences and the philosophy of value." See Edel, "Social Science and Value," in *The New Sociology,* ed. Irving L. Horowitz (New York: Oxford University Press, 1964), p. 218; Edel, *Exploring Fact and Value* (New Brunswick, N.J.: Transaction, 1978); and Dante Germino, "The Fact-Value Dichotomy as an Obstacle to the Development of a Critical Science of Politics," (Paper presented at the Seventy-Fourth Annual Meeting of the American Political Science Association, New York, August 31, 1978).

21. See the works of Jürgen Habermas: *Theory and Practice* (Boston: Beacon Press, 1973); *Knowledge and Human Interests* (Boston: Beacon Press, 1971); *Communication and the Evolution of Society* (Boston: Beacon Press, 1979); and *Legitimation Crisis* (Boston: Beacon Press, 1973). Students and critics of Habermas will criticize my failure to explicate his work in a more complete and systematic fashion, especially given the professed enthusiasm for his contribution. The primary reason for the absence of such a discussion is that the study is directed to a policy-oriented audience. It therefore adopts the language and problems of the social and policy sciences to promote a dialogue with those groups, eschewing the complex and often convoluted language of critical theory. At the same time, however, the study has attempted to pay its debts to Habermas at the essential points in the argument. This hopefully provides solid ground for further thought and research by enticing readers to seek out the works of Habermas on their own.

22. See Bernstein, *The Restructuring of Social and Political Theory.*

23. Stephen Toulmin, *The Uses of Argument* (Cambridge: Cambridge University Press, 1958); Kurt Baier, *The Moral Point of View: A Rational Basis of Ethics* (New York: Random House, 1965); Paul W. Taylor, *Normative Discourse* (Englewood Cliffs, N.J.: Prentice-Hall, 1961).

24. C. W. Churchman, *The Design of Inquiring Systems* (New York: Basic Books, 1971), and Duncan MacRae, Jr., *The Social Function of Social Science* (New Haven, Conn.: Yale University Press, 1976).

25. Ralph S. Hambrick, Jr., "A Guide for the Analysis of Policy Arguments," *Policy Sciences* 5 (December 1974):469–478.

26. It is important to clarify the usage of the word "normative" in this study. It is employed in the traditional sense used in political theory. A normative judgment is fundamentally a judgment about which goals and values to select. In modern policy literature, under the influence of the fact-value dichotomy, the term "normative" policy methodology is frequently used to refer to techniques designed to facilitate judgments about the selection of efficient and equitable means to goals. In this study, both the selection of means to goals and the selection of the goals themselves are inherent components of a normative judgment and both require evaluation.

2

The Fact-Value Debate and the Search for Methodology

The distinctive characteristic of a problem of social policy is indeed the fact that it cannot be resolved merely on the basis of purely technical considerations which assume already settled ends. Normative standards of value can and must be the objects of dispute in discussion of a problem in social policy because the problem lies in the domain of general cultural values.

—Max Weber[1]

The Fact-Value Dichotomy and Social Relevance

In recent times, the study of politics has been embroiled in an epistemological dispute over the role of values in political inquiry. Although aspects of the dispute date as far back as the turn of the century, the specific origins of the modern debate stem from the adoption of behavioral science methodology over the past thirty years. The principal purpose of the "behavioral movement" in political science has been to bring the rigorous empirical methods of the physical sciences to the study of political and social phenomena—an approach that is an outgrowth of logical positivism and its variants. By restricting the investigator's focus to the nonsubjective (observable) side of human behavior, the goal of behavioral science methodology is to uncover the empirical causes and effects that govern and explain behavior and to organize them into lawlike factual statements subject to verification by objective observers.

The behavioral project rests on several fundamental epistemological assumptions of positivism. Social actors are held to encounter, through their social-psychological perceptions and experiences, an extant social life-world that is independent of their beliefs, attitudes, and values. It is a world that, from the social actor's position, is "out there." As such, knowledge about it can be derived independently of the actor's sense perceptions or emotional framework. Moreover, the objectivity of such knowledge can be tested through controlled observation and the principles of formal logic, induction and deduction. The truth of a hypothesis, measured as validity and reliability, can be verified by evidence gathered by a neutral investigator from the objective world of facts.

Such knowledge is organized as propositional knowledge about the factual world—defined as empirical statements about the relationship of two or more variables. Ideally, such knowledge is general or nomothetic in character, in contrast to contextual or ideographic information about specific times, places, and circumstances. In the positivist view, the possibility of producing propositional knowledge about, say, the behavior of chief executives or decision-making processes is the basis for qualifying political science as scientific. What is more, the production of propositional knowledge is the basis for the belief that the social sciences can generate reliable empirical data for solving societal difficulties. If, for instance, a political scientist commands a body of scientifically tested propositions about the concepts and variables that cause political revolutions, he or she can utilize such data to help either contain or promote revolutions. For the positivist, however, the question as to whether to contain or promote a revolution is a value question that falls beyond the realm of political science, which is organized around the search for causal knowledge. The development of causal theory is the dominant concern of mainstream political science.[2]

At the same time, however, behavioral political science has never been able to fully silence its critics.[3] From the very beginning of the methodological venture, prominent members of the academic ranks have refused to accept the wisdom of shaping political methodology with positivistic physical science procedures. Today, many younger members of the discipline are unwilling to adopt the commitment to behavioralism, especially those influenced by physical scientists who have begun to question their own methods.[4] During the past decade, this reaction to behavioral science has at times taken the form of protest.

Behavioral science's plea for value neutrality has been one of the steadiest sources of tension. Based on metaethical noncognitivism, which holds that values are not scientifically provable, behavioral science methodology has relegated values to "the intellectual limbo of personal preference."[5] Ethical or value neutrality in mainstream social science is traced to the writings of Max Weber, particularly his essay on the relationship between social science and social policy. Weber pointed out that advocacy or affirmation of value judgments introduces bias, contaminating or transforming the perceptions of the phenomena under investigation. To avoid bias or misjudgment, the study of politics and society is best promoted by suspension of value orientations. As public citizens, scientists are free to adopt value-oriented positions. In their role as scientists, they may not prescribe norms or values as a result of their research investigations. Regardless of how detailed or comprehensive their factual results are, the scientists are in no special position to draw conclusions about what ought to be done. In the final analysis, the value judgments of the scientist, like those of the layperson, rest on irrational components.

Weber founded his position on a distinction between formal and substantive rationality. Formal rationality is the procedural rationality of the scientific method. The task of the social scientist is to investigate those aspects of the social world that lend themselves to formal procedures. Substantive rationality, in contrast, is identified with specific contents—such as propositions about the ontological nature of reality and statements of value. These are relegated to the province of philosophy and metaphysics. In social science and policy evaluation, the only admissible value statements are those based on formal rationality. Weber set forth three categories of admissible statements: (1) the explication and elaboration of the internal consistency of value judgments, which determine alternative attitudes, along with an examination of their conceptual implications for thought and action; (2) the investigation of the factual premises and their empirical consequences; and (3) the determination of optimal means-ends relationships between goals and the methods of achieving them.[6] What science cannot do, Weber argued, is establish the truth or validity of values. Discussion of normative principles leads to "a bottomless morass."[7] As there is no rational way to resolve fundamental goal conflicts, the only thing the social scientist can do is determine normative axioms and assumptions, explicate their implications for action, investigate their logical consistency, and continue with the empirical assignment.

Harold Lasswell, one of the founders of modern policy science, presented a clear picture of the policy analyst's orientation to values: "In his role as scientist, a policy scientist does not perceive himself as qualified to pass judgment on the validity of competing claims of a transempirical character." The analyst's "competence is restricted to the confirmation (or disconfirmation) of statements about the perspectives or operational events in social processes."[8] The only judgments capable of confirmation are empirical or mathematical judgments. Emotive, subjective statements about values are beyond the reach of the policy scientist's methods.

This does not mean that analysts are to naively disassociate themselves from value orientations. Even though professional analysts are precluded from "arbitrating among the conflicting assertions of theology and metaphysics," they are not precluded from identifying with goals and values. "On the contrary, we interpret problem orientation as requiring [the analyst] to clarify his goal preferences, since he is bound in some measure to affect value realization."[9] At some point in their analyses, policy scientists must consider themselves to be the object of inquiry. Utilizing all of the techniques available to them, they must engage in a full exploration of the factors, past and present, that predispose them to certain commitments influencing their judgments. This, however, is not to be misconstrued as justification for these judgments; such judgments cannot be justified by giving reasons. The basis for this position, according to Lasswell, is Weber's fact-value separation.

This value-neutral view provides the groundwork for a policy science that emphasizes empirically oriented technical criticisms of means designed to achieve presupposed goals or ends.

When this instrumental conception of policy science is carried to a logical extreme, technical efficiency is posited as the essence of rational social action. Ludwig von Mises, an ardent advocate of this view, argued that "the economic principle is the fundamental principle of all rational action, and not just a particular feature of a certain kind of rational action—all rational action is therefore an act of economizing."[10] The policy scientist functions as a social engineer whose task is to calculate the costs and benefits of alternative means for achieving goals hammered out by the political processes. The value implications associated with goals do not enter the calculations. The legitimacy of value implications—if not validity—is established by consensus in the political system.

To a growing number of political and social theorists, this conception of rationality places severe limitations on the development of the social sciences. Applicable only to means, the criterion of efficiency is inappropriate for dealing with the most important questions that plague decision makers—questions concerning which goals and ends to pursue. Such questions, in the standard conception of policy science, must be left to the political processes and dictated by power, arbitrary preferences, or cultural determinism. As one critic suggested, "it seems unfortunate to have rational procedures available for the relatively less important decisions of life and to have none for dealing with the most important decisions."[11]

In the late 1960s, the fact-value dichotomy was singled out for renewed criticism. The social unrest that characterized the second half of the decade provoked a protest movement within the social sciences that indicted behavioral methodology for "social irrelevance." Behavioral science is portrayed as hiding behind the principle of value neutrality and therefore incapable of evaluating contemporary political realities or prescribing socially relevant solutions. At the root of the problem, there is a disjunction between behavioral theory and political practice. David Easton, one of the leading advocates of behavioral political science, was himself compelled to criticize political science for wearing "collective blinders" that hinder the discipline's ability to perceive the nature of political reality. In his 1969 presidential address before the American Political Science

Association, Easton asked how the current behavioral interpretations could fail to identify, understand, or anticipate the kinds of domestic problems that began to generate political demands in the sixties: "How can we account for our neglect of the way in which the distribution of power within the system prevents measures from being taken in sufficient degree and time to escape the resort to violence in the expression of demands, a condition that threatens to bring about the deepest crisis of political authority that the United States has ever suffered?"[12]

Behavioral methodology deals inadequately with both the values of the behavioral investigator and the values of the social actors under observation. The methodological protest advocated renewed attention to the admonishments of writers such as Marx and Mannheim, who emphasized the fundamental role of value assumptions in the conduct of social research, a role shaping problem selection at the outset and data interpretation at the conclusion. As a movement, the protest railed against social scientists for continuing to approach their data and interpretations as if they possessed a pristine purity untarnished by the value premises that underlay their research. As Easton said, "We do not consistently ask the question central to the sociology of knowledge: To what extent are our errors, omissions, and the interpretations better explained by reference to our normative presuppositions than to ignorance, technical inadequacy, lack of insight, absence of appropriate data and the like?"[13]

This reaction was embodied in a call for a "new political science." In the subfield of public administration, Victor Thompson described the reaction as a "drastic attack" not only on existing governmental priorities, but on the very principle of administrative impersonality and objectivity around which the discipline is organized. Especially among the younger academic members of the discipline, there is a rejection of the possibility of a value-free political science. Many declare that "quantifiable, observable aspects of human relations and behavior are only partial descriptions and leave out the more important aspects of meaning and feeling."[14]

From this view, a value-neutral conception of political

science is either too simplistic or impossible. Not only does it fail to conform to an array of commonsense evidence, it ignores the findings of psychological research that show the influence of attitude on perception. In contrast to the positivistic orientation in behavioral science, facts are inherently dependent upon attitudes, values, and beliefs. Facts are not "out there" in the social world, nor are political and social problems independent of subjective attitudes. Based on an alternative epistemological tradition stemming from the writings of Hegel, Marx, and Mannheim, and more recently Ludwig Wittgenstein, Michael Polyani, and Thomas Kuhn, the basic themes of a value-oriented epistemology are succinctly summarized by Gresham Riley. The first is the "belief that perception, rather than being conceptually neutral, is structured by both linguistic categories and the mental attitudes and interests of the observers." Second is the epistemological assertion that "the categories in terms of which experience is organized and, in turn, known, as well as canons of truth and validity, reflect the values and interests of different groups at different times in history." Third is the claim that the social actor "does not encounter reality as uninterpreted but rather as something mediated or constructed by conceptual schema," whether paradigms, ideologies, or language games. In sharp opposition to positivism, which emphasizes scientific description and discovery of the world as it exists, this epistemological tradition has fostered the emergence of an emphasis on political and social involvement. From this position, the proper goal of the social sciences is not just to explain the social world but also to change and improve it.[15]

The search for a new value-oriented basis for political and social science came to be known, at least in political science, as "post-behavioralism."[16] There is no one particular orientation that embodies the full thrust of post-behavioralism, although some of its variants have been more widely accepted. Three approaches, alike only in their concern for a new value-oriented base for political and social science, are of particular significance: post-behavioral policy analysis, phenomenology, and political philosophy. The post-behavioral policy orientation, at least as Easton defined it, is the dominant alternative in political science. It represents an effort to modify the behavioral project by introducing a new value consciousness to empirical research. While retaining the basic foundations of the behavioral science orientation, the researcher is obliged to direct the methodology toward "socially relevant" questions. In contrast, the other two alternatives call for the discarding of behavioral science as a methodological foundation—one advocating a phenomenological reconstruction of the discipline and the other viewing the proper course as a return to the traditional methods of political philosophy.

In more vitriolic moments, the clash between these three competing methodologies has often been suggestive of the kinds of epistemological disputes that tend to accompany periods of normative malaise. The rise of conflicting normative perspectives often leads to a reciprocal distrust between co-existing groups, each questioning the basic integrity of the other. Long established as a topic in the sociology of knowledge, normative conflict is particularly familiar in the political arena. By contrast, Karl Mannheim has pointed out that in academia, "where normative expectations are somewhat more restraining, it leads to reciprocated ideological analyses and a renewal of epistemological questions."[17] The debate in contemporary political theory has often centered around this type of epistemological renewal. Bruce Wright has expressed it quite succinctly: "Political science is once again in a real state of ferment. The old 'behavioralists,' 'empiricists' or 'positivists,' especially when parading under the banner of liberal-pluralism, are under attack by the Young Turks, Caucusites, neo-traditionalists, 'third clats' or post-behavioralists."[18] The clash centers around the implicit conservative support of the status quo that results from the behavioralist's refusal to take a value position. The goal of the challengers is to develop a socially relevant discipline attuned to the normative malaise that underlies contemporary political issues.

Although in recent years the overt temper of the debate has tended to be more subdued, the critical tensions generated by the fact-value problem remain central issues in the discipline. More and more writers have begun to recognize the need to confront directly the problem of political value judgments and are advocating the study of political evaluation. It is easier, however, to agree on the need for political evaluation than it is to construct the required methodology. A political methodology for the evaluation of public policies is intricately tied to issues raised by all three competing methodologies. In the ensuing pages, I will show that an adequate concept of political evaluation can be built only with a methodology capable of incorporating insights from all three approaches.

The Epistemological Debate:
Post-behavioral Policy Analysis

Even though all three methodological approaches have at times laid claim to the title of "post-behavioralism," in the interest of clarity the term will be used here only to denote the dominant post-behavioral policy orientation.

For the post-behavioralist, the call for a new approach is not a wholesale rejection of behavioral science methodology. For instance, in writing about public administration, George Frederickson explained that the movement can be described as a "second generational behavioralism." The post-behavioralist, unlike his or her progenitor, "accepts the importance of understanding as scientifically as possible how and why organizations behave as they do but . . . tends to be rather more interested in the impact of that organization on its clientele and vice versa."[19] Refusing to accept the facade of value-neutrality, the analyst employs her or his scientific training to determine alternative forms of organizational behavior and the public policies that result from them. As Frederickson said, "The second generation behavioralist is less . . . 'institution oriented' and more client-impact oriented, 'less neutral' and more 'normative,' and, it is hoped, no less scientific."[20]

The impetus of post-behavioralism is thus not an attack on the scientific thrust of behavioralism but rather a shift in emphasis. It is viewed as an attempt to alert behavioralists to contemporary social-value problems and to urge redirection of their scientific tools toward the types of political and social difficulties that confront contemporary society. For post-behavioralists, the ethical neutrality of the political analyst is seen as a "cop-out." Rather than lend support to the status quo, the political science profession should devote its energies and resources to the development of the kinds of factual information necessary to inform the search for alternative political systems that more effectively satisfy the needs of citizens. Where behavioralists have held out for the long-term fruits of basic or "pure" scientific research, post-behavioralists call for an inclusion of the more immediate empirical requirements of applied political research. As one writer stated, "The problems which cry out for solution are here and now, and cannot wait for the slow wheels of science to grind out final answers."[21] Moreover, the benefits of applied political research are not to be extended only to those who can pay for them—the elites of business, government and the military—but also to the members of the lower, oppressed classes who are of particular concern to the post-behavioralists.

For the post-behavioralist, applied policy research is the key to social relevance. According to Easton, "The critics are correct in their description of the problems that the urgent crises of society revealed in the body of knowledge produced by contemporary social science. . . . The policy analysis movement represents the beginnings of our latest response."[22] Given the underdeveloped state of behavioral science, the political analyst is at times forced to make a choice between science and relevance. Policy analysis is the bridge across this gap. The basic difference between behavioralists and post-behavioralists centers around the issue of social relevance. Where behavioralists never sacrifice science to relevance, post-behavioralists are willing to concede that in the study of public policy, science must at times take a less important role.[23] The long-term goal, however, remains the same: a scientific approach to the explanation of political behavior. In the future, basic and applied political research will merge into a unified policy science capable of taking its place beside empirical value theory. Post-behavioralist Maria Falco expressed the objective this way:

> The problem for moralists, value theorists, policy scientists, post-behavioralists, or all those who would hope to establish a single value hierarchy for society or to ease the human condition through humane or progressive policy proposals, is an empirical one rather than a

logical or a philosophical one. Not only must research into the extensiveness to which certain values are maintained be conducted (e.g., how widely held are the taboos against murder, incest, robbery, rape, slavery, gambling, homosexuality, abortion, premarital sex, etc.), but the relationship between values and their functions for individuals and societies must also be extensively explored. Investigations should try to determine under what conditions certain values will be held by certain individuals and societies, and what consequences for these individuals and societies each value judgment may have.[24]

The scientific task is to discover the causal links between value judgments and consequences. In this respect, the task bears a close resemblance to the attempt to develop a social welfare function in modern economic theory. In similar fashion, the study of values in policy science should evolve as a system-oriented empirical theory. The basic difference between the present task of a policy-oriented value theory and its future assignment rests on determining the distinction between what "should" be the goals of society, what value configurations will appear in the social system as a response to specific needs (psychological, social or political), and what alternative policy or action can be proposed for the satisfaction of these needs. Rooted in a naturalistic perspective, the policy scientist, as value theorist, will discover the "laws" of these value responses and assess the most efficient course of action that will effect these goals. As Falco explained:

> "Should" therefore becomes reduced to a prescription for action rather than an absolute imperative. And the payoffs can then be rationally calculated even on a social level so that the choice itself becomes rational. Thus the question "What should our goals be," in an absolute sense, is replaced by the questions, "Under certain circumstances what should our goals be?" and "How are we most likely to attain them?" Probability theory is thus introduced into the equation and in this way logic and rationality are made an inherent part of the social value science (policy science) enterprise, as well as the science of individual ethics.[25]

Like the construction of a social welfare function in economic theory, a scientific theory of value remains a theoretical contribution rather than a practical policy methodology. A scientific value theory for policy science confronts serious practical problems when faced with real-world applications. Such a science depends on the ability of researchers to gather, classify, and elaborate an overwhelming amount of empirical information and place it in an explanatory hypothesis capable of specifying the weights and distributions of causal variables of all types—cultural, psychological, political, environmental, and so on. These would then have to be linked to a larger unified theory of social behavior that bears directly on policy decisions and their underlying value judgments. As one writer asserted, "Empirical investigators do not have available to them a conceptual apparatus suitable even for specifying the values, value systems, or value orientations of particular individuals or societies, at any given time, or changes in these values taking place over a period of time, let alone any understanding of how to assess the desirability or undesirability of any anticipated changes in such values which would enable those in charge of our destiny to take appropriate steps at least to avert disaster if not lead us to the Great Society."[26]

The Phenomenological Approach

Post-behavioral science is advanced in the face of major challenges to behavioralism by phenomenological social scientists and political philosophers. Both groups have long taken a back seat to the "behavioral revolution," remaining on the fringes of the discipline and chiseling at the foundations. Easton has made it quite clear that his post-behavioralism makes no concessions to phenomenologists and political philosophers. Although he has never rejected their basic criticisms, particularly the point that analytical models of behavioral science fail to capture reality as an integrated experience of the whole, he dismissed them as a return to intuition, the long-standing enemy of empirical science.[27]

For phenomenological social scientists and political philosophers, the normative deficiencies of behavioralism penetrate deep into the methodology itself. Pointing to the unique normative dimensions of the social world, these writers raise serious questions about the ability of physical science methodology to explain value-laden social problems. The challenge rests on a reassertion of the prolonged debate between the two fundamental traditions of explanation—causal explanation and social understanding.[28] As a methodological tradition, each possesses its own requirements to count as adequate explanation. Causal explanation is associated with physical science and the behavioral approach to social science. Social understanding rests on teleological explanation, based on goals or purposes, and is identified with the social world and *verstehen* sociology. Causal explanation aims at the empirical explanation and prediction of behavior, while *verstehen* explanation attempts to render facts understandable by interpreting them in light of relevant goals and values.

Although the label "phenomenologist" captures a mixed group containing many variants, by and large the works of Alfred Schutz have been seminal in their exploration of the epistemological debate with the behavioral approach. In view of the prevailing behavioral orthodoxy, the special value of the phenomenological movement is its reassertion of fundamental questions about the nature of social science inquiry itself.[29] Perhaps no other group has devoted as much energy as the phenomenologists to the explication of the distinction between the social and physical worlds and the methodologies appropriate to each. What is particularly unique about this group is that they are not just political and social philosophers. Today they are practicing social scientists.

The crucial question of phenomenology in social science revolves around the applicability of objective, empirically oriented methods to the subjectively based problems of the social world.[30] Concerned fundamentally with the role of "social meaning," the phenomenologists' complaint against the use of physical science techniques is that the physical world possesses no intrinsic meaning structure. Schutz stated this clearly:

> It is up to the natural scientist to determine which sector of the universe of nature, which facts and which events therein, and which aspects of such facts and events are topically relevant to their

specific purpose. These facts and events are neither pre-selected nor preinterpreted: they do not reveal intrinsic relevance structures. Relevance is not inherent in nature as such, it is the result of the selective and interpretative activity of man within nature or observing nature. The facts, data and events with which the natural scientist has to deal are just facts, data, and events within his observational field but this does not "mean" anything to the molecules, atoms, and electrons therein.[31]

The social realm, unlike the physical realm, is inherently involved with subjective meaning. For the social scientist, the observational field is not without structure. According to Schutz, "It has a particular meaning and relevance structure for the human beings living, thinking, and acting therein." As social actors, "they have preselected and preinterpreted this world by a series of commonsense constructs which determine their behavior, define the goal of their actions [and] the means available—which help them find their bearings in their natural and socio-cultural environment and to come to grips with it."[32] Thus, the social world is an "organized universe of meaning" experienced and interpreted by everyday social actors. Social knowledge is the product of these commonsense or everyday interpretations that, when combined with the social actor's personal experience, forms an orientation toward the everyday world that is "taken for granted."

The social actor's construct is a "first-order" construct of social reality that poses a fundamental methodological implication for the social scientist: Unlike the physical scientist, the social scientist cannot establish from the outside which events and facts are interpretationally relevant to the actor's own specific purposes.[33] The constructs of social science must take the form of "second-order" constructs, i.e., social science constructs of the social actor's constructs. The crux of the problem revolves around two interrelated methodological requirements: the distinction between the social scientist's second-order explanations and the everyday first-order explanations of the social actor, and the establishment and maintenance of a systematic relationship between them.

Behavioral science's failure lies in its inability to incorporate an adequate account of the social actor's subjective under-

standing of the situation. By focusing on the observable dimensions of a social phenomenon, the behavioral scientist and the
social actor observe the social world from different angles. As
a consequence, the behavioralist's theoretical models tend to
be constructed around his or her own implicit assumptions and
value judgments about reality. The behavioralist drifts astray
by tacitly substituting his or her own view of the relevant aspects
of the situation for the social actor's own view of that reality.
These tacit value assumptions are usually difficult to observe
since they are buried in the foundation of the behavioralist's
theoretical model.

To accurately explain social phenomena, the investigator
must attempt to "understand" the meaning of the social phenomena from the actor's perspective. Such an understanding is
derived by interpreting the phenomena against the social
actor's own motives and values. This is accomplished through
the process Weber called *verstehen,* a concept that has been
subject to much misunderstanding. For many, including Easton,
it signals a return to an explanatory technique based on empathy
or intuitive understanding of the motives and reasons behind
observed social action. From Schutz's perspective, *verstehen*
is not an instrument of explanation but rather a process of concept formation employed in arriving at an interpretive understanding of social phenomena.[34] The focus of the interpretive
process is on the social actor's meaning rather than the intuitive
or empathetic mental processes of the observer. By treating the
"subjectively intended meaning" of action as a problem in concept formation rather than a problem of how knowledge is
known, it is possible for proponents of interpretive explanation
to agree with behavioralists on a number of crucial aspects of
social explanation. Schutz, for example, has agreed with behavioralists that all empirical knowledge depends upon discovery through processes of controlled inference and that it
must be verified by properly executing the appropriate experimental test. In this respect, interpretive explanation does not
obviate the need for scientific verification, as implied by the
introspection or intuition conception of *verstehen.* Instead, it
only calls to attention the fact that any scientific method that
permits the observer to select and interpret social facts in terms

of his or her own private value system can never produce a
socially relevant, valid theory. Interpretive explanation is aimed
at developing concepts that are understood in terms of the
social actor's motives and values rather than those of the
scientific observer. In this perspective, scientific explanation
and *verstehen* are answers to two different types of questions
that complement each other—one concerned with causal explanation, the other with social understanding.[35] Here phenomenology need only be opposed to the uncritical acceptance of
meaning structure that occurs when the procedural rules of the
physical sciences are naively applied to the social world. The
phenomenologist's purpose is to map out crucial limitations of
behavioralism, pinpointing its blind spots.[36]

Despite this emphasis on subjective meaning, *verstehen* is
not to be understood as an uncontrollable or indeterminable
aspect of social discourse. Interpretive explanation is a process
of mutual understanding made possible through commonly
shared social learning and acculturation. Such understanding
must ultimately be subjected to tests of valid inference like any
other judgment. Schutz suggested that this point can be illustrated with a courtroom analogy.[37] In a court trial, subjective
perceptions of facts and reasons are submitted to a number of
inferential and documentary tests. The judge and jury, for
example, do not simply impute reasons and motives to the defendant, however plausible they may sound. Documentary
evidence and testimony must be produced in support of an
explanation formulated in terms of "reasons" for behavior
rather than "causes" in the strict sense of the term. The verdict
is reached by bringing together the external evidence and the
defendant's publicly stated subjective intentions. It is the task
of the judge and the jury to interpret the defendant's social
behavior against a reconstruction of the facts.

Following this line of argument, it cannot be said that interpretive explanations are arbitrary. Although answers are not
worked out by rigid adherence to the scientific methods of
demonstration and verification, interpretive explanations are
based on the giving of reasons and the assessment of arguments.
In such explanations one is attempting to show how certain
circumstances logically entitle a specific opinion or way of view-

ing things. The relationship of the belief to a decision or action is not external and contingent (like causes) but internal and logical.[38] To be sure, such argumentation is not based on certainty in the scientific sense, but it is possible to have a degree of confidence in a well-reasoned practical argument.

A couple of illustrations may help to clarify this point. If the behavioral political scientist wants to explain why Mr. X is more actively engaged in politics than Ms. Y, he or she might appeal to an empirically established causal finding in the behavioral literature: "Men are more active politically than women." The phenomenologically oriented political scientist, however, is likely to ask whether this type of causal reference really provides sufficient information to enable one to understand the situation. Most people confronted with this question would ask to be supplied with additional information: What are Mr. X's reasons and motives for his political involvement? Does he want to gain moral approbation? Is he determined to protect certain beliefs that he strongly holds? Does he think political involvement will further his business career? The limitation of a causal explanation is even better illustrated in historical situations, such as the case of Neville Chamberlain's action at Munich in 1938. Would it be productive to ask, "What always causes a Chamberlain at a Munich of 1938 to do exactly the sort of thing the actual Chamberlain did there and then?"[39] The phenomenologist's contribution here is to show that the historian would attempt to marshal the facts and norms of the situation to illustrate that Chamberlain's actions can be explained as the logical outcome of a specific configuration of factors. The task is to demonstrate that, given certain motives and purposes, it was (or was not) logical for the man to act in a specific way in such a situation.

During the epistemological dispute in the late 1960s and early 1970s phenomenology and the *verstehen* method attracted renewed attention among many social scientists.[40] In a society experiencing social crises—poverty, war, and racial riots—phenomenology is seen as an alternative to a behavioral methodology that (in Easton's own words) cannot foresee a "major crisis in public authority." Radical political scientists such as Marvin Surkin see in phenomenology the possibility of uniting thought with action and theory with practice. Surkin has argued that phenomenology represents a radical humanistic alternative because its view of the world encompasses social reality as a whole, including the commonsense reality of the man on the street. In the process, it draws attention to the multiplicity of conflicting perspectives and their implications for social change.[41]

In more methodological terms, Gibson Winter has criticized the behavioral approach to public policy from the phenomenological perspective. Winter stressed public policy's fundamental roots in the practical life-world of social action. He defined policy as a conscious and formalized statement of goals to be pursued in the world of "commonsense" opinion and argued that the policy analyst must assume a role altogether different from that of the theoretical behavioral scientist. Insofar as policy gives shape to society's norms and values, providing imperatives for social action and guidelines for decisions, the policy analyst works at the intersection where empirical social science meets empirical social ethics.[42]

Jürgen Habermas posited phenomenological analysis as a dialectical "moment" in the development of a critical theory. Drawing on Marx's concept of *praxis,* rooted in Hegel's phenomenology, Habermas illustrated how empirical theoretical knowledge and practical social knowledge are aimed at two fundamentally different purposes. Where theoretical knowledge is designed to explain causal relationships that govern objective reality (the question of "what is the case?"), phenomenologically oriented practical knowledge is addressed to the norms of social action (the question of "what ought to be the case?"). Behavioral science's mistake lies in its failure to recognize the need to mediate between these two epistemological spheres—i.e., to transpose theoretical causal knowledge into practical life-world meanings. Theoretical knowledge, verified by the rules of scientific procedure, must be validated in the practical world through normative discourse carried out by the relevant participants. Such discourse involves a dialectical interaction between facts and values. It is the core process of representative institutions aimed at a "discursive formation of public will." For Habermas, science must be anchored to a "pragmatistic model" of decision that governs a practical discourse between scientific experts, politicians, and the public. Without such practical discourse, science is tacitly planned and controlled by the dominant ideology of the hierarchical decision structure and the experts who direct it.[43]

The Critique in Political Philosophy

Political philosophy has been calling attention to the unique character of the social world and its special epistemological requirements even longer than phenomenological social science. In this respect, it is important to remember that phenomenology is still taught as a branch of philosophy. Although political philosophy has suffered a long decay under the aegis of the "behavioral revolution," in the 1960s political philosophers reasserted themselves forcefully in the controversy over ethical neutrality and the separation of facts and values. Especially important in the debate have been the writings of such theorists as Leo Strauss, Sheldon Wolin, Eric Voegelin, and Jürgen Habermas.

Strauss organized his epistemological polemic around four principal arguments: (1) ethical neutrality itself must be considered a value orientation, as it has clear implications and consequences for evaluation; (2) insofar as every political action is purposeful, the investigation of political phenomena must unavoidably assume a value orientation; (3) there is no language available for the study of political events that is inherently non-evaluative; and (4) the very process by which social scientists establish the concepts to be employed in their examination of particular actions or events rests upon implicit value judgments.[44]

Like the phenomenologists, Strauss directed his criticism at the behavioralists in no uncertain terms: "The modern approach to political science is 'diabolic'; it has no attributes peculiar to fallen angels . . . nor is it Neroian." Nonetheless, while Rome burns, behavioralism fiddles. "It is excused by two facts: it does not know that it fiddles and it does not know that Rome burns."[45]

To understand the normative malaise of the present age, according to Strauss, one must turn to the questions and methods of the political philosophers of the past, especially the classical tradition. Only through the classical tradition can the modern social sciences reunite theory with practice and fact with value. Classical political philosophy was built on the recognition that political action rests on the participants' value judgments. To examine politics through the lens of the fact-value dichotomy is to perpetrate a fundamental distortion.

For political philosophy, like phenomenology, action is guided by the actor's thoughts about what is good and bad, better and worse. As Strauss explained, political action "has in itself a directedness towards knowledge of the good: of the good life, or the good society."[46] Even the most practical political action, therefore, is based on an evaluation or value judgment. Action and judgment are inherently linked. Beyond this point, however, political philosophy begins to diverge from phenomenology. Where the phenomenologist focuses on the actor's account of his or her behavior, the political philosopher attempts to penetrate these everyday beliefs to get at the "underlying truths." For Strauss as well as others, such as Voegelin and Perry,[47] the phenomenologist is destined to fall "victim to every deception and self-deception of the people one is studying." By emphasizing the social actor's value judgments, the phenomenologist formulates an analysis that is trapped in the conceptual framework of the actor's own society and historical setting. The result is social and historical relativity.[48] To escape the pitfalls of relativity, theorists must make value judgments of their own about the subject matter. It is here that the questions and methods of political philosophy take on special relevance.

The pursuit of basic values that lie beneath everyday belief systems requires a special diagnostic tool.[49] The basic analytical tool is an ideal model of society. Employing intuition, insight, and imagination, the political philosopher's primary task is to construct an ideal model of society that provides evaluative standards or principles against which empirical reality can be judged. The justification of such ideal constructions—for example, Plato's Republic, Hobbes's Leviathan, or Marx's communist society, along with their respective moral principles— is established if they pass the test of generalization or universalization. The moral principle that can be generalized is one that is free of logical inconsistencies and self-contradictions. It is the principle that can be demonstrated to hold in all cases, not allowing for exceptions. Kant's "categorical imperatives," for example, were taken to be rationally demonstrable because they could be logically generalized without inconsistency and self-contradiction. It was their capacity to be generalized that established their moral claim.

Strauss argued that modern theorists must engage in these classical exercises if they are to come to grips with the contemporary crisis of values. Political philosophy's ability to transcend the everyday reality of the political system gives it a special "diagnostic" character. In fact, for this reason, political philosophy has tended to flourish in times of political crisis. In periods of severe social and political disorder, political philosophy becomes a practical tool for exposing basic assumptions and conceptualizations that underlie the social turmoil. During the social crises of the late 1960s, Eugene Miller, following Strauss's tradition, reasserted the role of traditional political philosophy in a major symposium on political inquiry. For Miller, only political philosophy can formulate a new mode of inquiry capable of doing justice to behavioralism and phenomenology while avoiding the pitfalls of positivism and social relativity. Such an attempt to restore political philosophy, he asserted, "can best be understood as a response to the social and intellectual crisis that Easton himself has spoken of in his early writings and again in his presidential address."[50]

Like Strauss and his followers, Sheldon Wolin has also been a forceful critic of "behavioral methodism," indicting it for lack of concern for the normative questions of the "epic theorists."[51] In order to make explicit their judgments of what ought to be done in politics, political scientists should adopt the "vocation of political theory." The job of the epic theorist is to provide arguments for the choice of one theory over another. For Wolin, the reintroduction of this function requires that behavioral methodism be replaced with political wisdom derived from "tacit" political knowledge and "vision." Such vision or imagination, however, is not something that can be judged against the kind of empirically rigorous standards sought by behavioral political science. Instead, vision depends on other extrascientific

sources for its richness. Such sources are more explicitly identified as "the stock of ideas which an intellectually curious and
broadly educated person accumulates and which come to
govern his intuitions, feelings, and perceptions." Seldom are
they specifically acknowledged in the formal theory of political
science, even though they provide the inspiration for its creation. "Lying beyond the boundaries circumscribed by methods,
technique, and official definition of the discipline, they can be
summarized as cultural resources and itemized as metaphysics,
faith, historical sensibility, or more broadly as tacit knowledge."
To behavioral political science, this is the stuff of "bias." Much
of the history of the behavioral approach can be described as
an attempt to rid political science of such knowledge.

If the job of the political theorist is to provide arguments for
the choice of one theory over another, the Frankfurt School
and Jürgen Habermas represent one of the most penetrating and
sustained epistemological achievements in modern political
philosophy.[52] Anchored in the dialectical tradition of Hegel and
Marx, the Frankfurt School has attempted to recover and
defend the critical impulse that must underlie an adequate political theory. Drawing on Marx's understanding and use of "critique," Horkheimer, Adorno, and Habermas have advanced
critique as a practical interest in the quality and fate of political
life. Moving beyond the phenomenological interpretation of the
social life-world, these theorists have attempted to posit critical
theory as a genuine force for the self-awareness of the social
actor.[53] Following Marx, the critical theorist's thinking is designed to further human emancipation. Reaching beyond a
merely negative stance toward existing social conditions, the
critical theorist must, in the words of Horkheimer, form "a
dynamic unity with the oppressed class, so that his presentation
of societal contradictions is not merely an expression of the historical situation but also a force within it to stimulate change."[54]
Habermas has attempted to specify the methodological foundations of such a critical theory. His project, as shown in Chapter 5, represents a methodological synthesis of three knowledge-
constitutive interests involved in a full evaluation: empirical
behavioral science, phenomenologically based interpretation,
and critical reflection. The undertaking is one of the most im-

portant epistemological efforts in modern times.[55]

Finally, it is important to recognize that the concerns outlined above have filtered down through political science to some of the field's most practical areas of research. In public administration, for instance, William Scott and David Hart argued that administrative policymaking should be rephased by casting it in the context of political philosophy and moral discourse.[56] Modern society, they maintained, confronts an "administrative crisis." Where most writers stress the need for better administrative management, Scott and Hart locate the problem in the value structure of the administrative elite that directs the modern technologically oriented managerial society. Subscribing to an administrative metaphysic based on an instrumental conception of knowledge and reason, the premises that inform this elite's decisions and behavior remain unarticulated and, hence, unexamined. The administrative crisis is essentially a "neglect of metaphysical speculation" about goals and values. Where speculation of this type has occurred in other disciplines, two essential aspects of moral discourse have been brought into play: a vision of man's moral nature and the normative criteria required to judge the morality of social action. Pointing out the implications of these aspects of moral discourse for contemporary administrative practice, Scott and Hart insisted that moral discourse be made a part of intellectual discussion in the policy-oriented managerial sciences. Administrative theorists, they maintained, must turn to political philosophy to begin such moral discourse.

Many political scientists and sociologists—probably the majority—express doubt about how this concern for speculation advances political analysis. For behavioral scientists, this approach is devoid of systematic or coherent methodology and seems to offer merely a program of liberal education. Political philosophers, the behavioralists argue, appear to imply that the analyst must seek political wisdom from the writings of the classical political theorists and employ intuition and reflection to determine the proper course of political action.[57] This much seems certain: both political philosophers and phenomenologists have neglected the behavioralists' principal objective— rational procedures governing intersubjective communication and verification of political knowledge.

At the same time, however, many social scientists concede that phenomenologists and political philosophers raise important epistemological questions that the behavioral scientists—including Eastonian post-behavioralists—fail to deal with satisfactorily. Although the challengers do not necessarily question the use of such tools as survey research or regression analysis, they have raised serious questions about the fundamental logic of the behavioral perspective. Within theoretical circles of the discipline, some writers now call for a "multimethodological" approach to political analysis.[58] A growing number recognize the need to pay more attention to the connections between empirical political theory and the interpretive models of political inquiry, especially political philosophy.[59] Political evaluation, in short, requires a unified theory of these several methods of explanation.

It is clear that the attack on behavioral science methodology cannot be sidestepped by merely reorienting inquiry to policy issues.[60] Evidence for such a conclusion is found in the fact that the value problem begins to crop up in discussions among behavioralists who have redirected their energies to policy analysis. Many of the same questions arise, although frequently under different labels or categories. In policy analysis, the problem of values has reasserted itself through the concept of "political feasibility" and the methodological implications that surround it.

The Fact-Value Problem in Policy Methodology

Following the lead of Easton and other post-behavioralists, policy analysis moved into the forefront of political science. As Kenneth Dolbeare reported, "Meetings of political scientists have heard in plenary sessions and elsewhere that the study of domestic policy consequences will be a central factor in a 'post-behavioral revolution' in political science—a move toward the social use of the skills developed by the behavioral movement."[61] In political science, it has become an organizing concept in the curriculum.

Spurred by the vast amount of social legislation in the 1960s and 1970s that carried a policy analysis requirement (particularly in the areas of education, manpower training, community action, and racial segregation) numerous governmental study commissions were set up to analyze the role of behavioral science in policy analysis.[62] Although these initiatives have created a small industry of academic and private consultants engaged in policy and program analysis, the substantive outcomes have been less than optimistic. In terms of practical contributions to program or policy decisions, the history of these efforts is disappointing. Few examples of significant contributions can be cited.[63] There has been, as a consequence, a slow but growing recognition in the policy analysis literature that data on efficient means and program performance provide an insufficient base for a successful intervention strategy. Even though everyone appears to be in favor of more policy analysis, there are very serious questions about the ability to translate its findings into useful information for political decision making. Charles Schultze summarized the dilemma:

> It is somewhat of a paradox that in precisely those programs . . . where there are relatively good data, where market prices can provide at least an initial guide to the evaluation of output, and where a long tradition of theoretical and empirical work exists that program analysis is faced with the greatest political constraints. On the other hand, in those growing social programs whose very newness offers a wider range of political options, analysis is faced with severe constraints by the scarcity of data and by rudimentary theoretical background. What we can do best analytically we find hardest to achieve politically.[64]

Those seeking to take politics out of the policy decision-making process are generally disappointed. Decision making within every policy area is motivated by the political processes of negotiation, compromise, and accommodation. Facts, as one writer has said, "have an impact [only] to the extent that program effectiveness—inevitably and justifiably—competes for influence on decisions with considerations of acceptability, feasibility and ideology."[65] Leading policy analysts have become much more aware that attention must be paid to the political dimensions of policy decision making, especially the recognition of diverse political values, recruitment of political support, and accommodation of contradictory goals and objectives. Meltsner argues that the policy analyst's focus on the political dimensions of policy will inevitably be the lever that secures the researcher's role in the policy decision-making process.[66]

This raises the theoretical question of how a particular policy relates to the existing structure of social values. To determine the "political feasibility" of a policy, the analyst must ascertain its ability to generate support for the particular institution or agency that promotes it. The policy analyst must explore for each alternative a series of conditional statements: If A is recommended, will B support it and C oppose it? Empirically, this involves an exploration of operating beliefs and values in the relevant political environment. Specifically, Yehezkel Dror has emphasized "the need for evaluation of the probability that a policy will be sufficiently acceptable to the various secondary political decision-makers, executors, interest groups and publics whose participation or acquiesence is needed for it to be translated into political action."[67]

The scientific logic of the task is clear: The policy analyst must sort out the political norms and values that bear on a particular policy problem and relate them to empirically established causal knowledge about the problem's underlying social processes. The policy scientist can rely on techniques such as value mapping.[68] The task is to determine the compatibility of a desired goal with other accepted goals in a normative framework. If there is goal conflict, the analyst must decide which to accept or eliminate, under which circumstances, and to what extent or degree. After establishing a congruent pattern of goals, the analyst must determine which variables within the decision maker's control operate as causes contributing to the desired goal. The search is for causal regularities with practical consequences for the achievement of the goal. Once a cause-and-effect relationship is identified, it can be mapped into the normative framework of goals and values.

Such an approach is essentially governed by the logic of scientific methodology. In this framework, values are integrated into the policy model as causal variables related to specific empirical conditions and consequences. A methodology of political acceptability or feasibility is translated here into a scheme for modeling and prediction. The ideal, according to Meltsner, is an analytical integration of political categories and data into the structure of a mathematical policy model.[69] Similarly, Dror and Majone stated that political feasibility should be expressed as a "probability distribution" of each policy alternative.[70] Conceived within the framework of a mathematical model, the influence of political knowledge will depend on political science's ability to quantify political factors.

However, Meltsner, Dror, and Majone are aware of the major dilemma posed by the scientific ideal. Even if it is theoretically possible (a subject of contemporary debate), it suffers the empirical limitations of a scientific value theory in general. Given the state of the art of quantification, the scientific approach is far beyond the reach of contemporary social science. First, it requires the ability to quantify normative political variables without distorting their fundamental or essential characteristics. Generally, analysts must rely on the use of indirect proxy variables designed only to estimate normative characteristics. Values usually emerge from the process as conceptually static and noncomplex. Second, the scientific approach implies the possibility of integrating these quantified normative variables into an empirically grounded theoretical model of the underlying social process, a model capable of connecting cause-and-effect relationships with means-ends relationships. The explanatory power of the available policy models is far from the level needed to provide the foundation for the design and development of effective intervention strategies. Such models can retrospectively isolate variables that assist in explanation, but are far too imprecise to generate predictive or causal knowledge. (See Appendix, p. 219.)

Equally important, the failure of the analytic process is also fostered by the overly simplistic conception of values and value clarification that lies behind it.[71] Peter Brown and Martin Rein attributed this failure to misleading positivistic assumptions, based on the fact-value dichotomy, that underplay the complexity of the nature of values and the character of normative relationships.[72] Under positivistic assumptions, the task of normative analysis, borrowed and adapted from Weber, is limited to the explication and elaboration of the consistency of value judgments and the examination of their logical implications for social action. For the policy analyst, this means tracing the relationship of an established goal to a fixed or static web of values surrounding a social problem. Once this is accomplished, normative variables can be quantified and plugged into the larger empirical model, which specifies the causal relationships that underlie the desired social action. Beyond these formal tasks, which are to a large degree technical in character, little further reflection about values is required.

Examination of the actual policy research process, however, shows the analytic approach to be a misleading simplification if not a fundamental epistemological mistake. Value positions in policy research seldom prove to be static conceptions that remain fixed and unchanging; rather, they tend to shift iteratively as the analyst moves through the phases of data collection, analysis, and interpretation. New data and knowledge frequently have a direct impact on the content and desirability of normative policy goals. Normative analysis, therefore, becomes an ongoing process that continues to occur throughout the phases of empirical policy research.

In large part, the failure of the analytic process is the result of the tendency to treat values as external to the particular social and material conditions that give rise to them in the first place. In actuality, as phenomenologists point out, values are internally related to specific life understandings.[73] Rather than entities located "out there," which can be abstracted from specific empirical relationships, values are part of the conceptual system (or world view) employed in constructing—and reconstructing—the social world of which they are a part. As such, they can be properly understood only from within a particular social context or situation.

Under value mapping, then, which separates empirical and normative investigation, the analysis of values remains peripheral to the social process. Values in policy evaluation are treated as a web or network that externally "surrounds" a social problem rather than as an internally related characteristic that exerts its own causal force. As an internal dimension of the social problem, values are already implicitly embodied in the construction of the causal policy model itself. In value mapping, therefore, the policy analyst is in the curious position of attempting to fit values (conceived as external and independent) into a causal model that (assuming the model is properly constructed) already houses the particular value relationships that belong to it.

In part, the policy analyst's problem is one of looking for value relationships in the wrong place. By treating values as external, the normative relationships logically explicated to fit the causal policy model tend to be the values ascribed by outsiders. The implications for action derived from the process are generally the formal logical implications deduced from the external point of view rather than the results drawn from informal discursive logic geared to the internal dialectical processes that motivate and move the social system. In phenomenological terminology, the positivist produces a reified second-order construct of the social actor's values.

As normative variables detached from the dialectical tensions of the social processes, these second-order constructions—proxy variables in the language of statistics—emerge as ephemeral shadows that fail to convey, let alone predict, the deeper processes that underlie social action. This, of course, largely occurs by epistemological design. Based on the tenets of moral relativism in value noncognitivism, it is the result of a rejection of the possibility of deeper social processes. Under moral relativism, values, like any other variable, can in the final analysis be manipulated as interchangeable symbols in an equation. Any particular value can be assigned or attached to any factual situation. Insofar as a factual proposition does not entail a particular value, value judgments are held to depend upon an independent, external set of values that each actor (for reasons that may be unique to him- or herself) brings to the situation. Independent of the empirical world, divorced from the construction of the causal policy model, one value therefore has as much status as another.

On an operational level, then, normative analysis is more complicated than it first appears. What is worse, when reduced to the epistemological level, the question of how to relate qualitative political norms and values to quantitative program performance data turns out to be a technical version of the fact-value problem. At this point, the policy analyst's concern with facts and values converges with the epistemological fact-value questions raised by phenomenologists and political philosophers. Although the similarity of the concerns is not generally recognized in the policy literature, policy analysis confronts the same methodological questions about how to relate facts to values and causes to reasons. Rein is one of the few policy writers who have recognized the underlying significance of this problem in policy science. He contended that the future of a relevant policy science hinges on the methodological integration of empirical and normative judgments.[74]

The policy analyst encounters a dilemma here: The methodological tools for both the empirical and normative dimensions of a value-mapping process are underdeveloped. Causal models can locate variables that assist in explaining social observations, but their margins of error are too wide to be useful in policy decision making. At the same time, the methods of normative analysis rest on simplistic assumptions about the role of values in the social process.

In recognition of these methodological limitations, a number of writers—particularly Dror, Majone, Meltsner, and Rein—have attempted to provoke discussion about the development of a political methodology for policy evaluation. Aware that the scientific model leaves analysts without reasonable prospects of developing a methodology for political evaluation, they have advocated the development of less rigorous but more practical approaches to normative policy analysis. These theorists have suggested that at least during the interim stages of scientific development, the policy sciences should further explore the use of scenario writing, the Delphi method, and other techniques based on trained insight, imagination, and conjecture (terms reminiscent of the phenomenologist's and philosopher's concepts of *verstehen,* vision, speculation, and so on). To compensate for the limited state of the policy sciences, policy analysis programs should supplement scientific methodology with training in the art of "political judgment."[75]

An appeal to political judgment is an interesting suggestion, especially coming from scientifically oriented writers. However, these writers provide little indication as to how this advances the search for a policy methodology. As a suggestion, it only turns the policy analyst to the normative side of the fact-value dichotomy, where he or she is the impoverished legatee of the underdeveloped normative methods of value-free behavioral science.

An Alternative Approach

The urgency and complexity of this methodological problem has led some theorists to renew epistemological exploration within the policy sciences. Ian Mitroff and Louis Pondy, for example, maintained that new methodological directions "can only be gotten outside the usual modes of thinking by going to fields of inquiry, like the philosophy of science, which traditionally have been conceived to be far removed from the concerns of both organizational theory and policy analysis."[76] Similarly, Charles Anderson suggested that the development of a "logic of policy evaluation" must draw as much from the philosophy of science as from established social science methods.[77] Policy scientists must begin to explore policy evaluation as a mode of inquiry with its own rules and procedures.

One of the most interesting directions to emerge from such explorations is that of a "forensic" social science. Writers such as C. W. Churchman, Duncan MacRae, Jr., Alice Rivlin, and Peter Brown have suggested that normative analysis can be facilitated by an organized dialogue between competing normative positions.[78] In such a scheme, policy analysts and decision makers would each take on the assignment of preparing briefs for and against the particular policy positions. As Rivlin suggested, they would "state what the position is and bring together all the evidence that supports their side of the argument, leaving to the brief writers of the other side the job of picking apart the case that has been presented and detailing the counter evidence."[79]

Such policy argumentation starts with the recognition that the participants do not have solid answers to the questions under discussion, or even a solid method for getting the answers. With this understanding the policy analyst and decision maker attempt to develop a meaningful synthesis of perspectives. Churchman and his followers suggested that the procedure should take the form of a debate.[80] They maintained that the problem posed by the absence of appropriate evaluative criteria can be mitigated by designing rational procedures to govern a formal communication between the various points of view that bear on the decision-making process. Such a procedure is based on an awareness of the symbiotic relationship that exists between the various functional components in an organization or social system. The fact that normative-oriented decision makers and empirical policy analysts have fundamentally different approaches to problem solving does not lead to an irreconcilable situation. Where the qualitative decision maker attempts to coordinate relevant interests around specific norms and goals, the quantitative analyst's task is to provide information about the probable success of various means to these goals. In organizational terms, these are the respective functions of the "manager" and the "expert."[81] Much unused or unusable analysis is often simply the result of a lack of communication between quantitative and qualitative decision makers. By establishing an understanding based on their separate perspectives, Churchman suggested that decision makers and analysts can work out a functional synthesis through a "dialectical communication" based on the rules and procedures of formal debate.[82]

In such a debate, each party confronts the other with counterproposals based on varying perceptions of the facts. The participants in the exchange organize the established data and fit it into the world views that underlie their own arguments. The grounds or criteria for accepting or rejecting a proposal must be the same grounds for accepting or rejecting a counterproposal and must be based on precisely the same data. Operating at the point where theory and science confront practice and ethics, both policy analysts and decision makers can explore and compare the underlying assumptions being used. Such a debate would help eliminate a common scenario: the policymaker presents the analyst with a problem, the analyst returns within a specified period with an evaluation, and the policymaker ignores the outcome.[83] Moreover, this procedure would not need to be confined to the interaction between organizational decision

makers and policy analysts. Ideally, as Churchman and Schainblatt have pointed out, it could be extended to the widest possible range of differing viewpoints drawn from the policy
environment.[84]

In this scheme, the formalized debate itself is seen as the
most instructive part of the analytical process. The technique
is designed to clarify the underlying goals and norms that give
shape to competing world views, and enables qualitative judgment to be exercised in as unhampered a way as possible. The
free exercise of normative judgment, released from the restrictions of the formal policy model, increases the chance of developing a synthesis of normative perspectives that can provide
a legitimate and acceptable basis for decisions and actions based
on the strongest possible argument. Even if analysts and decision
makers cannot agree, the forensic approach provides a procedure
for probing the normative implications of recommendations and
for indicating certain favored normative conclusions. At the
minimum, the technique goes a great distance toward removing
the ideological mask that often shields policy analysis from
genuine objectivity.

At this point, the relationship of the phenomenologist's
practical life-world to the behavioral scientist's empirical framework begins to become more apparent. Where behavioral science
attempts to adapt qualitative data about norms and values to an
empirical model through quantification, the forensic model
reverses the process by fitting the quantitative data into the
normative world view. In the latter case, pragmatic validity is
tested, criticized, and interpreted by qualitative arguments
based on value perspectives or world views. Here the locus of
the interpretation process is shifted from the scientific audience
to the practical-world audience. In the transition, the final
outcome of evaluative inquiry shifts from scientific demonstration and verification to the giving of reasons and the assessment
of practical arguments. In the earlier discussion of interpretive
explanation (where Schutz suggested a courtroom analogy),
the valid interpretation is the one that survives the widest range
of criticisms and objections. In the proposed debate model,
each participant would cite not only causal relationships, but
also norms, values, and circumstances to support or justify a

particular decision. As practical arguments, such interpretive evaluations connect policy options and situations by illuminating the features of those situations that provide grounds for policy decisions.

The forensic or communications approach is an important step toward the development of a dynamic methodology designed to facilitate complex dialectical value exploration throughout the policy research process. Like any step forward, however, it brings the methodologist to the next set of hurdles. The logical question that arises is this: If both analysts and decision makers must employ the same grounds or criteria in their respective arguments, what are these criteria? Here the technique encounters the fundamental fact-value problem of normative criteria: Are there criteria or grounds for mediating normative-based practical discourse? Practical debate brings the value dimensions of policy into sharper focus, but this is not to be confused with methodology per se. Given the long history of arguments in philosophy and the social sciences about value judgments, it is reasonable to surmise that the methodological success of the forensic model ultimately rests on the elaboration of rules that govern the exchange of normative arguments. Rational inquiry—whether scientific or normative—depends upon the availability of standards and rules that can serve as criteria for valid judgment (i.e., operational rules permitting the formulation of more or less general propositions or conclusions that are not specifically included in the data but legitimately deduced, inferred, or extracted from them).[85] In a normative exchange, it is often easy to agree that one argument is more persuasive than another, but it is not always clear how that is known. It is the absence of such normative judgments that has led to the epistemological demise of normative theorizing in the contemporary social sciences.

Several writers have recognized this problem, at least indirectly. One approach is to extend the legal-oriented analogy of brief writing to include the concept of "rules of evidence."[86] By studying the rules and procedures that govern legal argumentation in the courtroom, the policy sciences might gain insight into rules of argumentation that can be adapted to the policy deliberation process. Such an approach would permit the policy analyst to concede the limitations of formal social science models as decision-making tools but, at the same time, salvage the insights that they do offer. By combining empirical analysis, forensic policy debate, and the development of rules of evidence, policy scientists can potentially move the policy evaluation process toward a judicious mix of pragmatism and rigor.

The Nobel Prize–winning economist Kenneth Arrow, noted for his work in quantitative model construction, and Duncan MacRae, Jr., are among those who have stressed the value of supplying the policy sciences with a regulated discourse that commands the kind of rigor found in law.[87] The advantage of regulated communication, according to MacRae, is that it stands "apart from the discourse of ordinary life in several attributes such as precise definitions, stress on written rather than oral communication, and limitation of meaning to what has been specified in advance."[88] In such a discourse, a statement or judgment can be given a precise definition and interpretation by a larger audience. A legal essay, for instance, written by trained legal specialists, directs the attention of similarly trained readers to statements and conclusions that can be systematically reexamined by shared rules and methods.

The concept of rules of evidence in law suggests the development of logical rules for policy argumentation. Both MacRae and Anderson urged policy scientists to explore the possibility of borrowing and adapting the rules of normative analysis employed in political philosophy (the third methodology in the epistemological dispute). As Anderson stated, policy analysts fail to recognize that "their concern with cost-benefit analysis is only an episode in a long Western tradition of defining principles appropriate to judge the legitimacy and propriety of political activity."[89] (At the same time, political philosophers are able to examine the policy of representation in the eighteenth century but seem incapable of scrutinizing the problem of participation in modern-day economic planning.)

As a suggestive attempt to bridge this gap, MacRae introduced three logical tests that are employed in political philosophy: logical clarity, logical consistency, and generality.[90] Logical clarity refers to "the capacity of a verbal or symbolic expression to indicate precisely those observations or actions to which it would or would not apply, independently of the speaker, the listener, or subsequent explanation." Logical consistency refers to the capacity of "a set of principles to withstand searching scrutiny and to reveal no instances in which its implications are contradictory." Generality refers to the "breadth of application" of the principle across a wide range of arguments or ethical positions. MacRae presented these tests in three basic procedural rules:

a. Lack of generality. The proposed system fails to apply to a choice about which both discussants have moral convictions and to which the critic's system does apply.

b. Internal inconsistency. The proposed system makes contradictory prescriptions in a situation suggested by the critic, in which the critic's system is self-consistent.

c. Inconsistency with presumably shared moral convictions. The proposed system makes a prescription which, in a specified "conflict situation," conflicts with moral convictions presumably shared with the discussants, while the critic's system does not lead to such conflict.[91]

These are essential principles and rules of normative analysis that belong in policy deliberation. MacRae is correct in stating that policy arguments are seldom proposed with the degree of clarity and consistency that his scheme provides. Indeed, such arguments usually amount to little more than idiosyncratic criticisms advanced in ad hoc fashion. Policies would clearly benefit from a rigorous application of these logical procedures; unfortunately, they remain too abstract to serve as a basis for a policy methodology. It is not clear from MacRae's work what the operational rules for analytical layout and interpretation of policy arguments are, especially arguments involving both facts and values.

A second approach to the development of analytical rules in the literature refers more directly to the practical aspects of policy methodology. Writers such as Hambrick, Brock, Chesebro, Cragen, and Klumpp have sought the logical structure of policy arguments by studying policy discussions. For Hambrick, the task was to explicate the propositional components that constitute a logically complete policy argument. With the

TABLE 1
Hambrick's Policy Components

1. Action Proposal:	A statement specifying a proposed policy action.
2. Policy Proposition:	A statement indicating both the action(s) and goal(s) believed to lead to the policy action.
3. Grounding Proposition:	Definitional or conceptual statements stipulating a proven or assumed empirical claim that lays a foundation for the policy proposition.
4. Normative Proposition:	A statement specifying the positive or negative value derived from the policy goals.
5. External Impact Proposition:	A statement describing the policy action's impact on other than the intended goal(s).
6. Causal Proposition:	A statement specifying the immediate cause-and-effect relationship that results in the goal.
7. Instrumental Proposition:	A statement that turns the independent variable in the causal proposition into a dependent variable in the evaluation.
8. Time-Place Propositions:	Statements establishing the temporal and spatial configuration of variables providing an empirical base for assessing the need for policy intervention.
9. Constraint Proposition:	A statement of factors that potentially alter the instrumental or causal propositions.
10. Comparative Proposition:	A statement about the efficiency or effectiveness of the policy action.

Source: Ralph S. Hambrick, Jr., "A Guide for the Analysis of Policy Arguments," Policy Sciences 5 (December 1974). Used by permission of the author and publisher.

assistance of such components, it is possible for the analyst to determine the kinds of evidence needed to support, reject, or modify a policy proposal.[92] In Table 1, Hambrick offers ten propositional components as a logical structure for policy analysis.

Brock, Chesebro, Cragen, and Klumpp approached the problem from the point of view of argumentation theory in public speaking and the systems perspective.[93] Designed specifically as a tool for research and analysis in forensic debate, they offered a series of question formats for the description and evaluation of policy alternatives organized around a systems framework. Like Hambrick, they suggested a useful line of investigation. These schemes, however, are limited by their emphasis on the empirical, technical questions that underlie policy arguments—questions about cause and effect, costs and benefits of alternative means, and unanticipated impacts. While they avoid the methodological abstractions of political philosophy, they fail to deal adequately with the task of normative analysis. Still missing is a statement of logical structure that relates factual evidence to normative deliberation.

The question, then, is how to develop a practical framework that integrates both empirical and normative judgments. It is quite similar to the question posed by ordinary-language philosophers who study practical reason in everyday life. The similarity of concerns, in fact, suggests practical reason as a potential avenue of methodological exploration for policy evaluation. Before proceeding with an explication of practical reason, however, it is important to clarify what is involved in a "political" evaluation and the problem of rational judgment associated with it.

Notes

1. Max Weber, *The Methodology of the Social Sciences*, trans. and ed. Edward A. Shils and Henry A. Finch (New York: Free Press, 1949), p. 56.

2. Evron M. Kirkpatrick, "The Impact of the Behavioral Approach on Traditional Political Science," in *Essays on the Behavioral Study of Politics,* ed. Austin Ranney (Urbana: University of Illinois Press, 1962),

pp. 1–30; and George J. Graham, Jr., *Methodological Foundations for Political Analysis* (Waltham, Mass.: Xerox College Publishing Co., 1971). For an epistemological discussion of the relationship of causal knowledge to social intervention, see Brian Fay, *Social Theory and Political Practice* (New York: Holmes and Meier, 1975), pp. 18–48.

3. See, for example, Charles A. McCoy and John Playford, eds., *Apolitical Politics: A Critique of Behavioralism* (New York: Thomas Y. Crowell Co., 1967).

4. Because the nature of physical or natural science research methods has increasingly been criticized by leading scientists, there is some confusion associated with the use of the term "physical science methods." To avoid this problem, the term is employed here to refer to the general methodological traditions aligned with the Newtonian, positivistic, or logical empiricist conceptions of physical science, unless otherwise specified. In the physical sciences, see Gary Zukav, *The Dancing Wu Li Masters: An Overview of the New Physics* (New York: William Morrow & Co., 1979); and Imre Lakatos and Alan Musgrave, eds., *Criticism and the Growth of Knowledge* (Cambridge: Cambridge University Press, 1970). In the social sciences, see Richard J. Bernstein, *The Restructuring of Social and Political Theory* (New York: Harcourt Brace Jovanovich, 1976).

5. T. D. Weldon, *The Vocabulary of Politics* (London: Penguin Books, 1953).

6. Weber, *Methodology*, pp. 49–112.

7. Eugene J. Meehan, *Contemporary Political Thought* (Homewood, Ill.: Dorsey Press, 1967), p. 354.

8. Harold Lasswell, *A Pre-View of the Policy Sciences* (New York: American Elsevier, 1971), p. 41.

9. Ibid.

10. Ludwig von Mises, *Epistemological Problems of Economics* (Princeton, N.J.: D. Van Nostrand Co., 1960), p. 148.

11. Paul Diesing, *Reason in Society: Five Types of Decisions in Their Social Contexts* (Urbana: University of Illinois Press, 1962), p. 1.

12. David Easton, "The New Revolution in Political Science," *American Political Science Review* 63 (December 1969):1057.

13. Ibid.

14. Victor A. Thompson, *Without Sympathy or Enthusiasm: The Problem of Administrative Compassion* (University: University of Alabama, 1975), p. 65.

15. Gresham Riley, "Introduction," in *Values, Objectivity and the Social Sciences,* ed. Gresham Riley (Reading, Mass.: Addison-Wesley Publishing Co., 1974), pp. 3–6. See also Israel Scheffler, *Science and Subjectivity* (New York: Bobbs-Merrill Co., 1967); and Thomas S. Kuhn,

The Structure of Scientific Revolutions (Chicago: University of Chicago Press, 1970).

16. George J. Graham, Jr., and George W. Carey, eds., *The Post-Behavioral Era: Perspectives on Political Science* (New York: David McKay Co., 1972).

17. Karl Mannheim, *Ideology and Utopia* (New York: Harcourt, Brace and World, 1936), pp. 13–54. For a discussion of the historical background against which these disputes take place, see Ralf Dahrendorf, "Values and the Social Sciences: The Value Dispute in Perspective," in *Essays in the Theory of Society*, ed. Ralf Dahrendorf (Stanford, Calif.: Stanford University Press, 1968), pp. 1–18.

18. Bruce E. Wright, "Normative Principles and Prescription in Political Theory," *Bucknell Review* 19 (Fall 1971):3; and Michael Haas, "Three Types of Science," *PS* 2 (Fall 1969):598–599.

19. H. George Frederickson, "Toward a New Public Administration," in *Toward a New Public Administration*, ed. Frank Marini (Scranton, Pa.: Chandler Publishing Co., 1971), pp. 315–316.

20. Ibid.

21. Maria J. Falco, *Truth and Meaning in Political Science* (Columbus, Ohio: Charles E. Merrill, 1973), p. 97.

22. David Easton, "Commentary on Lane's Paper," in *Integration of the Social Sciences Through Policy Analysis*, ed. James C. Charlesworth (Philadelphia: American Academy of Political and Social Science, 1972), p. 92.

23. Philip L. Beardsley, "A Critique of Post-Behavioralism," *Political Theory* 5 (February 1977):7.

24. Falco, *Truth and Meaning*, p. 110.

25. Ibid., p. 111.

26. Kurt Baier, "The Concept of Value," *Journal of Value Inquiry* 1 (Spring 1967):1.

27. Easton, "Commentary on Lane's Paper," pp. 91–92.

28. George Henrik von Wright, *Explanation and Understanding* (Ithaca, N.Y.: Cornell University Press, 1971).

29. Alfred Schutz, *The Phenomenology of the Social World*, trans. George Walsh and Frederick Lehnert (Evanston, Ill.: Northwestern University Press, 1967).

30. See David Silverman, *The Theory of Organizations* (New York: Basic Books, 1971), pp. 126–127, for a good summary of the phenomenological position.

31. Alfred Schutz, *Collected Papers*, vol. 1 ed. Maurice Natanson (The Hague: Martinus Nijhoff, 1962), 1:5.

32. Alfred Schutz, *Collected Papers,* vol. 2 ed. Avrid Brodersen (The Hague: Martinus Nijhoff, 1966), 2:5-6.

33. David Walsh, "Sociology and the Social World," in Paul Filmer et al., *New Directions in Sociological Theory* (Cambridge, Mass.: M.I.T. Press, 1972), p. 18.

34. Arthur Kalleberg, "Concept Formation in Normative and Empirical Studies: Toward a Reconciliation in Political Theory," *American Political Science Review* 63 (March 1969):31; and Alfred Schutz, "Concept and Theory Formation in the Social Sciences," *Journal of Philosophy* 51 (April 1954):265.

35. Leon J. Goldstein, "The Phenomenological and Naturalistic Approaches to the Social," in *Philosophy of the Social Sciences,* ed. Maurice Natanson (New York: Random House, 1963), pp. 386-401.

36. See Hwa Yol Jung, "The Political Relevance of Existential Phenomenology," *Review of Politics* 33 (October 1971):551.

37. Schutz, "Concept and Theory Formation," p. 264.

38. See Walsh, "Sociology and the Social World," p. 29.

39. These examples were borrowed from K. W. Kim, "The Limits of Behavioral Explanation in Politics," in McCoy and Playford, *Apolitical Politics,* pp. 52-53.

40. Berger and Luckmann's "dialectical phenomenology" is an important case in point. See Peter L. Berger and Thomas Luckmann, *The Social Construction of Reality* (New York: Doubleday & Co., 1967). For a full discussion of this trend see Robert W. Friedrich, *A Sociology of Sociology* (New York: Free Press, 1970).

41. Marvin Surkin, "Sense and Nonsense in Politics," *PS* 2 (Fall 1969): 581; and Marvin Surkin and Alan Wolfe, eds., *An End to Political Science* (New York: Basic Books, 1970).

42. Gibson Winter, *Elements for a Social Ethics: The Role of Social Science in Public Policy* (New York: Macmillan, 1966).

43. Jürgen Habermas, *Toward a Rational Society* (Boston: Beacon Press, 1970), pp. 62-122.

44. Leo Strauss, *What is Political Philosophy?* (Glencoe, Ill.: Free Press, 1959), pp. 9-55; also, for an excellent introduction to the problem see John G. Gunnell, *Political Theory* (Cambridge, Mass.: Winthrop, 1979).

45. Ibid.

46. Ibid., p. 10.

47. In addition to Strauss, see Eric Voegelin, *The New Science of Politics* (Chicago: University of Chicago Press, 1952); and Charner Perry, "The Semantics of Political Science," *American Political Science Review* 44 (June 1950):398.

48. Leo Strauss, *Natural Right and History* (Chicago: University of Chicago Press, 1953).

49. J. Donald Moon, "The Logic of Political Inquiry," in *The Handbook of Political Science*, ed. Nelson W. Polsby and Fred D. Greenstein (Reading, Mass.: Addison-Wesley Publishing Co., 1975), 1:210; and Thomas A. Spragens, Jr., *Understanding Political Theory* (New York: St. Martin's Press, 1976).

50. Eugene F. Miller, "Positivism, Historicism, and Political Inquiry," *American Political Science Review* 66 (September 1972):817.

51. The following comments are from Sheldon S. Wolin, "Political Theory as a Vocation," *American Political Science Review* 63 (December 1969):1073-1074.

52. Martin Jay, *The Dialectical Imagination* (Boston: Little, Brown and Co., 1973).

53. Max Horkheimer, *Critical Theory* (New York: Seabury Press, 1972); Jürgen Habermas, *Theory and Practice* (Boston: Beacon Press, 1973); and Max Horkheimer and Theodor W. Adorno, *Dialectic of Enlightenment* (New York: Herder & Herder, 1972).

54. Horkheimer, *Critical Theory*, p. 215.

55. Habermas, *Theory and Practice.*

56. William G. Scott and David K. Hart, "Administrative Crisis: The Neglect of Metaphysical Speculation," *Public Administration Review* 33 (September–October 1973):415–422. For a related discussion, see Walter A. Weisskopf, *Alienation and Economics* (New York: Dell Publishing Co., 1972), pp. 116-151.

57. Wright, "Normative Principles," p. 9.

58. Michael Haas and Theodore L. Becker, "The Behavioral Revolution and After," in *Approaches to the Study of Political Science*, ed. Michael Haas and Henry Kariel (Scranton, Pa.: Chandler Publishing Co., 1970), pp. 479-510.

59. Moon, "The Logic of Political Inquiry," p. 209. He states, "One of the most vexing issues in the methodology of political science is the relationship between empirical inquiry and theory, on the one hand, and political philosophy and political evaluation, on the other."

60. Wright, "Normative Principles," p. 6.

61. Kenneth M. Dolbeare, "Public Policy Analysis and the Coming Struggle for the Soul of the Postbehavioral Revolution," in *Power and Community: Dissenting Essays in Political Science*, ed. P. Green and S. Levinson (New York: Random House, 1969), p. 85.

62. See, for example, National Science Board, *Knowledge Into Action: Improving the Nation's Use of the Social Sciences* (Washington, D.C.: 1969).

63. Carol H. Weiss, *Evaluation Research: Methods of Assessing Program Effectiveness* (Englewood Cliffs, N.J.: Prentice-Hall, 1972), p. 3. See also Weiss, "Improving the Linkage Between Social Research and Public Policy," in *Knowledge and Policy: The Uncertain Connection,* ed. Laurence E. Lynn (Washington, D.C.: National Academy of Sciences, 1978), pp. 23–81.

64. Charles L. Schultze, *The Politics and Economics of Public Spending* (Washington, D.C.: Brookings Institution, 1968), p. 89.

65. Weiss, *Evaluation Research,* pp. 3–4.

66. Arnold J. Meltsner, "Political Feasibility and Policy Analysis," *Public Administration Review* 32 (November–December 1972):859.

67. Yehezkel Dror, *Public Policymaking Reexamined* (San Francisco: Chandler Publishing Co., 1968), p. 35.

68. Martin Rein, *Social Science and Public Policy* (New York: Penguin Books, 1976), pp. 43–58; also see Paul Kecskemeti, "The 'Policy Sciences': Aspiration and Outlook," *World Politics* 4 (October 1951):523–524.

69. Meltsner, "Political Feasibility."

70. See Yehezkel Dror, "The Prediction of Political Feasibility," *Futures* 1 (June 1969):282–288; and Giandomenico Majone, "On the Notion of Political Feasibility," in *Policy Studies Review Annual,* ed. Stuart S. Nagel (Beverly Hills, Calif.: Sage Publications, 1977), p. 82. For an illustration of an attempt to quantitatively integrate social value judgments and scientific information, see Kenneth R. Hammond and Leonard Adelman, "Science, Values and Human Judgment," in *Judgment and Decision in Public Policy Formation,* ed. Kenneth R. Hammond (Boulder, Colo.: Westview Press, 1978), pp. 119-141; and Douglas Rae and Michael Taylor, "Decision Rules and Policy Outcomes," *British Journal of Political Science* 1 (January 1972):71–90.

71. For a guide to some recent controversies about value clarification, see John S. Stewart, "Problems and Contradictions of Value Clarification," in *Moral Education . . . It Comes with the Territory,* ed. David Purpel and Kevin Ryan (Berkeley, Calif.: McCutchan, 1976), pp. 136-151; and Andrew Oldenquist, "Moral Education Without Moral Education," *Harvard Educational Review* 49 (May 1979):240-247.

72. Peter G. Brown, "Ethics and Policy Research," *Policy Analysis* 2 (Spring 1976):325–340; and Rein, *Social Science and Public Policy,* pp. 37–95.

73. See, for example, Walsh, "Sociology and the Social World," p. 29.

74. Rein, *Social Science and Public Policy,* p. 249.

75. Dror, "The Prediction of Political Feasibility"; Majone, "On the Notion of Political Feasibility"; Meltsner, "Political Feasibility"; and Rein, *Social Science and Public Policy.* Meltsner put it this way: "Simple political

sensitivity is not enough. If the analyst is going to have a political orientation toward his work, he should be taught to use his knowledge of politics
and to exercise his political judgment. The point is that the student must
analytically engage in politics himself: learning about the political process—
that there is a President, a Congress, and that policy making is complex—
is interesting but insufficient." See also Ralph H. Huitt, "Political Feasibility," in *Political Science and Public Policy,* ed. Austin Ranney (Chicago:
Markham, 1968). On making policy judgments, see Sir Geoffrey Vickers,
The Art of Judgment (New York: Basic Books, 1965).

On the Delphi method, see Harold A. Linstone and Murray Turoff,
eds., *The Delphi Method* (Reading, Mass.: Addison-Wesley Publishing
Co., 1975). The Delphi method is a technique designed to aid decision
makers in forecasting events. It involves the repetitive use of a controlled
questionnaire administered to selected experts who serve as an advisory
committee. The purpose is to develop consensus in a given area about
anticipated events where no previous consensus existed.

76. Ian I. Mitroff and Louis Pondy, "On the Organization of Inquiry:
A Comparison of Some Radically Different Approaches to Policy Analysis," *Public Administration Review* 34 (September–October 1974):513–514.

77. Charles W. Anderson, "The Logic of Public Problems: Evaluation in
Comparative Policy Research," in *Comparing Public Policies: New Con-
cepts and Methods,* ed. Douglas E. Ashford (Beverly Hills, Calif.: Sage
Publications, 1978), pp. 19–42.

78. C. West Churchman, *The Design of Inquiring Systems* (New York:
Basic Books, 1971); C. West Churchman and A. H. Schainblatt, "PPB:
How Can It Be Implemented?" *Public Administration Review* 29 (March–
April 1969):178–189; Duncan MacRae, Jr., "Scientific Communication,
Ethical Argument and Public Policy," *American Political Science Review*
65 (March 1971):38–50; Alice Rivlin, "Forensic Social Science," *Perspec-
tives on Inequality,* Harvard Educational Review Reprint Series, no. 8
(Cambridge, Mass.: Harvard University Press, 1973); Gordon Bermant and
Peter Brown, *Evaluating Forensic Social Science* (Columbus, Ohio:
Academy for Contemporary Problems, 1975); and Peter Brown, "Ethics
and Policy Research."

79. Rivlin, "Forensic Social Science," p. 25.

80. See note 78 above. Ian I. Mitroff, "A Communication Model of
Dialectical Inquiring Systems—a Strategy for Strategic Planning," *Manage-
ment Science* 17 (June 1971):B634–B648; and Richard O. Mason, "A
Dialectical Approach to Strategic Planning," *Management Science* 15
(April 1969):B403–B414.

81. See Amitai Etzioni, "Authority Structure and Organizational
Effectiveness," in *Organizational Decision Making,* ed. Marcus Alexis

and Charles Z. Wilson (Englewood Cliffs, N.J.: Prentice-Hall, 1967), pp. 14–28.

82. Churchman, *The Design of Inquiring Systems.*

83. Churchman and Schainblatt, "PPB: How Can It Be Implemented?"

84. Ibid., pp. 178–189.

85. For a discussion of inference in the social sciences, see Daniel Lerner, ed., *Evidence and Inference* (Glencoe, Ill.: Free Press, 1959).

86. See, for example, Glen G. Cain and Robinson G. Hollister, "The Methodology of Evaluating Social Programs," in *Evaluating Social Programs: Theory, Practice, and Politics,* ed. Peter Rossi and Walter Williams (New York: Seminar Press, 1972), pp. 135–136. They put the case this way: "Higher standards of evaluation will lessen the role of 'hearsay' testimony in the decision process, but they are not meant to provide a hard and fast decision rule in and of themselves. The public decision-making process is still a long way from the point at which the evidence from a hard evaluation is the primary or even the significant factor in the totality of factors which determine major decisions about programs. . . . But if standards for the acceptance of evaluation results are viewed in terms of the 'rules of evidence' analogy, we can begin to move toward the judicious mix of rigor and pragmatism that is so badly needed in evaluation analysis."

87. Remarks by Kenneth Arrow during a National Bureau of Economic Research conference concerned with the economics of public output; cited by Cain and Hollister, "The Methodology of Evaluating Social Programs." See also MacRae, "Scientific Communication, Ethical Argument and Public Policy," pp. 38–50.

88. Duncan MacRae, Jr., *The Social Function of Social Science* (New Haven, Conn.: Yale University Press, 1976), p. 85.

89. Anderson, "The Logic of Public Problems," p. 22.

90. MacRae, *The Social Function of Social Science,* p. 93.

91. Ibid.

92. Ralph S. Hambrick, Jr., "A Guide for the Analysis of Policy Arguments," *Policy Sciences* 5 (December 1974):469–478.

93. Bernard L. Brock et al., *Public Policy Decision-Making: Systems Analysis and Comparative Advantages Debates* (New York: Harper & Row, 1973); and Douglas Ehninger and Wayne Brockriede, *Decision by Debate* (New York: Harper & Row, 1978).

3

Political Evaluation and the Problem of Rational Judgment

Even if it should prove that certain philosophic doubts cannot be eliminated, combining the arguments about facts, consequences, and principles . . . it is clear that there is a significant place for reason in the consideration and decision of moral questions. . . . [P]ractical men can, at least within some limits, rest their commitment to moral rules and their evaluations of particular consequences on rational considerations, and can discourse concerning them in a reasoned manner.

—Richard E. Flathman[1]

Political evaluation has received little systematic attention in the social science literature, especially the policy literature. Although a full analysis of the concept is beyond the scope of this chapter, it is important to sketch out a framework for the basic methodological task of this study. My purpose is to illustrate the nature of the problem and to set out requirements toward which a political methodology must strive.

This discussion is not offered as an attempt to solve or settle the long and complicated debate about the nature of the "political" and how to define it, nor does it resolve in any final way the problem of rational judgment. Its purpose is only to establish an agenda for further thought and investigation; in this sense, the discussion is programmatic.

An analysis of political evaluation in public policy must focus on when and how the concept is used and how it relates to other concepts in policy evaluation, especially the concept of rational political judgment. Toward this end, political evaluation is examined in terms of the following issues: the role of values and norms in evaluations, the nature of a "political" evaluation, the problem of rational inference in political value judgments, and the use of "informal" logic as an alternative approach.

Evaluation, Values, and Goals

In a study of evaluation and values, the clarification of essential concepts is crucial. The starting point must be the concept of evaluation itself. An evaluation is essentially the assignment of value to things—in short, the determination of whether they are good or bad. The concept, however, is subject to a "process-product" ambiguity.[2] It may refer to the process of evaluation, appraisal, or criticism of something, or it may refer to the product of the process. The process of evaluation consists of trying to determine the value of something. As a product or outcome of that process, an evaluation is a settled opinion that something has a certain value; this product is a value judgment.

The term "value" is also caught in the process-product ambiguity. A value is defined as an abstract and generalized behavioral ideal to which group members "feel a strong, emotionally toned commitment and which provides a standard of judging specific acts and goals."[3] One usage of the term refers to the specific product of the evaluation. For instance, it might be argued that "no other piece of music is as pleasant to listen to as this one," or "financial success brings well-being." These value judgments indicate the outcome of an evaluation, but do not specify the criteria involved in the process of making them. The second usage of the term refers to values as process criteria— standards or rules—that serve as a basis for these judgments. In this case, it might be asserted that "music is pleasant to listen to because it is harmonious," or that "financial success brings well-being because it leads to personal freedom." For political analysis, the use of values as criteria is generally the more important of the two analytical distinctions.

Values are closely related to norms, both conceptually and empirically.[4] In conceptual terms, norms are logically related to values, which serve as ideal criteria for assessing their validity. Empirically, norms are more concrete, situation-bound specifications that mediate between action and values and as such tend to be more imperative than values in the social world. Normative statements prescribe specific rules or principles of conduct against which behavior "ought" to be judged and approved or disapproved. For example, "honesty" is a generalized value that requires specific norms for concrete situations, such as rules governing student behavior on examinations, standards for establishing financial accountability in banking practices, or rules governing voting procedures at the ballot box. Norms in this sense are shared cultural definitions of behavior and are learned by individuals through socialization. By definition, they are shared by two or more individuals. Some norms are particular to quite small groups, such as husband and wife, while others are shared by entire nations.

Together, values and norms are the sources of the ends that are pursued. Based on their level of generality, ends can be differentiated as ideals, goals, or objectives. According to Kaplan, these three levels of generality constitute the "directions, regions and points in the value space."[5] Ideals are like horizons, permitting a continuous progression in their direction, but are always receding. Goals refer to attainable ends—"ends-in-view," to use Dewey's term—but lack the full specificity of concrete objectives. Objectives, the most concrete of the three levels, are blueprints or programs for carrying out an end. They specify exactly how the project is to be carried out—how much is to be spent, who gets it, what they're supposed to do with it, and so on. For example, ideals—such as maximum economic welfare—are never wholly attainable. Full employment, however, is an attainable goal toward that end, while the Humphrey-Hawkins Senate bill specifies concrete objectives for pursuing full employment. Such objectives must be based on measurable intermediate goals. In turn, these goals, anchored to the interests that individuals and groups regard as beneficial in their specific situations, must be aligned with higher ideals.

Evaluations are crucial to all forms of human action. Any decision, whether it be to accept a professorship, to vote for a candidate, to purchase a dishwasher, to take a leave of absence, or to live in a socialist country, involves making evaluations. Moreover, in the abstract, all of these evaluations follow the same principles. Michael Scriven succinctly stated this point in his widely cited essay on the methodology of evaluation: The underlying task "is essentially similar whether we are trying to evaluate coffee machines, teaching machines, plans for a house, or plans for a curriculum. [The activity involves] the gathering and combining of performance data with a weighted set of goal scales to yield either comparative or numerical ratings, and . . . the justification of (a) the data-gathering instruments, (b) the weightings, and (c) the selection of goals."[6] In each type of evaluation, the content will differ widely. Evaluative decisions about school curricula or coffee machines will not employ the same kinds of data. The mixture of empirical data and normative information, as well as the quality of the judgments inferred from them, will vary significantly. The evaluations upon which these judgments rest may be highly complex or relatively simple, explicit or implicit, heavily influenced by empirical data, or predominantly shaped by speculation and intuition.

Risk and uncertainty are key factors that determine the character of evidence in the evaluation process. The results of problem complexity, limited information, and time constraints on the evaluation process, they have become the subjects of a vast literature in the economic and management sciences. Much of this work has focused on the development of mathematical models of decision and game theories designed to guide decision making to the best solution under risk and uncertainty. With the assistance of such models, the analyst can compare, for example, the choice between an alternative that appears to present a fifty-fifty chance of complete success or total failure and a second alternative in which the probability of succeeding is nearly certain but the reward from succeeding is quite small. Logicians and statisticians have devoted a substantial amount of time and energy to formulating criteria for determining the rational decision in such cases.

However, the development of such decision strategies has not proved successful in the most important social questions confronting the policy sciences. Although the decision models of writers such as Arrow, Harsanyi, and Raiffa have unmistakable heuristic value in a range of social problems,[7] they can generally provide solutions only in well-defined technically oriented problems of tactics and strategy that lend themselves to quantification and calculation. In social policy, they can calculate solutions only under restricted circumstances such as uncomplicated situations with quick and easy information or perhaps where calculations are based on preemptory values.[8] As Robert Dahl has said, the more sophisticated and compelling the mathematical formulation, the more it tends to apply to less controversial technical questions. It is not that such questions are unimportant but rather that they are less relevant to the normatively complex problems of social life that press for answers.[9]

In a complex social world, it is fair to say that a policy science that remains methodologically limited to these less important questions has a small future. To overcome this barrier, at least in practice, analysts turn to a range of less rigorous methods. Given the complexity of policy problems, which generates risk and uncertainty, evaluative decisions must frequently be based on estimates, best guesses, or even hunches that specific outcomes will result.[10] Even when highly sophisticated evaluative decisions can be approached through statistical techniques, the introduction of crucial assumptions resting upon intuition, common sense, or personal values is unavoidable.[11] Awareness of this reality has led some policy writers to search for more practical strategies based on a wider mix of factual and normative information.[12] A first step in this search must be an analysis of evaluative methodology itself. To determine its strengths and weaknesses as an analytical process, evaluation methodology must be divided into its empirical and normative components and examined against the requisites of policy decision making.

Such exploration shows that both empirical and normative analyses in policy evaluation fall short of the requirements. On the empirical side, technical criticisms of means designed to achieve alternative courses of action and the assessment of the consequences of such policy actions are evaluated in terms of the extent to which they achieve their stated goals. Such evaluations can be organized around the concept of efficiency, the positivist's standard for rational decision making. Policy outcomes are stated as probabilities that provide the basis for subsequent predictions: if X occurs, then Y will (probably) occur. Empirical analysis, however, is unable to produce valid predictions. The quality of the available predictive knowledge required for political decision making is low. As most existing political information is nonscientific, political decision makers must generally rely on commonsense knowledge and tutored intuition drawn from unanalyzed experiences. Politicians who chose to make decisions based only on scientifically verified empirical data would find themselves straightjacketed. To avoid inaction, decision makers are forced to rest their judgments on limited or incomplete data. Such uncertainty is a rule in political life.

On the normative side, investigation turns to the analysis of the assumptions about the standards of value or worth against which policy efficiency is measured empirically. In a normative appraisal of the goals themselves, evaluation can no longer be based on the instrumental standards of efficiency employed in empirical analysis. Information about the efficiency of achieving the goals can only contribute to resolving secondary considerations in a larger practical question about "what ought to be done." To answer this question, it is necessary to decide which goals are the best to pursue. While a course of social action (like a manufactured article) can be judged by its ability to serve the purpose for which it has been designed, such a judgment is only provisional. It does not provide sufficient information to determine which course of action is best.[13]

Analysis of the best action to pursue requires a criterion— or criteria—that can be used to determine which action is the good one. The evaluator must consider the problem of justifying the normative principles as well as the application of particular normative principles to each course of action. Here there are no clear evaluative tests capable of performing the functions that efficiency and predictability serve in empirical analysis. There is profound disagreement as to whether such criteria exist—one of the traditional questions in the history of political theory and philosophical analysis that remains unresolved. Essentially, the controversy rests on the fact-value problem, raising methodological questions concerning how facts and values are to be integrated in a full-scale political evaluation. Before exploring the alternative solutions to this problem, it is important to show its close relationship to a concept of the "political" in a political evaluation or value judgment.

A Concept of "Political" Evaluation

There is no shortage of attempts to define the "political," but no definition has been universally acclaimed as accurate or adequate by modern political theorists. In large part, this is due to the internal complexity of the concept. Considering the broad and variable set of concepts implicated in an understanding of politics—decision, institution, issues, options, outcomes, power, conflict, consensus, values, desires, intentions, interests, and goals—it is perhaps best understood as a "cluster concept."[14] Various theorists weigh the importance of the several concepts differently. In developing a methodological framework for "political" evaluation in policy analysis, it is useful to start with the notion of political activity as the pursuit of individual or group goals. The pursuit of goals is the primary focus of the policy analyst.[15] The fundamental question that confronts political evaluation in policy analysis is the acceptability of policy goals to the political interest groups and other publics whose participation and agreement are required to translate them into political action.

Viewed as the pursuit of goals, politics is frequently defined as the process by which values—things or relationships that people would like to enjoy—are allocated to the society as a whole in an authoritative manner.[16] Specifically, politics commences when actors have two or more conceptions of goals or values. If these conceptions cannot be carried out at the same time, they conflict and constitute a political issue. The political process, then, is "the activity (negotiation, argument, discussion, application of force, persuasion, etc.) by which an issue is agitated and settled."[17]

Politics is inevitable by simple virtue of the plurality of interests and values that exist in societies. Societies and individuals cannot live by any single value alone. Life requires a plurality of values that are stressed differently at various times.

Politics unavoidably arises from the fact that different individuals and groups are competing for different values that are not necessarily compatible with each other. The result is political conflict, which has been called the "universal language of politics."[18]

Harold Lasswell suggested that there are at least eight basic values that people pursue: power, wealth, enlightenment, wellbeing, skill, affection, rectitude, and deference.[19] Although they are pursued with varying degrees of interest, no one can generally do entirely without them in either politics or life. Social organization, in fact, is developed around these basic values and the norms derived from them. As organized sets of norms, social institutions tend to be "clustered into statuses, and interrelated sets of statuses are organized around main foci of values and interests in recurrent situations, for example, birth of children, allocation of scarce means, and use of power."[20] Such organized networks of norms constitute the main societal structures: family, economy, education, political system, and so on.

As a social structure, a political system can be either a formal governmental institution or an informal organization such as a neighborhood political association. Whether formal or informal, a principal task of a political system is to function as a decision-making structure for resolving conflicts that result from competition over desired goals. Public policy and law are the end products of society's institutionalized political decision processes. Policy represents the actual authoritative decisions by which available values are distributed among the demanding, supporting, and often conflicting elements of society's citizenry. The outcome of policy processes in pluralistic systems can at times be viewed as a "score card" of political struggle, recording the victories of winning coalitions on each policy debate and decision. As a political statement, policy specifies the operating norms of behavior posited by the dominant groups for society's preservation and operation.

In institutional terms, a political decision-making structure is an orderly and more or less formal collection of human habits, expectations, and roles. Paul Diesing has listed three essential elements characterizing such a decision-making structure. The first is a discussion relationship—i.e., a relationship for talking and listening, asking and answering questions, and suggesting and accepting courses of action—that will be more or less institutionalized, depending on the complexity of the society. The second element is a set of roles defining the participants in the discussion relationship and their manner of participation. The third is a set of beliefs and values generally held in common by the participating members—beliefs establishing the types of factual propositions that are admissible to the participants, and values determining acceptable goals and objectives.[21]

Viewed in this way, the decision structure refers in essence to the set of sociocultural determinants of practical reason—determinants that organize both thought itself and the system of communication within which the particular habits of thought are applied to materials to result in decisions.[22] In this respect, the organizational relationships that underlie a decision-making structure are basically epistemological relationships in the practical world of affairs. The elements of the structure (the discussion relationship, the rules defining who participates, and the belief and value systems that govern the admissibility of evidence) form a communication process that establishes and certifies practical social knowledge and goals.

At this point, it becomes easy to introduce a second major function of a political system. The capacity to resolve goal disputes is also the capacity to determine which goals are chosen and followed. Beyond the resolution of disputes, the political system is also involved in deciding fundamental questions about "what ought to be done." In fact, without the specification of basic value commitments, the political system would possess no framework of values and goals for deciding disputes.

Political decisions about fundamental values establish a framework or context within which all subsequent reasoning about goals takes place. The authority to specify basic commitments is the capacity to generate all other types of values and goals— economic, social, technical, legal, aesthetic, and so on. This has led Diesing to define the politically effective decision as one that makes "possible an attack on any other problem." Insofar as a political deficiency can impede or block all other problem solving, Diesing has contended that the effective political decision is one that preserves or improves the capacity to make future decisions.[23]

Preserving the capacity to make future decisions emphasizes the integrative character of political deliberation. Unlike the instrumental decision, the integrative decision is not based solely on its contribution to goal achievement. First and foremost, it is based on its ability to secure normative acceptability or agreement on those objectives important to the various participants involved. In questions of efficient achievement of objectives "the best available proposal should be accepted regardless of who makes it or who opposes it." But in a political judgment, "action should be designed to avoid complete identification with any proposal and any political point of view" regardless of how popular or good. "The best available proposal should never be accepted just because it is best; it should be deferred, objected to, and discussed until all major opposition disappears."[24] Although decisions based on compromise are generally less than acceptable in nonpolitical decisions, they can represent the essence of wisdom in political judgments. Only political decisions that have eliminated major opposition—regardless of efficacy—contribute to the preservation and improvement of decision structure integration.

Diesing suggested four general criteria for judging the effect of a political decision on the normative decision structure: (1) the ability of the decision to reconcile or harmonize conflicting factors that blocked decision making; (2) the ability of the decision to increase toleration between various groups and their respective beliefs and values; (3) the decision's ability to establish equilibrium between opposing forces in a destructive struggle with each other; and (4) the decision's ability to reject, repress, or otherwise exclude the threatening factors from the decision problem.[25]

Once this normative dimension of a political judgment is fully appreciated, it is easier to see the interpretive character of political evaluation. In addition to an assessment of the process by which a political judgment is determined, the evaluation of the judgment must also include an assessment of the goals it posits. Unlike instrumental decisions, political judgments must be evaluated in terms of how the goals they propose or accept are interpreted by the various parties subject to them (interest groups and other members of the public whose support or acquiescence is needed for action). Political decisions thus rest on normative explanations, which require the giving of reasons rather than causes. In appealing to reasons (motives, purposes, or intentions) for adopting a course of action, the political actor exhibits the actions or policy in the light of political norms that are considered appropriate to the circumstances of the situation. The relevant norms and particular circumstances are presented in such a way as to demonstrate that a conclusion for or against the policy is warranted or entitled. This is a process of showing how a political judgment is to be justified.[26]

The exploration of this process has been facilitated by social scientists who have recognized the relationship between the concerns of phenomenological sociology and ordinary-language analysis in philosophy. Based on the insights drawn from these relationships, analysts are able to portray actors engaged in political evaluation as pursuing "moves in a language game."[27] Each participant, evaluating the alternative interpretations of a political action, attempts to uncover and probe the logics utilized by other participants to judge relevance or value. As an implication of this perspective, John Gunnell suggested that the critical assessment of political action can profitably be viewed "in terms of an analogy with the rational justification of value judgments."[28]

The usefulness of the approach becomes even clearer in the context of the relationship of politics to morality. Political decisions, as normative judgments designed to establish harmony in decision structures, can in the ideal be conceived as "morality enlarged."[29] By their very nature, however, political decisions seldom even approximate the ideal. Only rarely do they rest on consensus free of all opposition, and even less commonly are they the outcomes of rational discussion alone. The reason for this stems from the collective character of political decisions. Where moral deliberation may involve a single individual, political deliberation involves a range of groups from across the society; where the philosopher may have time and resources to pursue a question to philosophical certainty, the politician generally operates under the pressures of "forced choice," dictated by the constraints of power, time, knowledge, and resources.[30] It is, in fact, the nature of the political decision that motivates the introduction of governmental authority and power. To prevent the decision-making structure from being immobilized by disagreement and conflict resulting from forced choice, pluralist systems grant authority and power to those who coordinate and direct the activities of political deliberation. Political evaluation, in this sense, is a limited form of the normative ideal.

To properly understand the nature of political deliberation, it is essential to recognize the dialectical conflict between normative consensus and the exercise of political power. As the organization of force underlying a governmental structure, political power can be defined as the ability of governmental decision makers to carry out goals or policies and to control, manipulate, or influence the behavior of others, whether or not they wish to cooperate. Political power mediates the transactions that occur in the decision-making structure. Its existence and exercise makes possible, in the face of major or minor opposition and disagreement, the rendering and enforcing of decisions. It permits those who hold the principal roles in the decision structure to crystallize the process in the form of decisions at key points. This is ensured by providing various types of sanctions to back up such decisions, which in governmental decision structures (unlike other decision structures, such as labor unions or religious organizations) includes the use of physical compulsion.

However, in the process of facilitating decisions the exercise of power also breeds countercurrents of alienation and political conflict. In this sense, political power is no simple resource. The fact that it permits one group to make the final decisions, even after deliberation, and to back them up with force, introduces political domination and its potential for generating conflict ranging from opposition to revolution. Such conflict is essentially the by-product of political alienation experienced by those excluded from the decision-making structure. Etzioni captured this double-edged character of political power from the point of view of the political decision maker: "The dilemma of power is how to increase the capacity to act without generating counter-currents so that the very movement forward will not reduce the capacity to move on this and future occasions."[31] Such resistance is generated by power exercised to overcome resistance. Some degree of alienation and resistance inevitably accompanies the use of power. It is, in fact, the inevitability of alienation and resistance that underlies the Marxist theory of class struggle. Where policy writers tend to discuss the exercise of power from the standpoint of the rulers, Marxism is a theory of power from the view of the ruled.

The resolution of the dilemma posed by power, therefore, is not simply a question concerning the effective operation of a political system. As the dilemma is never completely resolvable, those who hold power in political systems must continually seek to minimize opposition, resistance, and alienation. Thus, a central question that has dominated the minds of political thinkers is: which type of power generates the weaker counter-forces? The long-standing answer to the question is "legitimate power" based on normative consensus—consensus about values and goals.

For Max Weber, legitimate power was the thread running through the action of a democratic political system, providing its special quality, importance, coherence, and order.[32] Power is legitimated when those who exercise it seek to justify their decisions and actions in the context of commonly accepted beliefs and values internalized by society's members. Although some social scientists argue that legitimacy and consensus are not prerequisites for political action, it is generally recognized that some degree of legitimate consensus is a requirement for effective action in the long run.[33] In this view, legitimate consensus need not involve complete agreement.

Most of democratic political theory in pluralistic societies has anchored the concept of legitimate consensus to the concept of a rational political process, defined in terms of free group competition. In this view, a rational decision process is one that is free of distracting or distorting pressures that prevent calm, clear observation and sober reflection. By linking the operation of a rational decision process to the concept of a political marketplace of ideas (an analogy taken from Adam

Smith's theory of competition) political theorists portray the competitive interaction of existing political groups as a beneficient process operating through a kind of "invisible hand" mechanism. Legitimate consensus, in this scheme, can rest on the free interplay of the participants' beliefs and values (beliefs establishing the factual propositions that are admissible, and values determining the goals and objectives that are acceptable). By viewing politics as process, modern political behavioral scientists can train the focus of their investigations on the objectively available empirical measures of the political processes—such as the amount of consensus present, the number of participants, or the levels of conflict—leaving justification of values to the processes of political competition. Working within this tradition, writers such as Diesing have attempted to connect the concept of "political rationality" itself to the rationality of the decision-making structure, defined in procedural and institutional terms.[34]

By the late 1960s, the normative limitations of this approach became quite apparent. In a society plagued with social and political unrest, the explanatory difficulties of the process model of political evaluation could be directly traced to its failure to deal with the substantive dimensions of values and goals. Indeed, most of the epistemological dispute in the sixties was predicated on this divergence of process-oriented behavioral theory from political reality. During that period, the process approach and its accompanying pluralistic outlook were constantly embarrassed by the results produced by the processes of existing regimes. This disparity between theory and practice was the primary impetus behind the search for alternative methods of evaluation.

In general, the principal objection to the process model is that it fails to adequately account for the fact that a decision-making structure is always built upon specific social and economic conditions, which are reflected in a specific set of values that govern the deliberation processes. For example, in a mass industrial society, where the decision-making structure is a multilayered hierarchy, most decisions are either carried out or monitored by a powerful, centralized elite group. As the primary participants in the decision-making processes, the function of the elite group is to ensure decisions that reflect and perpetuate the distribution of values established by the underlying social and economic relations. Therefore, decision making at this level, for political purposes, is specifically designed to exclude certain relevant social beliefs and values that would require attention in a fully legitimate process of consensus formation.

By focusing on the formal or established decision-making structures, process theorists tend to overlook or underestimate the significance of minorities and other groups without political power. Even more important, they tend to avoid the more basic question of how general participation in consensus formation is structurally possible in a complex industrial society, especially where elites can establish and legitimate goal consensus by the use of persuasive techniques.[35] Through the control of communications channels, particularly the mass media, those in power can exploit ignorance or lack of awareness at the lower levels of the hierarchy. The social-psychological nature of the process requires the introduction of a notion of "societal consciousness." Drawing on Marx's conception of "false consciousness," Etzioni has attempted to confront this problem by introducing the concept of societal consciousness in his analysis of political decision structures. Societal consciousness is designed to refer to "the level, extent and topics of attention, which can be limited, misdirected or unfocused."[36] Such a concept addresses the subjective dimensions of decision making that are beyond the methodological reach of a behaviorally oriented emphasis on the objective, empirical dimensions of the decision processes.

Habermas's analysis of the legitimacy of decision structures in modern industrial society traces the normative problem to Weber's theory of legitimacy. Weber's conception of legitimate decision making, as Habermas showed, tends to confuse a belief in the legitimacy of a procedurally established legal order with its potential for justification or truth. The difficulty with Weber's conception is that the normative laws of the legal order that form the basis for legitimacy are in reality established by the dominant ruling groups rather than the citizenry as a whole. Moreover, the submission to such laws and norms does not solely reflect a belief in their legitimacy by those affected.

Instead, it "is also based on fear of, and submission to, indirectly threatened sanctions, as well as on simple compliance engendered by the individual's perception of his own powerlessness and the lack of alternatives open to him."[37] What is controversial here to Habermas is not Weber's description of legitimacy in political systems but, rather, the relation of this concept of legitimacy to truth.[38] For Habermas, the legitimacy of such consensus is based on the "systematically distorted communication" that characterizes decision making in modern mass industrial societies.[39] The dominant ruling classes, he argued, eliminate normative opposition by setting up barriers to consensus-forming communications that extend beyond the ideological limits of ruling system norms or world perspectives. As ideology, the ruling beliefs and values restrict certain types of factual propositions from the deliberation processes and refuse to admit values that lead to goals and objectives that are "inadmissible." Legitimate consensus, then, measured against epistemological criteria for establishing validity, can be "false consensus."

Further discussion could be devoted to this point showing that consensus on goals can be founded on irrational or emotional bases, but the point is generally not an unfamiliar one. In the policy literature, it has led writers such as Grauhan and Strubelt to contend that policy scientists should not capitulate to a restricted evaluative frame of reference based on process or structural criteria but rather must ask whether they can identify criteria for the rational evaluation of the goals.[40] Where writers such as Diesing have linked political rationality to an evaluation of the political process, Grauhan and Strubelt asked analysts to develop rigorous evaluation methods that go beyond deficient structural and process criteria by including the evaluation of goal content. Similarly, Barry and Rae concluded that policy arrangements must in the final analysis be judged by the content of the decisions they bring about.[41] In light of the role of social class domination, institutional loyalties, political emotions, physical coercion, and so on, the operation of the decision-making process itself can be only a secondary consideration in political evaluation.

In this view, political rationality requires an assessment of the outcomes of the decision-making process. Such an assessment must aim at determining the "right" or "good" decision. It implies the possibility of arriving through reason at judgments about policies that, in turn, can be validated by all who agree to assume a rational posture. This, of course, raises the question of how to assign value to policies, decisions, or laws.

The task of assigning political value has long been a primary intellectual objective of political philosophy. Whether in a family or a political system, the most obvious way to create consensus about values is to establish commonly accepted aims or goals. Political philosophy's mission is to uncover fundamental rules or principles that provide a valid basis for common aims.[42] One such principle is social justice; another is the public interest. For illustrative purposes, we shall consider the case of the public interest.

The public interest is advanced as a fundamental political principle. As an ethical criterion for governing deliberation about the pursuit of interests and ends, its classical formulation, as stated by John Stuart Mill, is: "In any political election the voter is under an absolute moral obligation to consider the interests of the public, not his private advantage, and give his votes, to the best of his judgment, exactly as he would be bound to do if he were the sole voter, and the election depended on him alone."[43] The state, according to this principle, is neither owned by nor designed to serve any particular interest. No one citizen can justifiably call it his or her own, nor can any group of citizens claim it to be theirs. Although composed of a compound of private interests, the public interest refers to the common good of the community as a whole, and, as such, can be employed as a standard for evaluating specific policies and decisions.

The difficulty of establishing the validity of such principles is clearly gleaned from the debate generated by the concept of the public interest. Even though the concept has been the subject of a voluminous literature in political science, there exists no generally accepted definition of the public interest—not to mention an operational definition providing empirical indicators for deciding if a policy meets the requirements.[44] In fact, this inability to develop substantive criteria for the evaluation of goal content has been a mainstay of the behavioralist's position, namely, that nothing rational can be said about political value judgments. In the absence of such criteria, most modern political theorists have abandoned the concept and focus instead on the operation of the political process itself, where empirically verifiable criteria (measures of consensus, levels of conflict, number of participants, and so on) are more readily available.

At this point, the search for substantive criteria has returned to the fundamental problem that impedes rational deliberation about value judgments in general. There is no agreement about how to validate a political value judgment. In the case of the public interest, one might identify it as the outcome of the democratic process; another might hold that it is based on higher motives and interests, such as justice, equality or freedom; and a third might identify it with the realization of God's "will on earth." All three are value judgments. How is the decision maker to judge? What constitutes rational inference in such decisions? Is there a logical or methodological basis that can serve as a foundation for systematic reasoning about political value judgments?

Value Decisions and Rational Judgment

The question of how to make valid judgments about norms and values takes the discussion back to the contemporary epistemological debate, this time to the very roots. The traditional behavioral scientist, it will be recalled, adopts the noncognitivist position. Essentially, rational inference about value judgments is ruled out. Unlike objective facts, value judgments are assertions of opinion, belief, intention, or orientation toward the social world. Ultimately they must be reduced to emotional responses conditioned by the individual's life experiences. Lacking the cognitive status of objective propositions, they cannot, according to the noncognitivist, be true or false, valid or invalid.

If there is no logical way of resolving value judgments, the most the analyst can do is explicate the value assumptions that underlie empirical work, draw out their implications, and proceed with the empirical assessment. As it is impossible to supply basic principles applicable to vastly different cultural, social, and political contexts, the discipline must be limited to an analysis of what ought to be done after the nonrational acceptance of normative principles has taken place. Sidestepping the possibility of justifying the norms or goals behind recommendations, the normative task of political theory is restricted to the study of instrumental rationality. The classical search for general principles is replaced by models of rational decision making in the context of specific circumstances. The only basis available for the evaluation of such norms is the consequences that follow from them.[45]

Basic noncognitivist tenets are not easily refuted. Not only is it difficult, for example, to supply normative principles that are relevant to all social contexts, it is also quite difficult to prove value judgments. This, however, does not invariably lead to the noncognitivist conclusion that normative criteria cannot be dealt with in a rational, cognitive manner. Even if it proves impossible to validate fundamental principles, it does not follow that normative deliberation proceeds without rational or systematic methods. Overextension or misapplication of noncognitivist conclusions has generally led to underemphasis of important aspects of normative inquiry that have great bearing on the status of value judgments. Taking issue with noncognitivism, others point to a significant degree of reasoned discourse that does take place in politics and practical affairs. Even in the face of philosophical problems, reason plays an important role in moral and political judgments.[46]

There are two approaches to value judgments that contrast sharply with noncognitivism. One constitutes a scientific approach to ethics and value theory and represents the epistemology upon which the policy-oriented post-behavioral critique is generally founded. Called scientific "naturalism," it attempts to derive rational judgments about values from the factual side of the continuum. The second approach, called "practical discourse," is drawn from philosophical analysis on the value side of the dichotomy and is concerned with ethical and normative discourse as they occur in practical deliberations.

Scientific Value Theory

The dominant position of noncognitivism has begun to yield to the scientific or naturalistic approach to values and ethical principles, especially as constituted in scientific post-behavioralism. In its most rigorous form, naturalism holds that certain moral principles or value statements are true because they describe universal properties that can be determined scientifically. They can be established as factual propositions subject to empirical verification. Taking very seriously the idea of natural law as the basis of a rational science of values, Arnold Brecht was probably the most systematic naturalist in modern times, envisioning extremely rigorous conditions for such a science. Its purpose is to empirically establish the existence of natural laws by comparing past and present behavior in all known societies to discover common principles operating in them. Brecht believed that universally recognizable principles may well exist and proposed a number of hypotheses for investigation.[47]

The establishment of natural principles of value would provide the basis for the construction of a rational moral code. All lower norms, standards, and rules could be organized and evaluated as means to ends in a hierarchy of norms that connect with ultimate values. John Dewey was one of the most sophisticated theorists in this tradition. For Dewey, the difference between ends and means was essentially a question of where one leaves off in the means-ends chain that constitutes the value hierarchy. The scientific task, according to his "instrumental" theory of value, was to discover the causal links in the chain—links between value judgments and consequences.[48] Modern welfare economics, particularly the attempt to construct a social welfare function, rests on such a means-ends chain.

However, the possibility of a scientific value theory is clearly beyond reach. The amount of empirical data that would have to be amassed to carry out such a project reaches far beyond present capabilities. Even if such an enterprise could be carried out, it is not clear that such a grand theory would represent more than sweeping generalities that are too broad to be of practical value. If one of the tests of a proposed value principle is that it must, without exception, be recognized by all past and present social groups, it would probably be so devoid of content as to be meaningless in practical decision making. Take, for instance, the proposition that "like cases should be treated alike."

Such a value principle does not help with the crucial problem of which cases are alike.[49]

Equally problematic is the development of a logical, practical, empirical moral code rationally deduced from first principles.[50] The multiplicity of existing values, coupled with the manifold ways in which they may be expressed, renders the ideal model of logical deduction infeasible. In reality, the problem for an evaluator is not which value provides the underlying basis for decision but rather which mixture of available values is best. The question of how to form a single group preference by combining sets of individual preference scales (the "aggregation problem") can be considered *the* political problem.[51] Employing indifference curves and the concept of trade-offs between competing values, modern economic theory has struggled at length with the problem without positive, practical results. Both theoretical and operational difficulties stand in the path of constructing a solution to the aggregation problem. Indeed, Kenneth Arrow received the Nobel Prize for his theoretical work showing that it is impossible, under reasonable circumstances, to develop a "social choice function" capable of aggregating individual preferences into a set of collective preferences.[52]

In policy analysis, such work must at present be valued for its heuristic contribution, rather than its practical empirical achievements.[53] For post-behavioral scientists attempting to base value-laden policy evaluations on empirical verification, the prospects are dimmer than the rhetoric. Falco's contention, for instance, that the policy scientist will be able to discover the "laws of value response," which can be reduced to prescriptions for policy, can be interpreted as optimistic thinking: it bears no relationship to the existing state of policy science. There are, however, several less dramatic but nonetheless essential contributions made by the scientific approach to value theory. Of particular importance is the attention given to system interrelationships between value conditions and responses and the clarification of the role of empirical methods in identifying their functional bases.

To explore the empirical patterns of value orientations and their social consequences, the contemporary behavioral sciences draw assistance from the systems approach to policy analysis, a basic methodological technique utilized in rational-comprehensive decision models in economics.[54] Easton, Dror, and others in political science have elevated the systems perspective to the status of a leading theoretical paradigm in political theory and policy analysis.[55] In the policy sciences, systems analysis can be adapted to situations that do not have the clearly definable objectives required for rigorous value maximization. Although the technique utilizes quantitative methods, it reserves them for selected phases of a problem. Mixing quantitative calculations with commonsense reasoning, the policy scientist uses the systems perspective as a guide to structure thinking about complex decision problems.[56]

Scientific value theorists can employ systems methods to assist in modeling the connections between organized sets of norms and institutions and their functional interrelationships to other values, interests, and goals in recurrent situations.[57] Societal structures such as economy, government, schools, and family can be mapped out as networks of norms and values. Empirical relationships between normative inputs and outputs constitute data for the potential development of the post-behavioral lawlike causal theories of value conditions and responses. Although rigorous empirical connections between value theory, systems research techniques, and policy formulation are beyond reach, the heuristic value of logically tracing these interrelationships is crucial to policy thinking. Linking value judgments to functional bases tends to reduce the often mysterious and arbitrary characteristics associated with values, a point that receives further attention in Chapter 5.

As a systems perspective, post-behavioral naturalism is also capable of directing research to crucial questions about basic human needs and underlying values. Empirical knowledge about needs and values, linked to the functional bases of society, provides a foundation for developing criteria for judgment in normative inquiry and evaluation. Even though empirical inference cannot establish the full validity of basic value judgments, it can bring useful—and often essential—factual information to bear on the evaluative process. For this reason, writers such as Abraham Kaplan have contended that scientific naturalism is the epistemological position most suited to modern social science.[58]

In its most cogent form, naturalism is seen as an empirical supplement to qualitative judgment. It recognizes that valuative imperatives cannot be deduced from purely nonevaluative factual premises, at least not given the present state of science. In this form, naturalism is in agreement with noncognitivism about the inability to verify ultimate values, but unlike noncognitivism, it emphasizes the overlooked factual aspects of evaluation. Essentially, it avoids the noncognitivist error of turning to an overly instrumental conception of rational value inquiry by stressing "normative facts" as crucial factors in value judgments. Toward this end, Paul Kurtz delineated six types of descriptive knowledge that can be used to ground value judgments: (1) knowledge of available means, (2) knowledge of consequences that flow from action alternatives, (3) knowledge of the particular facts of the situation, (4) knowledge of general causal conditions and laws relevant to the situation, (5) knowledge of the established values and norms that bear on the decision, and (6) knowledge of the fundamental needs of man. Moral and political theories of decision criteria, Kurtz explains, generally err by considering only one or two of these factual data.[59] What is needed is a way of unifying these separate types of factual knowledge into a comprehensive theory. Separately they are narrow and partial—not of great value as decision criteria—but their synthesis would provide considerable aid in value decisions.

Practical Discourse

A second approach to rational value judgments that has appeared in the epistemological debate attempts to establish rational judgment through the logical analysis of normative concepts and rules employed in practical discourse. Such an approach emerges with the revitalization of political philosophy but veers sharply from the classical notion that value judgments are validated through intuitive transcendental principles, a position that has encountered even more objections than scientific naturalism. In place of the pitfalls presented by insight and intuition, practical-discourse philosophers find the key to the fact-value problem and political evaluation in the rules of normative-based practical argumentation.

In recent decades, as Fred Dallmayr explained, "philosophical trends in a variety of contexts have pointed toward a revival of normative arguments even in the absence of cognitive premises; by means of a careful and critical scrutiny of normative statements, philosophers of different persuasions have progressively uncovered the distinctive and autonomous status of moral and normative discourse vis-à-vis empirical propositions."[60] Stimulated by linguistic analysis—especially the ordinary-language approach—these normative political theorists seek knowledge about values through a "metaethical" analysis of the structure of normative arguments in politics.[61] The primary purpose of metaethics is to explicate the distinctive logic of practical discourse to determine how people make reasoned judgments—i.e., how they choose and systematically employ rules and standards as criteria to arrive at conclusions. The basic aim in metaethics is to come to a clear understanding of what it means to be rational in the process of dealing with values and norms.[62] Where conceptual analysis focuses on the definitions and meanings of the concepts employed in practical discourse, metaethics examines the nature of the judgments in which normative concepts are used; inquires about the logic of practical discourse that governs reasoning about values; and asks whether value judgments can be justified, proved, or shown to be valid.

Strongly influenced by the later work of Wittgenstein, these investigations revealed the idea that there are different regions of language for dealing with different kinds of reason and application of an inappropriate language will lead to confused inquiry. In their search for rigor, the positivists, according to this view, lose sight of the fact that value judgments can be discussed rationally in everyday discourse. While such discourse cannot be conducted with scientific rigor, the conclusion that little or nothing of value can be said about value judgments is unjustified. Such a conclusion is arrived at by employing an inappropriate language in practical discourse. To rely on the language of the empirical sciences to explore the normative domain is as fundamentally absurd as using the language of chemistry to discuss the aesthetics of a painting. The principal aim of ordinary-language writers is to clarify and enrich normative discourse by increasing understanding of the language and logic employed in the discussion of practical questions.

The interest in a logic applicable to the practical realm is motivated by recognition of the epistemological impasse that confronts traditional attempts to establish validity in value judgments. Of particular importance is the tension between the noncognitivists (who hold that nothing can be said) and the naturalists (who claim that facts alone can perform the evaluative task). Kurt Baier has captured the essence of the problem:

> It is unfortunate that the means-end model has dominated philosophical thinking in this field. It has led some philosophers, maintaining (rightly) that we can ask which is the best thing to aim at in these circumstances, to conclude (wrongly) that there must be an *ultimate* aim or end, a *summum bonum*, to which all ordinary aims or ends are merely means. Hence, they claim, whether this or that is the better end to aim at must be judged by its serving the ultimate end or *summum bonum*. Other philosophers, maintaining (rightly) that there can be no such ultimate end or *summum bonum*, have concluded (wrongly) that we cannot ask which is the better end to aim at. They have claimed that reason can tell us only about what are the best means to given ends, but that ends themselves cannot be determined or judged by reason.[63]

The dilemma here is located in the idea that the goal or end itself determines the reason for acting in a certain way. The problem, according to Baier, is misconstrued. It is based on the failure to understand that a reason for or against an aim is determined independently of what is actually being aimed at. "The best course of action is not that course which most quickly, least painfully, least expensively, etc., leads to the gaining of our ends, but *it is the course of action which is supported by the best reasons.*"[64]

Baier's position—that a reason for doing something is independent of what is actually aimed at—indicates the point of departure for a logic of practical deliberation. Although the search for criteria in practical discourse has been carried out from a number of theoretical vantage points, making it difficult to single out one representative view, the concern here is restricted to the "good-reasons" approach stemming mainly from the writings of Toulmin, Baier, and Taylor. Their work involves an effort to explicate the "informal logic" of normative reasoning. It is motivated by the recognition that (1) in practical affairs people do, in fact, reason about values, even if the kind of rigor found in science is not employed, and (2) value judgments cannot be justified in some ultimate fashion. They stress that in moral discourse or political evaluation, as in science, there is a limited and distinctive mode of reasoning with its own pragmatic point or purpose. To understand the nature of normative reasoning in practical deliberations, attention must not be fixed only on the meaning of normative expressions or terms taken in isolation. It is also necessary to grasp the overall point or rationale of the discourse in question. Each mode of discourse is subservient to the overall purposes for which evaluative discourse exists but each has its own distinctive procedures. In accordance with these procedures, a judgment can be made as to whether something is or is not good evidence for a certain claim. Without such ground rules, it is not possible to speak correctly of evidence or reasons for or against a contention.

Toulmin likened moral or political discourse to a "jurisprudential analogy," pointing out its similarity to arguments used by lawyers in a courtroom.[65] Good lawyers do not simply present the facts but rather marshal them with persuasive language to stress those aspects of the situation that favor their client's case. With the jury and judge in mind, language and arguments are selected and designed to persuade or convince. Similarly, moral and political evaluations are statements in support of decisions that can be forcefully or poorly defended. Neither factual nor emotive statements per se, they are "like records of practical decisions or positions taken which can be defended or supported much like a lawyer defends his client."[66] Such evaluations are constructed rationally but are not proved inductively or deductively as is a scientific proposition. In this respect, science refers to the "proof" of the law of gravity but political philosophy refers not to Mill's "proof" of liberty but rather to his "magnificent defense" of it.[67] Toulmin argued that this distinction between scientific and normative discourse rests on purpose or function: The function of scientific judgments is to alter one's expectations about what *will* happen, while that of a moral or political evaluation is to alter one's feelings, behavior, and decisions about what *should* happen.[68]

Once it is recognized that normative political inquiry involves arguments much like those made by lawyers, it becomes important to know to whom an argument is addressed—i.e., what kind of jury must be convinced or persuaded. The force of a political judgment depends wholly on the "communicative power" it has for its audience.[69] It has been argued that it is just such communicative power that maintains the challenging and forceful tradition of "epic" political theory.[70] Although classical political philosophers failed to "prove" universal normative principles, their knowledge of the process of political argumentation and use of rhetorical techniques has often kept their works relevant and persuasive. Thus, while judgments of value may not be true or false in the ordinary sense of the term, decisions can be powerful and persuasive or weak and unconvincing; that is, choices can be better or worse for members of the audience. The fact that some arguments are more persuasive than others is a suggestive clue that can open the way to a metanormative approach to evaluative criteria. If it can be shown that there is an underlying logical structure (a metalogical structure) that gives the persuasive argument intellectual or moral force, then perhaps this logical structure (the logical structure of the rationally persuasive argument) might itself be the source of potentially useful criteria. With the aid of such a logic, it would be possible to take apart a normative argument in order to test its structure against the ideal criteria or to construct an argument that logically attempts to fulfill the requirements. For those who agree to submit their arguments to the tests of such a logic, it would be possible to speak of an argument's ability or power to rationally persuade. It is here that the attempt of the "good-reasons" philosophers to explicate the metanormative logic of practical discourse holds some interesting possibilities.

Toulmin's work on the informal logic of practical reason and his idea that the underlying properties of arguments might provide evaluative criteria for normative argumentation have not gone unnoticed. In these respects, Habermas's work is clearly the more ambitious. Although Habermas has not explicated

such a logic in accessible methodological terms, he has seen the
connection between Toulmin's work on "substantive" informal
arguments and his own effort to develop an epistemology for
his pragmatic communications model.[71] As seen in Chapter 2,
Habermas's communications model, like Churchman's formal
debate, was designed to test and judge substantive arguments
advanced from competing normative perspectives. In exchanges
between decision makers, policy analysts, and the political public, substantive arguments based on the logic of practical discourse have "the force to convince the participants in a discourse of a valid claim, that is, *to provide rational grounds for*
the recognition of validity claims."[72] Toulmin, he pointed out,
has located "the rationally motivating force of argumentation
in the fact that the progress of knowledge takes place through
substantial arguments."[73] A substantial argument, like all types
of arguments, is based on logical inference but is not restricted
to the deductive model of inference (the model of the syllogism)
that formally links propositional statements together as major
and minor premises. Instead, the substantial argument is a justification or explanation that connects sentences in everyday,
practical speech acts. The clarification and justification of these
linkages—that is, clarification of their underlying systematic
character—can be carried out only within the framework of a
logic of practical discourse.

Habermas stressed the distinction between scientific and
practical discourses. The important point is that the rules of
argumentation for theoretical scientific discourse (designed to
ground factual assertions) are different from those employed in
practical discourse (which serves to justify norms and recommendations). Only with an understanding of the distinctive
"formal properties" of these two types of arguments can the
inferential process be properly conducted. With the guidance of
the formal properties of practical arguments, the analyst can
recognize and separate the "valid" consensus from agreements
based on political pressure and manipulative persuasion. The use
of the formal properties of practical discourse as criteria makes
it possible to identify and sort out the constraining political
contexts and forces that impede valid judgments in the decision-
making process. In an ideal political discourse, the "bracketed"

validity claims of factual assertions and normative recommendations become the exclusive objective of the discussion. There are no restrictions on who participates or what themes and contributions may be submitted to test the validity of the goals or norms in question. The only force in the discourse would be the "force of the better argument."

Essentially, Habermas contended that argumentation under the conditions of ideal political discourse (characterized by debate between "hypothetically proposed, alternative justifications") can lead to the formation of a consensus that expresses a "rational" public will or commitment. Insofar as all participants who are affected have the opportunity to participate discursively in the practical deliberation, the "rationality" of the consensus is based on the validity of the common interests that emerge as a result of free discussion without deception or distortion. The common interests, which take on normative status as "reciprocal behavioral expectations" through mutual understanding, provide the grounds for normative validity claims. These interests are judged to be common on the basis of a constraint-free consensus process. Such a process can allow only what all participants desire or want. It is deception-free because even the interpretations of basic or fundamental needs can become the object of argumentation and discursive consensus formation.[74] Moreover, such discursive consensus formation is always open to reevaluation; common interests are always subject to reassessment through open practical discourse. If the things that all participants desire or want should change, either as a result of changing sociohistorical requirements or new scientific knowledge about human needs, a new consensus must be formed through the discursive processes.

For Habermas, this discursively formed consensus can be called rational because the "formal properties" of the ideal discourse and the characteristics of the ideal, constraint-free deliberative situation "sufficiently guarantee" that only a consensus based on "appropriately interpreted *generalized interests*" (which can be communicatively shared and mutually understood) can emerge from ideal discursive consensus formation. Such an ideal scheme does not imply that the pluralism of value orientations can be overcome; rather, it suggests that it is possible under ideal conditions to separate generalizable interests from those that are particular.[75]

Habermas's work offers epistemological support for linking policy argumentation with practical discourse. The possibility of sorting out the properties of substantive policy arguments is a compelling reason for pursuing the connection. Beyond providing epistemological grounding for the relationship, however, Habermas's efforts offer little that helps to show what such a methodology might look like. What is missing is a statement of the logic or rules that govern practical deliberations and how they might be translated into a method for policy evaluation. To move the discussion beyond the theoretical stage, the policy analyst must be supplied with those principles of practical thought that provide the basis for rational judgment. Embodied in a systematically organized, steplike set of questions, such a methodology would permit the analyst to organize relevant factual assertions and recommended norms into a formal decision framework capable of probing validity questions. It is to Taylor's work that this analysis turns in an attempt to develop such a method. Before confronting the task, however, it is important to have a better understanding of the "good-reasons" approach upon which Taylor's methodology draws.

Good Reasons

Practical deliberation is found to rest on an implicit network of rules that govern its conduct. These procedural rules are geared to a specific end. The primary purpose of practical statements is to suggest, advise, admonish, or protest. Unlike theoretical statements asserting that something *is* the case, practical knowledge is about what *should be made* the case. Knowing what to do requires that something be known about the case, but knowledge of the case does not (in and of itself) tell what must be done. For good-reasons theorists, there is no evidence backing the claim that investigations into what is to be done are irrational or hopelessly subjective. Such questions merely belong to a different type of inquiry.

Toulmin challenged the use of the positivist model in practical normative analysis on the ground that it rests on a limited conception of logic that is appropriate only to various stages of scientific inquiry. Stressing a distinction between "working logic" (logic in use) and "idealized logic" (reconstructed logic), he pointed out that reconstructionists are reluctant to grant any autonomy to working logic or in fact to recognize it at all.[76] As a result, they ignore many aspects of inquiry (including aspects of scientific inquiry) by characterizing explanations that do not approach the ideals of formal logic as imperfect or incomplete. From such a position, much of what constitutes explanation in history and political theory is considered to be merely an "explanation sketch."[77] In contrast, the completeness and perfection of an informal working logic explanation depends on context rather than universal standards.[78] Standards for judging the soundness, validity, cogency, or strength of these informal arguments are practical and context-bound. To neglect substantive contextual criteria by requiring that complete explanation rest on field or context invariant laws (logically symmetrical with predictive statements) is to impose standards too restrictive to include all of what scientific practice finds perfectly acceptable and too inclusive to admit assertions that in many instances do not count as relevant explanations. For Toulmin, the problem is resolved by taking account of the diversity of explanations actually used. Although formal deduction is one of the valid types of explanation, there is no reason why it should necessarily apply to detective work as well as physics. Deductive inference and the meaning of concepts such as "valid" and "certain" do not necessarily have to be interpreted in terms of formal logic. It is only one standard for judging the infinite variety of substantive arguments.

For present purposes, the importance of this approach lies precisely in the fact that it dodges the positivist thesis on empirical verification or final validity, the pitfall of traditional normative inquiry. Toulmin established this point by illustrating an important similarity between reasoning in ethics and science.[79] Like scientific investigation, practical inquiry is a rational pursuit in the sense that normative statements or propositions are supportable with reasons.[80] Rather than focus concern on the problem of empirically verifying the final validity of these statements (which Toulmin has seen as a misguided activity), what is important is how such statements are warranted by reasons. By substituting the concept "warranted by reasons" for verified truth, he has established the more tentative character of practical statements. They are warranted by certain evidence yet remain more subject to modification, correction, and rejection than verified statements.[81]

For example, the proposal of a more liberal welfare policy may be investigated to determine its worthiness or value. To the question "Why is this particular welfare policy good?" any reason offered as an answer may be subject to an evaluative study. But Toulmin was careful to establish the limit of such an evaluation: Beyond the point of evaluating the reasons offered in support of the particular welfare policy, practical inquiry becomes pointless. Like science, it has its own limits, determined by its own rules and purposes.[82] In practical normative inquiry the goal is social harmony. Although this purpose or goal is not as firmly anchored as the goal of explanation in science, Toulmin contended that moral and practical inquiry— i.e., ethics—are normally viewed as attempts to bring individual desires into a state of harmony. If a certain behavior is justified on the ground that it leads to a harmonious state of affairs, and the critics of this behavior ask for the justification for asserting the merit of this reason, they have in Toulmin's scheme stepped beyond the bounds of ethical inquiry. Such a question, for Toulmin, shifts the probe to another type of philosophical inquiry.[83]

For those students of ethics who ask whether social harmony is the only (or even appropriate) goal of moral inquiry, Toulmin's approach is problematic. On the other hand, if the scope of its application is restricted to the narrower normative requirements of policy evaluation, most of these philosophical criticisms can be sidestepped. Social harmony, derived through a fully legitimate political consensus, would appear to adequately capture the interests and objectives of the ethically oriented policy evaluator (a point that receives further attention in a later chapter).

From the point of view of policy evaluation, Toulmin's approach to practical discourse, of which political evaluation is a special form, offers the possibility of establishing a useful link between is and ought and fact and value. In the good-reasons scheme, as in policy evaluation, it is not necessary for the evaluator to consent to a fundamental or primary value. Practical deliberation, like scientific discourse, occurs within the framework of a set of rules. In practical discourse, these rules are derived from the cluster of social practices or activities that the members of the social group (or inquiring community) have come to agree upon. As such, they constitute a set of socially accepted normative rules that delineate duties or rights and proper or improper steps and procedures. Learned and shared by members of the community, the application of these rules permits certain normative conclusions to be deduced from factual evidence. This is not the rigorous kind of inference employed in formal logic, but it is capable of deriving normative judgments from descriptive statements. In this respect, the logical structure of the practical judgment bears a similarity to the naturalistic approach, although the inference is warranted by reasons rather than formal scientific deduction. In a practical judgment, the conclusion is based on a warranted inference derived from facts that serve as reasons in social practice.[84] By developing this approach, the good-reasons writers have succeeded in paving a path through the epistemological thicket of the fact-value debate. Good reasons do not answer the higher epistemological questions concerning ultimate validation, but these questions seldom arise in the context of everyday discussions or policy deliberations.

It is important to concede that the notion of an "informal logic" is not well received by all philosophers and logicians. Ordinary-language writers have not succeeded in convincing some philosophers that it satisfies the underlying epistemological dilemma associated with the validation of value judgments. Most of the disagreements tend to center around the question of whether values and norms are governed by a specific logic of their own.[85] Critics generally suggest that the use of the term "logic" in ethical or practical reasoning is misleading. Preferring to adhere to a strict definition of the term, logic for them refers only to formal deduction and induction. As rules of correct argument, deduction and induction are methodological principles that specify the logical structure of valid arguments.

Under these two principles, the form of the structure of an argument determines whether the conclusion is valid, that is, whether the conclusion can be logically derived from the given set of premises. Those skeptical of the idea of a practical or normative logic argue that such formal criteria are not found in ethical inquiry. In the strict sense of logic, the skeptics are of course correct. But, as other writers have pointed out, this conclusion (that normative inquiry is not governed by formal criteria) does not also establish the view that genuine reasoning cannot take place beyond the boundaries of formal logic. For many, including some of the more moderate skeptics, the informal approach has moved objective epistemological discussion forward in normative inquiry. Even though it may not be wholly satisfactory on the highest epistemological level, it certainly augments understanding of practical discourse.[86]

The most difficult question is posed by noncognitivists, or metaethical relativists, who accept the notion that practical deliberation has its own unique rules of reason (even an informal logic) but contend that it fails the test of objectivity. For the metaethical relativist, only the formal deductive and inductive logics governing factual judgments are valid across cultures. Normative rules are merely based on the rationalizations of social convention and custom.[87] From this perspective, the effort to evaluate the soundness of these social rules is misguided.

In certain respects, metaethical relativists are on solid ground. But their position holds up only insofar as the account of practical deliberation is limited to the rules of social conventions and practices. In the informal-logic approach, normative analysis need not terminate with the analysis of social rules and practices.[88] As Taylor's work shows, the social rules themselves may be submitted to two established tests of ethical analysis, the tests of utility and generalization.[89] Essentially, this involves subjecting the social practices that provide standards for everyday discourse to the tests of two higher standards. First, they can be analyzed in terms of their contribution to human welfare maximization. In moral analysis and political philosophy, this test is recognized as the principle of utility or consequences.[90] The second test is derived from the principle of generalization or universalization. Independently of what is justified as useful to human well-being, the moral point of view requires that well-being be distributed as equitably as possible.

However, unlike traditional political philosophers, informal-logic philosophers approach these two tests as procedural rather than substantive criteria. As a metaethical theory, informal logic is advanced as a description of how practical reason is carried out rather than as a prescription per se. It leads to no particular social or political outlook. The principle of utility is considered a rule of thinking, not a substantive ideal. Even though it cannot necessarily decide value judgments, good-reasons writers point out the fact that it is clear enough conceptually to be of use in a wide variety of specific situations. Rather than employing it to prove or justify value judgments, the utility principle is approached as a normative test for determining the warrantability of evidence in practical arguments. It is, in fact, the flexible application of this rule of thinking that makes the approach attractive to policy science.[91]

From the perspective of informal logic, then, value judgments fall into a middle ground. They can neither be dismissed as emotionally based responses nor be formally proved by scientific analysis: Value judgments are worked out and tested by the informal procedural rules that constitute and define practical discourse. In some cases, where the judgment is heavily dependent upon facts, it is possible to establish validity with a high degree of objectivity. In other cases, where such objectivity is more difficult, it is at least possible to sort out arguments that are more generalizable than others and to identify those that remain hopelessly particular. The point is this: There are value judgments that are not merely determined by cultural conditions or personal idiosyncracies. If decision makers agree to employ the procedural rules of practical deliberation, they can validate such value judgments on the basis of the relevant facts and norms. Even though normative assertions include emotionally conditioned attitudes, practical discourse constitutes a rule-governed process with a purpose.

In the next chapter, the focus turns to Taylor's logic of practical deliberation. As an evaluative framework based on informal logic, it provides a practical basis for developing a logic of policy evaluation. Toward this end, Taylor's logic of evaluation is examined against the methodological issues that arise in political and policy evaluation.

Notes

1. Richard E. Flathman, *The Public Interest: Essays on Normative Discourse in Politics* (New York: John Wiley & Sons, 1966), p. 153.

2. Paul W. Taylor, *Normative Discourse* (Englewood Cliffs, N.J.: Prentice-Hall, 1961), p. 3.

3. George A. Theodorson and Achilles G. Theodorson, *Modern Dictionary of Sociology* (New York: Thomas Y. Crowell Co., 1969), p. 455.

4. Robin M. Williams, Jr., "The Concept of Norms," *International Encyclopedia of the Social Sciences,* vol. 2 ed. David L. Sills (New York: Macmillan, 1968), pp. 204–208.

5. Abraham Kaplan, "On the Strategy of Social Planning," *Policy Sciences* 4 (March 1973):57.

6. Michael Scriven, "The Methodology of Evaluation," in *Evaluating Action Programs,* ed. Carol H. Weiss (Boston: Allyn & Bacon, 1972), p. 123.

7. Kenneth J. Arrow, *Social Choice and Individual Values* (New Haven, Conn.: Yale University Press, 1963); John C. Harsanyi, "Cardinal Welfare, Individualistic Ethics, and Interpersonal Comparisons of Utility," *Journal of Political Economy* 63 (August 1955):309–321; and Howard Raiffa, *Decision Analysis* (Reading, Mass.: Addison-Wesley Publishing Co., 1968).

8. On this point see Fred M. Frohock, *Public Policy: Scope and Logic* (Englewood Cliffs, N.J.: Prentice-Hall, 1979); and Giandomenico Majone, "The Feasibility of Social Policies," *Policy Sciences* 6 (March 1975):49–69.

9. See the chapter, "Political Evaluation," in Robert A. Dahl, *Modern Political Analysis* 3d ed. (Englewood Cliffs, N.J.: Prentice-Hall, 1975), p. 130.

10. Ibid., pp. 132–133. Dahl explained: "Ordinarily one cannot simply apply one's standards of value to the different possible results of a decision, determine which one is 'the best,' and then choose it. For if there is uncertainty about the outcomes, to choose 'the best' might be to adopt a strategy that most people on careful reflection would surely reject. For example, let us suppose that one *possible* outcome of foreign policy A is an international system that will ensure permanent peace; but the most *likely* outcome of this policy is thermonuclear war. On the other hand, the most likely outcome of foreign policy B is another decade of stalemate without war or guaranteed peace. The chance that B will produce an inter-

national system of peace and order is virtually zero, yet the chance that it will lead to war is rather low."

11. Charles E. Lindblom and David K. Cohen, *Usable Knowledge: Social Science and Social Problem Solving* (New Haven, Conn.: Yale University Press, 1979).

12. Ibid. See also David Braybrooke and Charles E. Lindblom, *A Strategy of Decision: Policy Evaluation as a Social Process* (New York: Free Press, 1970); and Giandomenico Majone, "The Uses of Policy Analysis," in *The Future and the Past: Essays on Programs,* ed. Russell Sage Foundation (New York: Russell Sage Foundation, 1977).

13. Kurt Baier, *The Moral Point of View: A Rational Basis of Ethics* (New York: Random House, 1965), pp. 24–28.

14. William E. Connolly, *The Terms of Political Discourse* (Lexington, Mass.: D. C. Heath & Co., 1974), p. 14.

15. On this point see Aaron Wildavsky, "The Political Economy of Efficiency: Cost-Benefit Analysis, Systems Analysis, and Program Budgeting," in *Planning Programming Budgeting,* ed. Fremont J. Lyden and Ernest G. Miller (Chicago: Markham, 1967), pp. 371–402.

16. David Easton, *The Political System* (New York: Alfred A. Knopf, 1953).

17. Edward C. Banfield, "Note on Conceptual Scheme," in Edward C. Banfield and Martin Meyerson, *Politics, Planning and the Public Interest* (New York: Free Press, 1955), p. 303.

18. E. E. Schattschneider, *The Semi-Sovereign People* (Hinsdale, Ill.: Dryden Press, 1960), p. 2.

19. Harold Lasswell, *Politics: Who Gets What, When, How?* (Cleveland, Ohio: World Publishing, 1958).

20. Robin M. Williams, Jr., "Individual and Group Values," *The Annals* 371 (May 1967):24.

21. Paul Diesing, *Reason in Society: Five Types of Decisions in Their Social Contexts* (Urbana: University of Illinois Press, 1962), pp. 171–172.

22. Ibid.; and Frederick C. Thayer, "Organization Theory as Epistemology: The Demise of Hierarchy and Objectivity" (Paper presented at the Seventy-Third Annual Meeting of the American Political Science Association, Washington, D.C., September 1, 1977).

23. Diesing, *Reason in Society,* pp. 169–234.

24. Ibid., pp. 203–204.

25. Paul Diesing, "Noneconomic Decision-Making," in *Organizational Decision Making,* ed. Marcus Alexis and Charles Z. Wilson (Englewood Cliffs, N.J.: Prentice-Hall, 1967), p. 196.

26. James Ward Smith, *Theme for Reason* (Princeton, N.J.: Princeton University Press, 1957), p. 14.

27. David Walsh, "Sociology and the Social World," in Paul Filmer et

al., *New Directions in Sociological Theory* (Cambridge, Mass.: M.I.T. Press, 1972), p. 30. Few social scientists have recognized the significance of the link between language and social action, although philosophers of the hermeneutic tradition have begun to explicate the relationship. See Maurice Roche, *Phenomenology, Language and the Social Sciences* (London: Routledge & Kegan Paul, 1973); and Paul Rabinow and William M. Sullivan, eds., *Interpretive Social Science* (Berkeley: University of California Press, 1979).

28. John G. Gunnell, "Social Science and Political Reality: The Problem of Explanation," *Social Research* 35 (Spring 1968):187.

29. Edmund Burke, cited by Brand Blanshard, "Morality and Politics," in *Ethics and Society*, ed. Richard T. DeGeorge (New York: Doubleday & Co., 1966), p. 4.

30. Brian Barry and Douglas W. Rae, "Political Evaluation," in *The Handbook of Political Science*, ed. Nelson W. Polsby and Fred D. Greenstein (Reading, Mass.: Addison-Wesley Publishing Co., 1975), 1:344.

31. Amitai Etzioni, *The Active Society* (New York: Free Press, 1968), p. 352.

32. Max Weber, *The Theory of Social and Economic Organization*, trans. A. M. Henderson and Talcott Parsons (New York: Oxford University Press, 1947).

33. For an interesting discussion of the problems involved in securing consensus for collective action, see Mancur Olson, Jr., *The Logic of Collective Action* (New York: Schocken Books, 1968).

34. Paul Diesing, *Reason in Society*, pp. 169–234.

35. For a discussion of exclusion of values from the political processes, see Harry S. Kariel, *The Decline of American Pluralism* (Stanford, Calif.: Stanford University Press, 1961). For a discussion of the structural possibilities of participation in industrial societies, see Robert A. Dahl, *After the Revolution* (New Haven, Conn.: Yale University Press, 1970); and Mihailo Markovic, *From Affluence to Praxis* (Ann Arbor: University of Michigan Press, 1974).

36. Etzioni, *The Active Society*, p. 228.

37. Jürgen Habermas, *Legitimation Crisis* (Boston: Beacon Press, 1975), pp. 95–143.

38. Weber himself recognized the nature of the problem. See Max Weber, *Economy and Society*, trans. G. Roth and C. Wittich (New York: Free Press, 1968), 1:241.

39. Jürgen Habermas, "Systematically Distorted Communication," in *Critical Sociology*, ed. Paul Connerton (New York: Penguin Books, 1976), pp. 348–362.

40. Rolf-Richard Grauhan and Wendelin Strubelt, "Political Rationality

Reconsidered: Notes on an Integrated Scheme for Policy Choice," *Policy Sciences* 2 (Summer 1971):270. Somewhat similarly, in his "mixed-scanning" approach to decisionmaking, Etzioni distinguished between the political objectives of interest groups and the normative objections to alternatives that violate "basic values." Although his analysis is vague on this point, he seemed to suggest that policy decision makers and analysts should be the contact point for introducing basic values into fundamental political decisions. In a footnote he stated that the "normative integrity" of these groups should be encouraged. Etzioni, *The Active Society*, p. 286.

41. Barry and Rae, "Political Evaluation," p. 340.

42. See Leo Strauss, "Natural Rights and the Distinction Between Facts and Values," in *Philosophy of the Social Sciences*, ed. Maurice Natanson (New York: Random House, 1963), pp. 419–420; and Felix E. Oppenheim, *Moral Principles in Political Philosophy* (New York: Random House, 1968).

43. John Stuart Mill, cited by Bernard Berelson, "Democratic Theory and Public Opinion," in *Theory and Practice of American Government*, ed. Fred Krinsky and Gerald Rigby (Belmont, Calif.: Dickenson, 1967), p. 125.

44. Barry M. Mitnick, "A Typology of Conceptions of the Public Interest," *Administration and Society* 8 (May 1976):5.

45. See, for example, Eugene J. Meehan, *Value Judgment and Social Science* (Homewood, Ill.: Dorsey Press, 1969); Fred M. Frohock, *Normative Political Theory* (Englewood Cliffs, N.J.: Prentice-Hall, 1974); and Felix E. Oppenheim, *Moral Principles in Political Philosophy.*

46. Flathman, *The Public Interest*, p. 153.

47. Arnold Brecht, *Political Theory: The Foundations of Twentieth Century Political Thought* (Princeton, N.J.: Princeton University Press, 1959); and Abraham Edel, *Ethical Judgment: The Use of Science in Ethics* (New York: Free Press, 1955).

48. For an excellent discussion of Dewey's contribution to behavioral science methodology, see Rollo Handy, *Value Theory and the Behavioral Sciences* (Springfield, Ill.: Charles C. Thomas, 1969).

49. For an illustration of this point see Frederick M. Watkins, "Natural Law and the Problem of Value-Judgment," in *Political Research and Political Theory*, ed. Oliver Garceau (Cambridge, Mass.: Harvard University Press, 1968), p. 64. Watkins wrote the following: "To those who believe in the common humanity of Jews and Gentiles, the slightest discrimination against a Jew as such will give rise to a sense of injustice; by the same token, a man who believes that Jews as such are enemies of the human race will deplore the injustice of any single act of clemency that permits a Jew to live. Since both, in their respective judgments, are appealing to the

principle that like cases should be treated alike, it may be said in a sense that the humanitarian and the anti-Semite are animated by a common sense of justice. To call this a principle of natural law is all very well in its way, but laws like this are too formalistic to have any real significance. Even if . . . it were possible to prove the universal validity of many such propositions, the result would be too trivial to repay so great an effort."

50. Braybrooke and Lindblom, *A Strategy of Decision*, pp. 1–57.

51. Abraham Kaplan, "Some Limitations on Rationality," in *Rational Decision*, ed. Carl J. Friedrich (New York: Atherton Press, 1967), p. 58. As Kaplan said, "Majority rule is not necessarily the rational procedure for such aggregation; it is easily shown that consistent individual scales do not necessarily yield a consistent scale for the majority. There is a related problem of dividing the loot among the members of a winning coalition. To my knowledge this problem has not been solved in game theory in any acceptable way: it is *the* problem of politics."

52. Arrow, *Social Choice and Individual Values*.

53. Lindblom and Braybrooke contended that Arrow's contribution to the construction of a social welfare function has been misunderstood by many policy writers. Its value is primarily heuristic rather than practical. As they explained, Arrow constructed his work principally as "an analytic aid to theorists," not as "a practical guide to policy analysis." Braybrooke and Lindblom, *A Strategy of Decision*, pp. 22–23. Heuristics is a generic term employed generally to refer to noncomprehensive analytic strategies of investigation designed to probe complex problems. See J. R. Slagle, *Artificial Intelligence* (New York: McGraw-Hill Book Co., 1971).

54. See Stanford L. Optner, ed., *Systems Analysis* (Baltimore: Penguin Books, 1973); C. West Churchman, *The Systems Approach* (New York: Dell Publishing Co., 1968); and Grace Kelleher, ed., *The Challenge to Systems Analysis: Public Policy and Social Change* (New York: John Wiley & Sons, 1970).

55. David Easton, *A Systems Analysis of Political Life* (New York: Alfred A. Knopf, 1965); and Yehezkel Dror, *Public Policymaking Reexamined* (San Francisco: Chandler Publishing Co., 1968).

56. See Bruce L. B. Smith, *The Rand Corporation* (Cambridge, Mass.: Harvard University Press, 1966); and Howard Raiffa, *Decision Analysis*.

57. For some illustrations and discussion, see Bertram M. Gross and Michael Springer, eds., "Political Intelligence For America's Future," *The Annals* 388 (March 1970).

58. Abraham Kaplan, *The Conduct of Inquiry: Methodology for Behavioral Science* (Scranton, Pa.: Chandler Publishing Co., 1964), p. 389. For a discussion of human needs and the systems perspective in the context of post-behavioralism, see Avery Leiserson, "Realism and Commit-

ment in Political Theory," in *The Post-Behavioral Era,* ed. George J. Graham and George G. Carey (New York: David McKay, 1972), pp. 144–170.

59. Paul Kurtz, *Decision and the Condition of Man* (New York: Dell Publishing Co., 1965), p. 247.

60. Fred R. Dallmayr, "Beyond Dogma and Despair: Toward a Critical Theory of Politics," *American Political Science Review* 70 (March 1976): 64–79.

61. The recentness of this approach can be observed in the fact that the discussion of political evaluation in the 1970 edition of Robert Dahl's *Modern Political Analysis* mentions only the clash between noncognitivism, naturalism, and intuitionism; Dahl states that the conflict seems "too fundamental to be resolved by general agreement," requiring the search for a new methodology for political evaluation. Six years later the revised version of the same passage includes a fourth approach, "one not entirely inconsistent with any one of the other three perspectives" that "has recently gained ground in political evaluation." The aim of this approach "is to enrich and clarify moral discourse and political evaluation by heightening our understanding of the language we use when we discuss moral questions." Even though a large amount of this conceptual approach is "tedious and often trivial," Dahl suggests that at its best it "seeks to restore the dignity and significance to political evaluation" that has been eroded as scientific naturalism and intuitionism have yielded to noncognitivism. Compare Robert A. Dahl, *Modern Political Analysis,* 2d ed. (Englewood Cliffs, N.J.: Prentice-Hall, 1970), p. 108 with Dahl, *Modern Political Analysis,* 3d ed. (Englewood Cliffs, N.J.: Prentice-Hall, 1975), pp. 135–136.

62. Taylor, *Normative Discourse,* p. viii.

63. Kurt Baier, "Reasoning in Practical Deliberation," in *The Moral Judgment,* ed. Paul W. Taylor (Englewood Cliffs, N.J.: Prentice-Hall, 1963), p. 278.

64. Ibid.

65. Stephen Toulmin, *The Uses of Argument* (Cambridge: Cambridge University Press, 1958), pp. 7–8. See also Chaim Perelman, *The Idea of Justice and the Problem of Argument* (London: Routledge & Kegan Paul, 1963). For a discussion of argumentation as a methodology in the social sciences see Derek L. Phillips, *Abandoning Method: Sociological Studies in Methodology* (San Francisco: Jossey-Bass, 1973).

66. Margaret MacDonald, "Natural Rights," in *Philosophy, Politics and Society,* ed. Peter Laslett (Oxford: Oxford University Press, 1953), pp. 53–55.

67. Ibid.

68. Stephen Toulmin, *An Examination of the Place of Reason in Ethics* (Cambridge: Cambridge University Press, 1970), p. 130.

69. Sheldon S. Wolin, *Politics and Vision* (Boston: Little, Brown and Co., 1960), p. 27.

70. Mark Gavre, "Hobbes and His Audience: The Dynamics of Theorizing," *American Political Science Review* 68 (December 1974):1543.

71. Habermas, *Legitimation Crisis*, pp. 95–143.

72. Ibid., p. 107.

73. Ibid.

74. Ibid., p. 108.

75. Flathman has advanced a similar argument in his attempt to adapt the logical rules of normative discourse to the concept of public interest policy arguments, although the significance of his contribution appears to have been partially lost because of its ties to the public interest concept, which still remain the subject of considerable debate. Flathman, *The Public Interest*.

76. Toulmin, *The Uses of Argument*, pp. 146–210. Reconstructed or formal scientific logic is based on the principles of induction and deduction. In scientific explanation, these two principles are linked through the "hypothetico-deductive method." A scientific explanation, in this sense, is defined as a deductively organized set of inductively tested empirical generalizations. Based on the formal "if-then" structure of the logical syllogism, which is similar to a mathematical model, the hypothetico-deductive method is tautological. All valid conclusions are based on the consequences of the initial generalizations. See also R. B. Braithwaite, *Scientific Explanation* (Cambridge: Cambridge University Press, 1953).

77. Ernest Nagel, *The Structure of Science: Problems in the Logic of Scientific Explanation* (New York: Harcourt, Brace and World, 1961), pp. 552–575.

78. The notion that explanation must be able to predict the state of the system at *any* moment from its state at *one* moment is an example of a universal standard. For further discussion, see Stephen Toulmin, *Foresight and Understanding* (New York: Harper and Row, 1961).

79. Toulmin, *An Examination of the Place of Reason in Ethics*.

80. A "reason" is defined as "a fact or circumstances forming, or alleged as forming, a ground or motive leading, or sufficient to lead, a person to adopt or reject some course of action or procedure, belief," etc. See Flathman, *The Public Interest*, p. 75.

81. Frohock has offered a useful example that captures the difference between the warranted-by-reasons approach and the positivist's verification position: "To the verificationist, the statement 'President Nixon is 60 years old' is a proposition to be proved true or false as it conforms to

experience." Good-reasons philosophers "will see the statement as a warranted assertion as evidence is brought to bear in support of it." Verificationists and good-reasons theorists hold essentially similar positions on this proposition. Consider, however, the proposition that matter is soluble: "Since this statement attributes a disposition to matter to perform in certain ways under certain conditions, and these conditions can never be exhausted, then the verificationist is stuck with a statement which is not verifiable. The 'good reasons' philosopher, on the other hand, will be content to see dispositional statements as more or less warranted in terms of the evidence at hand. No dilemma is presented with a dispositional [statement] because truth or falsity is not at issue. Now consider the statement 'All men ought to love their neighbor.' To the verificationist, this statement is meaningless because we have no means of verifying it. But the 'good reasons' philosopher will, again, be able to accept the statement as more or less warranted on the basis of supporting considerations, for example that following such a prescription will make for more congenial zoning policies, and so on. A 'good reasons' view of adequacy, then, escapes the verificationist critique of evaluative statements by replacing verification with the notion of supporting reasons." Frohock, *Normative Political Theory*, pp. 73–74.

82. For example, Toulmin has cited the classic illustration of light: Is it in reality a particle or a wave? Scientific method cannot answer. All that science can tell us is that light is at times viewed as a wave and at times as a particle. The determination of what light really is is beyond the scope of science. If one is looking for an authoritative statement about reality, or ultimate justification of explanation, it is necessary to turn to metaphysics. The instrumental nature of science rules out any such statements derived from its own methods. Similarly, normative inquiry is limited by its own purpose and rules, which identify it as a distinctive enterprise.

83. As Frohock explained, "The infinite regress of questioning is halted in the same way it is halted in science, by an identification of the purpose and rules of ethical inquiry and a further assumption that the purpose and rules of ethics marks off a form of activity which has its own limits to requests for justification." Consider the following illustration: "Suppose, for example, that I say, 'Joan, you ought to return the book to Jones,' and Joan asks why. Then I say, 'Because you promised to,' which is a perfectly good reason for carrying out the *ought* I have stated. Now if Joan then asks, 'Why ought I to keep promises,' she has, according to Toulmin, moved outside the ethical game of promising." An inquirer in ethics who probes the question back to the objective of ethical inquiry moves outside the field of ethics. Frohock, *Normative Political Theory*, p. 74.

84. One such social practice is "promising," involving public procedural

rules that are readily taught to all social members. When a promise is made, an agreement to operate within specific procedural rules is established. A promise to meet another person cannot be abrogated merely because it is decided subsequently that it would be more advantageous not to meet him or her. Such an excuse cannot be presented as a ground if the evaluator is still to be considered operating within the social practice of promising. It is possible to change the practice, but if it is accepted, some things must be done. Failure to do them either reveals that the practice is not really understood or that in actuality it was not accepted. Legitimate excuses (based on exceptional situations) can be advanced, but they are built into the very social practice itself. For a sociological account of social rules and practices, see Peter L. Berger and Thomas Luckmann, *The Social Construction of Reality* (New York: Doubleday & Co., 1967). Also, see T. S. Simey, *Social Science and Social Purpose* (London: Constable, 1968), pp. 149–174. For a discussion of the problem of deriving normative judgments from descriptive statements that considers its relationship to naturalism, see John Searle, "How to Derive 'Ought' from 'Is,' " in *The Is-Ought Question*, ed. W. D. Hudson (New York: St. Martin's Press, 1969), pp. 120–134.

85. For a range of perspectives on this issue, see Carl Wellman, *The Language of Ethics* (Cambridge, Mass.: Harvard University Press, 1961); Vere C. Chappel, ed., *Ordinary Language* (Englewood Cliffs, N.J.: Prentice-Hall, 1964); Arthur Edward Murphy, *The Theory of Practical Reason*, ed. A. I. Melden (LaSalle, Ill.: Open Court Publishing Co., 1964); and Paul Edwards, *The Logic of Moral Discourse* (Glencoe, Ill.: Free Press, 1955).

86. For two excellent recent discussions on this, see Thomas D. Perry, *Moral Reasoning and Truth* (Oxford: Clarendon Press, 1976); and David A. J. Richards, *A Theory of Reasons for Action* (Oxford: Clarendon Press, 1971).

87. For an interesting discussion of this point see J. H. Barnsley, *The Social Reality of Ethics* (London: Routledge & Kegan Paul, 1972). Barnsley accepts the view that values are relative but argues that this is not necessarily dysfunctional. It is, in fact, this reality that permits social groups to adjust to one another.

88. See Kai Nielsen, "Problems of Ethics," in *The Encyclopedia of Philosophy*, ed. Paul Edwards (New York: Macmillan, 1967), 3:130–132.

89. For discussion of these two principles see R. M. Hare, *The Language of Morals* (Oxford: Clarendon Press, 1952); and Marcus G. Singer, *Generalization in Ethics* (New York: Alfred A. Knopf, 1960).

90. A number of normative theorists are likely to point out the fact that the good-reasons approach is a form of rule utilitarianism, an ethical position that has drawn a good deal of criticism in recent years in the

writings of Rawls, Gewirth, and Dworkin. See John Rawls, *A Theory of Justice* (Cambridge, Mass.: Belknap Press, 1971); Alan Gewirth, *Moral Responsibility* (Lawrence: Department of Philosophy, University of Kansas, 1972); and Ronald Dworkin, *Taking Rights Seriously* (London: Duckworth, 1977). These writers, however, do not reject the utility principle as a tool in moral argument. Instead, they are concerned with its relationship to other principles, such as the principle of generalization. It is worth noting that good-reasons writers can consider Rawls to be a representative of their point of view. See Kai Nielsen, "History of Ethics," in *The Encyclopedia of Philosophy,* 3:110.

91. For a discussion of the utilitarian character of policy decision making see Ian Budge, "Representations of Political Argument: Applications Within Meta-Planning," *Political Studies* 27 (December 1978):439–449. Also, see Paul Kurtz, "Policy Decisions and Value in Metaeconomics," in *Human Values and Economic Policy,* ed. Sidney Hook (New York: New York University Press, 1967), pp. 150–156.

4

The Logic of Evaluation: Evaluation Research and Phenomenology

---

[What we need] is a language in which we may express our sentiments—approvals, disapprovals, evaluations, recommendations, advice, instructions, prescriptions—and put them out in the public arena for rational scrutiny and discussion, claiming that they will hold up under scrutiny and discussion and that all our audience will concur with us if they will also choose the same point of view.

—William K. Frankena[1]

A primary task of epistemology and methodology in philosophy and the social sciences is to analyze and clarify the basic concepts and rules that govern the logic of the discourse in which human beings do their thinking. The purpose is to obtain an understanding of what it means to be rational in the several types of discourse employed to explain social phenomena—scientific, mathematical, historical, or normative discourse. In social scientific discourse, analyses of what it means to be rational are quite familiar.[2] These investigations involve the explication of the rules of reasoning that govern the perception, organization, and communication of empirical results. In normative discourse, however, there has been less systematic inquiry into the actual rules of reasoning that govern rational thinking, although there is a growing belief that normative discourse is governed by its own unique rules, as seen in the previous chapter. The problem is that few analysts have said what these rules are, at least with enough precision to be useful. In this respect, Paul Taylor is an important exception. His book, *Normative Discourse*, presents a clear exposition

of the concepts and rules of reasoning employed in the evaluation of practical arguments.[3]

The Informal Logic of Evaluation

Thus far, this study has focused on the issues that generate
concern for political evaluation, the problems involved in the
formulation of the concept, and its methodological implications. At this point it is appropriate to present the "informal
logic" of evaluation[4] and examine it in relation to the methodological problems that arise in political evaluation. My purpose
is to show that this informal logic provides a methodological
framework that facilitates evaluative inquiry by organizing the
key epistemological questions raised by behavioral scientists,
phenomenologists, and philosophers.[5] Moreover, by showing
how facts bear on questions of value, I am suggesting an approach that avoids the practical dilemma posed by the fact-
value dichotomy.

Taylor is concerned fundamentally with two questions:
What is it to evaluate something? And how can such evaluations
be justified?[6] As an extension of the work of Toulmin and
Baier, Taylor's informal logic focuses on the rules implicitly or
explicitly followed in an attempt to judge a rule or standard to
be good, to justify a goal as right, or to show that a decision
to take an action ought to be made.[7] Essentially, the informal
logic provides the evaluator with two things: (1) the rules of
reasoning that demonstrate what makes a reason *relevant* to
validity claims (the "rules of relevance"), and (2) the rules of
reasoning that determine what makes a reason a *good* one in
support of such claims (the "rules of valid inference").[8]

Each universe or type of discourse has its own rules of
inference, although there are usually a number of subuniverses
of discourse within each type. Within evaluative discourse, for
example, there are the subuniverses of moral, aesthetic, religious,
legal, or political evaluation. Sharing the common rules of inference, each subuniverse involves making and justifying value
judgments.

The discussion in the previous chapter included an examination of a "political" evaluation. In metanormative terms, political

evaluation was seen to be a special case of practical moral discourse constrained by the requirements of power and authority, limited knowledge, scarce resources, and time. In the ideal, political evaluation remains subject to the logic of moral reasoning, although the realities of the political world limit the degree of rationality that can be achieved.

The nature of the logical relationship between evaluation in general and political evaluation in particular has been clearly expressed by Brian Barry: "Since every evaluation may be made from many different aspects, not every judgment that a situation is bad is a political judgment; in order to be a political judgment it must be connected (even if at some remove) to the judgment that some action of a political nature ought to be taken to improve it." He illustrated this with the following example:

> An evaluation of, let us say, newspapers, novels or television programmes to the effect that they are not all that they might be, is, so far, not a political evaluation. It becomes one (or, more exactly, it forms the grounds for one) if this state of affairs is attributed to the educational system and it is believed that the state has a responsibility for the condition of the educational system, or if it is thought that the state should do something about the subsidization of the arts, the ownership of newspapers or the control of television programmes. On the other hand, if such activities are thought to be no business of the state, the evaluation remains a full blooded aesthetic one but does not attain any political relevance.[9]

Political evaluation, as a subuniverse of evaluative discourse, specifies a "point of view." To adopt a point of view is to agree to accept the general "rules of relevance" that establish and govern the framework and purposes of the specific mode of reasoning. Such rules provide the contextual basis for deciding what makes a reason relevant when thinking within the point of view. The rules of relevance of a political point of view direct attention to questions concerning the criteria for determining the nature, content, and selection of goals and values governing collective decisions and action. By contrast, economists tend to consider the economic point of view as an emphasis on the means of achieving goals and values, rather than on the selection or character of the goals themselves. Within the social sciences, the proper delineation of particular points of view—political, social, or economic—remains the subject of varying degrees of controversy. Without accepting Diesing's attempt to explicate and compare the nature of political, economic, social, and legal rationality, it is possible to see it as an interesting exercise designed to uncover the rules of relevance that govern these points of view.

As contextual rules, the rules of relevance of a point of view do not establish the criteria for specific empirical or normative data. Within a point of view, there are many different possible value systems that specify criteria that can be employed in the judgment process. The admissibility of evidence within a point of view is determined by the adoption of a particular value system, i.e., an organized set of substantive concepts bound together by normative principles and value axioms. Value systems "offer the relevant rules and principles" that indicate what makes a reason in support of a claim a "good" reason. Political value systems—such as liberal democracy, Marxist socialism, or fascism—offer different standards and rules for judging the acceptability of political goals. Where the liberal might judge a policy or action against constitutional provisions, the Marxist will assess it in terms of its implications for the working classes. Employing alternative rules and principles, each infers a different conclusion concerning the normative validity of a particular political decision or action.

The metanormative task is to ask what sorts of reasons are good reasons for justifying a political value system within the political point of view. The purpose is to emphasize the logical structure and rules of inference governing the justification process, approached here through Taylor's informal logic.

Taylor has presented a general logical structure that governs rational judgment in evaluative discourse as a whole. It is germane to all types of evaluation—political, aesthetic, economic, religious, and so on—and is delineated in four phases: verification, validation, vindication, and rational choice. In epistemological terms, the four-phased logical structure cuts across the two fundamental levels of normative analysis, first- and second-order discourse. First-order discourse, verification and validation, involves decision making based on principles fixed in the value systems that govern the particular decision-making process in question. This is the level of discourse most familiar to contemporary social scientists. In verification, evaluation focuses on the empirical demonstration of whether the object under evaluation fulfills the requirements of the norms introduced by the decision maker; in validation, it asks whether the goal itself is compatible with the basic value systems that provide the competing criteria in the judgment process.

Second-order discourse, vindication and rational choice, is associated generally with the concerns of normative inquiry, in particular political and social philosophy. It involves choosing value systems by making "decisions of principle," i.e., deciding which value principles are to be adopted as guides in subsequent decision making. Here, the evaluator must ask if the basic value system is itself acceptable. In vindication, an effort is made to determine whether the value system is instrumental or contributive to the adopted way of life (or "culture," in the terminology of the social sciences). Finally, for a complete or full justification, it is necessary for the evaluator to attempt to show that the choice of the way of life was governed by rational processes in free and open deliberation. This last phase is called rational choice.

Each of the four phases contains specific requirements that must be fulfilled in making a complete justification of a value judgment. For a reason to be considered a "good reason," it must meet the requirements of the four-phased probe. Included in the requirements are the basic types of empirical data applicable to normative judgments.

The remainder of the discussion in this chapter is devoted to an examination of the first two phases of the logic of evaluation—verification and validation. Vindication and rational choice are discussed in the next chapter. In each phase, the analysis proceeds first with a presentation of the logic of evaluation, then illustrates the main points of the phase in a policy evaluation problem, and finally raises key methodological questions confronted in each phase—the questions posed by behavioral science, phenomenology, and political philosophy.

Verification

Verification is a first-order phase in the attempt to evaluate a value judgment. It is the simplest of the four phases to explain but is by no means easy to satisfy in the evaluation process. The basic question in this phase is whether or not an object under investigation (the evaluatum) does or does not fulfill a standard or rule that has been adopted as a criterion. Verification assumes the adoption of a standard and proceeds as an empirical assessment. To say that something fulfills or does not fulfill a standard is to render an empirical judgment.

Evaluation Research

Verification is essentially an appeal to the rules governing empirical demonstration in the behavioral sciences. It consists of finding out whether the evaluatum does or does not fulfill the given criteria to the degree stated in the judgment. In scientific terms, the crucial dimension is whether the judgment can be shown to be correct through publicly demonstrable procedures. As a basic concept of science, publicly demonstrable procedures stress intersubjectivity through tests capable of replicating the same results. Empirical testing and reliability of results are the concepts that epistemologically ground the activity.

The underlying assumption of the verification phase in a policy evaluation is that action programs are designed to achieve specific ends and that their success can be measured in terms of the extent to which these ends are reached. The question of how well a program fulfills a standard or goal is closely related to—at times synonymous with—the concept of efficiency in economic analysis (i.e., how well means achieve ends). In the classical formulation of policy decision making derived from positivist economics, efficiency in fact is the principal criterion for evaluation. In its purest form, efficiency is the meeting of objectives at the lowest cost or the obtaining of the maximum amount of an objective for a specified amount of resources.

The ideal methodological design for the evaluation of social action programs is the controlled experiment. Known as evaluation research (or applied action research) in the policy literature, it involves adapting the methods and tools of behavioral research to the action context of program evaluation. Emphasizing experimental design, evaluation research focuses on the identification of the aspects of the situation or target populations that are to be changed, the measurement of their state before introduction of the program, and measurement again after completion of the program. To assure that the effectiveness of the evaluatum (rather than other extraneous variables) is being measured, a control situation that does not receive the program is ideally introduced for the purpose of comparison. The primary difference between nonevaluative experimental research and evaluation research is that the dependent variable generally refers to the object of investigation in the former, with the hypothesis developed around the conditions and factors influencing the growth or attenuation of, say, poverty. In program evaluation, interest is directed to the program itself, which is an independent variable, and hypotheses are developed around the conditions and factors that bear on the successful implementation of the program and the efficiency of its impact on the dependent variable.[10]

A review of the recent spate of compendiums on evaluation research shows clearly that research design is the central focus.[11] The particular problems of experimental design and data analysis that stand out are: (a) specification of the research question(s) to be addressed; (b) selection of the appropriate population for testing the hypothesis; (c) selection, assignment, and maintenance of subjects in treatment categories; (d) designation of a system that provides for early estimates of immediate effects and estimates of long-range effects; and (e) selection of data sources and/or analytic procedures that can serve as correctives for defective design strategies arising from constraints on the research.

Volumes are devoted to the difficulties involved in developing criteria for empirical testing, especially the problem of operationalization, which is concerned with constructing empirical recording devices that can be both physically accomplished and epistemologically justified.[12] Many argue that the methods and tools of social research are intrinsically inhospitable to the action context of social programs—whether in

education, social welfare, criminal correction, health, job training, community action, or any other area. Bernstein and Freeman, for instance, do not consider evaluation studies to be
scientific research in the usual sense of the term. They defined
evaluation research as the "application of social science methodology to the assessment of programs in a way that allows one
to determine empirically their implementation and efficiency,"
but argued that "evaluation studies have a particularistic decision
focus, i.e., are designed to help decision makers faced with
practical action alternatives." Nonevaluative research studies,
in contrast, aim for empirical knowledge of a more "generalizable, less decision-oriented sort." In fact, to these writers the
very phrase "evaluation research" represents a "hybrid conceptualization" of pure and practical approaches.[13]

While textbooks typically present research methods designed
to determine statistical variance through experimental treatment, it is recognized in practice that program evaluation
research can seldom go about its business so systematically.
Evaluation is hobbled by the constraints of the field situation:
too few clients, demand for quick feedback of information,
inadequate funds, contamination of the special treatment
groups by receipt of other services, dropouts from the program,
lack of access to records and data, changes in programs, and so
on. But perhaps even more critical—certainly for the present
study—is the fact that evaluation research is hampered by difficulties involved in developing and operationalizing criteria.
As Rein and Weiss said, "Evaluation asks the extent to which
predetermined goals are reached. But how will such goals as
increased opportunity, a more responsive institutional system,
and a richer cultural atmosphere show themselves? What operations can be chosen, in advance, to decide whether these goals
have or have not been realized?"[14] The development of social
programs by political decision makers, unlike, say, the development of an electrical motor by an engineer, involves aims and
goals that are often so broad that it appears virtually impossible to measure their real effectiveness.

It is at the verification level of evaluation that traditional
means-ends behavioralists enter the epistemological debate.
For them, relevance rests on the ability of social scientists to

surmount the obstacles that impede the use of scientific measurement techniques in applied action research. Conceding that it will take some time before results from such work will be socially useful, behavioral scientists maintain that in the long run they will be more dependable. Such results will be grounded on statistical regularities and causal laws, which are themselves subject to verification.

The fact that behavioral science has not yet developed such causal knowledge should not overshadow the growing sophistication in measurement techniques in recent decades. Henry Riecken is correct in stating that "the major contribution of a socially useful character from the social sciences is in the mensurative or methodological realm."[15] Even though most verifications are not based on causal regularities, they nonetheless employ empirical measurement involving the methodological issues of validity and reliability.

Improvements in the techniques of measurement have contributed significantly to the development of reliable empirical indicators. In fact, the development of indicators has itself become a major methodological activity. Numerous economic indicators have achieved institutional status, such as the consumer price index, the unemployment rate, the gross national product, and the Dow Jones industrial averages. As empirical measures of reality, such indicators play an important technical and political role in modern society.[16] In the late 1960s, the growth of empirical evaluation research was reflected in the movement toward the development of a set of social indicators, although the effort was associated more with the systems-oriented post-behavioral perspective than with the traditional means-ends approach.

Verification Illustrated

The fact that verification is one of the most important and complicated phases in the evaluation process is clearly illustrated by the federal government's evaluation of the Head Start program, designed to help poor children compensate for learning disadvantages.[17] An evaluation research study, conducted by the Westinghouse Learning Corporation at Ohio University under federal commission, generated a sizable controversy that provides an excellent illustration of the problems confronting evaluation at the verification level.[18] These problems, as this case shows, principally revolve around the complex methodological questions associated with empirical assessment.

The Head Start program was seen by many to be a major innovation in social legislation designed to help the children of the ghetto poor. The program was an archetype of the war on poverty and had strong political support. Many saw it as a watershed in the struggle for social change. In 1969, however, President Nixon stated in his economic opportunity message to Congress that the results of the Westinghouse study showed that the long-term effects of Head Start appeared to be extremely weak. The terse announcement triggered a major public controversy through Congress, the executive branch, and the educational community. The question was this: Had the Learning Corporation succeeded in accurately verifying its evaluative judgment, namely, that there was little evidence that Head Start had shown long-term results? The *New York Times* reported that "a number of social scientists . . . have expressed fears that Congress or the Administration will seize upon the report's generally negative conclusion as an excuse to downgrade or discard the Head Start program."[19] Much of the debate focused on the esoteric techniques of modern statistical analysis and research design. Included in the criticisms were the following:

- The study is based on an *ex post facto* design which is inherently faulty because it attempts to generate a control group by matching former Head Start children with other non–Head Start children.
- The study tested the children in the first, second, and third grades of elementary school—after they had left Head Start. Its findings merely demonstrate that Head Start achievements do not persist after the children return to poverty homes and ghetto schools.
- The study fails to give adequate attention to variations among the Head Start Programs.
- The sample is not representative. Many of the original randomly chosen centers had to be eliminated.
- The test instruments used in the study, and indeed all existing instruments for measuring cognitive and affective states in children, are primitive. They were not developed for disadvantaged populations.[20]

These criticisms clearly involve questions of whether the claim that Head Start fails to fulfill cognitive and affective standards has been empirically verified. Where the study states that the standards have not been fulfilled, the methodological criticisms assert that the program's performance has not been adequately measured to justify the judgment. At this point in the evaluation process, a judgment can at times be thought of as true or false in the scientific sense of the term.

The debate over whether the standards have been fulfilled is a probe for the reasons behind alternative judgments. To probe for reasons in empirical verification is to seek out the list of "becauses" that normally lie behind a verdict. For example, a line of questioning concerning the Westinghouse study might proceed as follows:

Question: Why do you say that Head Start is only a limited success?

Answer: Because it does not appear to satisfy the criteria we've set up for such pre-school educational programs.

Question: You're saying you're convinced that according to acceptable standards of cognitive and affective learning you judge the program to be weak.

Answer: That is correct.

Question: But how do you *know* the program has not satisfied the criteria and that you are justified in stating that it is weak?

Answer: We've graded the program as weak because on all major criteria employed, and their corresponding standards, the programs appeared to be failing.

Question: But have you actually measured these criteria accurately? What about the fact that the study lumps the programs together into an overall average and does not explore what variation there may be in effectiveness as a function of differing program styles and characters? Also, your sample does not seem to be representative. I am very concerned about these methodological limitations and am wondering if, on this basis, you are fully justified in your judgment that Head Start is only a limited success?[21]

Validation

Assume it is decided that the Westinghouse judgment has, in fact, been empirically verified, that is, the Head Start program is weak on all criteria employed. The questioning then might take a different turn:

Question: But "weak" compared to what?

Answer: Weak compared to these criteria.

Question: But why these criteria?

Answer: Because . . .

The question "But why these criteria?" moves the probe to the second phase of the evaluation process, validation. In this phase, the task is to show why the criteria employed are the appropriate ones. Further exploration of the Westinghouse evaluation indeed reveals this second kind of criticism, thus directing attention beyond verification to the validation phase. Critics have argued:

> The study is too narrow. It focuses only on cognitive and affective outcomes. Head Start is a much broader program which includes health, nutrition, and community objectives, and any proper evaluation must evaluate it on all these objectives.[22]

Questions are raised here about the appropriateness of the evaluative criteria employed. Head Start, in effect, is a broadly aimed program; much more is involved than cognitive and affective outcomes. How can it be judged weak without considering these other criteria? Given the political climate of the war on poverty, some analysts in fact argue that its social-symbolic impact is as important a criterion as any other. They might conclude that the Head Start program is weak in terms of its cognitive and affective outcomes, but as a political commitment to impoverished people in the ghetto it has played a valuable role. In short, it would be a mistake to eliminate the program on the basis of these narrow criteria.

While verification attempts to show that an object fulfills or fails to fulfill standards, validation questions whether certain criteria are the ones that should be employed in that judgment. In validation, one is not concerned with the outcome itself, but rather with the criteria that were employed in making the judgment. For example, a validation of the Head Start program might follow the kind of dialogue Kelly has suggested for educational curricula in general.

Judgment: The educational curriculum is a good one.

Question: Why?

Answer: Because it provides these disadvantaged children with socially relevant experiences.

Question: But why does providing socially relevant experiences for such children make it a good educational curriculum?

Answer: Because whether or not a curriculum provides socially relevant experiences for children is a good reason for judging a curriculum good or bad.

Question: But what I want to know is why you think that reason is a good one?

Answer: Because providing socially relevant experiences for children is a good reason for judging educational curricula for disadvantaged children to be good, and the Head Start program is a curriculum of this type.

Question: Suppose I admit that this is an educational curriculum for disadvantaged children and that it does, in fact, provide socially relevant experiences for such children. But what I want to know is why providing socially relevant experiences for children is a good reason for judging the educational curriculum for Head Start to be good? I fail to see that you've answered that question yet.[23]

To say that a curriculum is good because it offers socially relevant experiences for children is to say that it satisfies a criterion. For instance, the reply to the last question above might have been: "Providing socially relevant experiences for children is a good reason for judging a curriculum 'good' because the goal of education is to train children for entrance into society. One of the illustrations of this training occurs in those curricula that provide socially relevant experiences. Thus, this educational curriculum is a good one insofar as it offers socially relevant experiences." The question that might follow is: "But why is preparation for a role in society the purpose of education?" If pursued, this line of questioning would force the defendant of the judgment to regress to first principles. Generally, only a tedious philosophical axe grinder is likely to push the inquiry to this level, shifting the argument from validation to vindication and rational choice.

Validation as a Logical Method

A fully justified answer to the question of validation requires proof showing that not only this particular evaluator but every evaluator is justified in adopting social relevance as a criterion for judging an educational curriculum such as Head Start. According to the general logic of evaluation, a complete validation of such a criterion involves the three following logical steps:

Step 1:   It must be demonstrated that the criterion for evaluation (standard or rule) is *relevant.* That is, its range or scope of application must include the class of comparisons of the given value judgment. As a result of this step, the evaluatum is established to belong to a class of things that are correctly judged by the criterion.

Step 2:   It must be demonstrated that neither the circumstances in which the evaluatum occurs nor anything out of the ordinary about the evaluatum (i.e., anything that distinguishes the evaluatum from the other members of the class of comparison) allows an *exception* to be made to the general application of the criterion determined in Step 1. As an outcome of this step, the evaluatum itself, not just the class of things to which it belongs, is determined to be properly judged by the criterion.

Step 3: It must be demonstrated that either no other valid criterion conflicts with the criterion being applied, or if there is conflict, the criterion that is being applied takes precedence over those in conflict with it.[24]

Each of these three steps must be probed with the assistance of three methods. Method A involves an appeal to the more general criteria from which the standards and rules under consideration are deduced.[25] This method is based on the principle of generalization. Method B, based on the principle of utility, is an appeal to standards for assessing the consequences of fulfilling or not fulfilling the criterion being probed. Method C is concerned with criteria for judging whether it is better to permit an exception to the standards or rules in question than it is to follow them and for judging the relative precedence of any criteria that are in conflict. Methods A and B are alternative methods for carrying out Step 1. Method C is used for carrying out Steps 2 and 3. All three methods must be engaged before the "reasonableness" of the entire process of validation can be fully demonstrated. The three steps and the methods by which they can be satisfied encompass the process of appeal to rules and consequences that characterizes normative justification in the validation phase.[26] Closely following Taylor's text, they are illustrated in the following discussion.

Step 1 is concerned with relevance. The first way to show that a criterion is relevant is to demonstrate that its range or scope includes the class of comparisons of the given value judgment. This is accomplished by Method A[27]—an appeal to a more general criterion from which the first criterion can be deduced (recognizing that the relevance of the more general criterion would itself eventually have to be validated by Methods A or B).[28] This entails a logical demonstration that the first criterion actually meets the requirements of the second criterion.[29]

In addition, the applicability or relevance of a standard can be determined by Method B. "One might argue," as Taylor

explained, "that liberality in giving to charity is a relevant standard for judging a man's character, because the over-all effects
of people's acts are *better* when it is fulfilled than when it is
not." That is to say, "the more widely the standard is adopted
in a society, and the more completely it is fulfilled by those
who adopt it, the *more ideal* the society will be."[30] A determination that one particular effect or consequence is better
than other consequences, or that a particular outcome is found
to be more ideal than others, is a value judgment itself. As such,
it too must be subjected to the tests of Methods A and B. If
the relevance of the second criterion is demonstrated, the original criterion can be accepted as relevant.

As a procedure for justifying criteria, Method B is recognized
in ethics as a form of "restricted utilitarianism." A rule validated
by Method B is justified by an appeal to the "utility" principle,
also known as the "greatest happiness" principle. Here the criteria themselves are the evaluata. "They are," as Taylor explained,
"judged as having instrumental value or disvalue to an inherently
valuable end (the greatest happiness of all sentient beings)."[31]

Step 2 is concerned with circumstances. An act can involve
breaking a rule without conclusively establishing that it must be
judged wrong. Taylor cited Toulmin's example about book
borrowing. If a person has borrowed a book from someone and
is asked why (s)he ought to return it, (s)he might reply:

> I ought to take it back to him, "because I promised to let him have
> it back before midday"—so classifying my position as one of type S_1.
> "But ought you *really*?", you may repeat. If you do, I can relate
> S_1 to a more general S_2, explaining, "I ought to, because I promised
> to let him have it back." And if you continue to ask, "But why
> ought you really?", I can answer, in succession, "Because I ought to
> do whatever I promise him to do" (S_3), "Because I ought to do
> whatever I promise anyone to do" (S_4), and "Because anyone ought
> to do whatever he promises anyone else that he will do" or "Be-
> cause it was a promise" (S_5).[32]

Beyond this line of argument—a Step 1 justification—the
question as to "Why ought I (you) to do this particular act in
these circumstances?" cannot again be advanced because, as

Toulmin put it, "There is no more general 'reason' to be given beyond one which relates the action in question to an accepted social practice." But what if it was to be assumed for a moment that the circumstances change in such a way that it seems appropriate to permit an exception to the rule or standard? At such point, it is not sufficient to appeal only to the rule or standard to accept the action. Another type of reason must be given. Consider Toulmin's book-borrowing example somewhat further:

> If I have a critically ill relative in the house, who cannot be left, the issue is complicated. The situation is not sufficiently unambiguous for reasoning from the practice of promise-keeping to be conclusive: I may therefore argue, "That's all very well in the ordinary way, but not when I've got my grandmother to look after: whoever heard of risking someone else's life just to return a borrowed book?"[33]

In the case of a critically ill grandmother, a person can be excused from his or her obligation to return the book on the appointed date. As Taylor wrote, "if keeping his promise to return the book involves risking his grandmother's life, we say it is right for him to make an exception to the rule: Always keep your promises."[34] Generally, the promise-keeping rule includes in its range of application provisions for promise breaking. In certain circumstances, in fact, promise breaking may become obligatory. A judgment that "failure to return a book is wrong" cannot, in such cases, be ethically supported. The behavior in question does not come under the rule that governs such judgments.

The grounds for justifying such an exception are provided by Method C. The case for an exception must be based on evidence showing that it is better to permit the exception than to fulfill the criterion. This involves a value ranking with a class of comparisons composed of (1) anything that satisfies the criterion, and (2) something that would, in the existing circumstances, constitute a violation or failure to fulfill the criterion.[35] "When the result of evaluating the members of this class of comparisions is such that the evaluatum in 2 is judged to have more value or less disvalue than instances of 1, then it is

legitimate to make an exception" to the criterion.[36] This judgment, of course, assumes that the validity of the second criterion
can itself be established (by use of the three methods).

Thus far, Steps 1 and 2 have been presented. Step 1 is concerned with ordinary circumstances. The evaluatum is judged to
fall—or not to fall—under the jurisdiction of a criterion. Step 2
examines the possibility that the evaluatum differs from the
other members of the appropriate class of comparisons or that
the circumstances in which it occurs are so different as to constitute a legitimate reason for making an exception to the criterion. This brings the discussion to Step 3.

Step 3 directs attention to the problem of conflicting criteria.
Criteria are in conflict with one another when an aspect of one
that is judged to be bad is considered to be good by the other.
To resolve such a conflict it is necessary to determine which of
the criteria takes precedence, a process involving a logical
appeal to a higher-order criterion. One standard (S_1) takes precedence over another standard (S_2) if something that completely
fulfills the first standard (S_1) is *better* than something that
completely fulfills the second standard (S_2).[37] Whether S_1 or
S_2 is better than the other is established by ranking them
according to a higher-order standard (S'). When one criterion
is determined to take precedence over the others, it can be said
that the first one has a "higher claim," or establishes a "heavier
obligation." Furthermore, it is possible to have criteria beyond
S' that can be appealed to for the validation of S' itself. Few
people, however, organize their lives around high-level, fundamental criteria. Reality, in fact, is characterized by conflict
among a great number of criteria. Ideally, it is possible to
arrange all criteria in a hierarchy, but the actual sets of criteria
used by people are never organized into neat, hierarchical value
systems.

High-level criteria do, however, play an important mediating
role in the lives of both individuals and social groups. To be
able to function at all, individuals and groups must develop a
way of resolving tension and conflict between criteria. This is
accomplished by establishing higher-order rules to which they
can appeal. The following example illustrates the process:
"Suppose an army unit has two rules: 'Always obey the com-

mands of a superior officer,' and 'No one is to enter this building without a pass.' If an officer without a special pass commands the soldier on duty to let him enter the building, which rule ought the soldier obey? A well-run army unit will specify the relative precedence of such conflicting rules by means of a [higher]-order rule. After the statement of the rule requiring a special pass, there might be added the [higher]-order rule, 'Absolutely no personnel of any rank will be exempted from this requirement.' "[38]

Before turning to the next section, it is useful to follow an evaluation through all three steps of validation. This can be done by returning to the Head Start curriculum illustration, where the question was brought to the validation level. The curriculum was judged to be a good one because it provided socially relevant experiences. In Step 1 of the probe of this judgment the question arises, "Why is socially relevant experience a good reason for judging the Head Start curriculum a good one?" Employing Method A, an appeal is made to a higher criterion concerned with society, namely, to ready children for entrance into society. Method A can be satisfied by showing that the educational principle concerned with preparing children for entrance into society includes in its range of application the class of things called curricula that are designed around socially meaningful experiences.

The value of socially relevant experiences might also be established through assistance from Method B by providing evidence about the consequences of fulfilling or not fulfilling the criteria. Here social experience is judged for its instrumental value. A principal concern of means-ends evaluation in behavioral science, the question focuses on the general causal conditions or laws bearing on the situation that might justify acceptance. In the present illustration, statistics might be collected on students who were exposed to socially relevant curricula and those who were not. If it can be established that those who were exposed are more effective in getting ahead in society, such evidence could be employed to satisfy Step 1 by Method B.

Step 2 of validation requires showing that the object under judgment does not exist in circumstances that would disqualify it from judgment by the standard in question. Such a demonstration focuses on the description and definition of the particular facts of the situation. In the case of the Head Start educational program, this issue has been frequently invoked by many as the critical point for public discussion and debate. Numerous leaders of the black and Hispanic communities have raised criticisms about the propriety of imposing educational programs based on middle class standards upon the disadvantaged children of the lower classes. This, in fact, was a key criticism of the Westinghouse study. Proponents of Head Start pointed out that the test instruments utilized in the study were statistically standardized on middle class children with social and educational experiences very different from less-advantaged minority children. Therefore, to conclude that no significant learning has occurred may only be the result of the use of criteria with which lower class children are less familiar. If measured in terms of criteria derived from their own cultural experiences, the program outcomes might well show substantial progress. Other critics question the value of a middle class way of life in general. In the present scheme, this question shifts the debate to the higher levels of discourse in the logic of evaluation, vindication, and rational choice.

Step 3, validation, asserts that the accepted criterion must not be in conflict with other relevant or applicable standards or rules. For instance, a question might arise as to whether socially relevant educational programs are more important than programs that embody the current knowledge of the subject matter.[39] For purposes of illustration, suppose the two programs can be judged as equally good in terms of academic standards and social relevance. In such a case, it might be possible to appeal to the "principle of human equality" to justify socially relevant programs over those that stress academic standards. The probe of this judgment might take the following course:

Judgment: Social relevance is a standard superior to academic respectability.

Question: Why is that the case?

Answer: Because the essential moral consideration in these
           matters (curricular concerns) is that of human equal-
           ity and the social relevance of a curriculum is an
           instance of the study and concern for human rights
           as they exist in society. Academic respectability
           does not provide such an instance and is inapplicable
           to this judgment.

Question: But how do you know that human equality is the
           principle that is applicable in this case? Couldn't
           one just as well entertain the principle that inquiry
           and scientific method are the things that man has
           to offer in his schools as the ways of learning how to
           deal with the problems of society? I mean, wouldn't
           that say something about the greater applicability
           of human knowledge, so defined, as a criterion
           superior to "social relevance"?[40]

At this point in the discussion, the two participants have
reached the upper limit of the validation phase. Further progress
can be made only by shifting to the next level of evaluation,
vindication, which requires a fundamental shift in the reasoning process.

Validation and Phenomenology

In Chapter 2, the phenomenological critique of behavioral
science was seen to rest on an alternative view of the nature of
social reality (ontology), which requires a different epistemology. The purpose of this section is to show that phenomenology and the validation phase of evaluative discourse are concerned with complementary aspects of the same basic questions.
Although phenomenologists and ordinary-language writers in
philosophy have begun to explore these parallels, the convergence of concerns at this level of evaluation has received very
little attention in the social science literature.

The first thing to recognize in moving from verification to
validation is that the epistemological relationships between
data shift from "explanation" to "understanding." Both facts

and values still constitute the data in the two phases, but a shift is made from reliance on empirical rules that characterize the verification phase to a reliance on normative rules that govern validation. In the first phase, where the goal is a valid judgment about the state of objective reality, normative standards and rules are imported into the empirical context as constants. In the second phase, where the purpose is to render an interpretative understanding of the meaning of an established objective reality, facts are brought to the normative context of standards and rules. In verification, the key relationships between empirical data are causal; in validation, the essential connections are logical.

In terms of social science methodology, Robert MacIver has provided a useful conceptual framework for comprehending this shift from verification to validation. The transition centers around his concept of a two-level analysis. For MacIver, the study of politics is first empirical. Statistical analysis and related techniques are employed to determine whether and to what extent the events under investigation are associated with other phenomena. All hypotheses must pass these tests before they can be considered at the next level. Once such relationships are established, they must be analyzed on a higher level to discover the meaning of the associations or correlations. As MacIver said: "We must here assay the task of projecting ourselves by sympathetic reconstruction into the situation as it is assessed by others."[41] This requires an examination of "the dispositions, avowals, confessions, justification, and testimonies offered by agents, participants, or witnesses" giving their answers or interpretations about motivation and meaning.[42]

In the phenomenological sociology of Schutz, these two levels are referred to as "causal adequacy" and "adequacy of meaning."[43] As a problem of *verstehen*, the second level, concerned with meaning, entails a logical shift from causal explanation to practical reasoning, which, as Gunnell pointed out, is an assessment analogous to the rational justification of a value judgment. As he explained, "One does not usually speak of 'testing' in a value judgment but rather of providing good reasons for or against its application or validity in a particular context or set of circumstances."[44]

For phenomenology, social action is "rule-governed." Instead of focusing on causal explanation, the phenomenologist explores the ways in which social actions can be seen to fall under the applicable social rules that are available to the members of society. It is in this sense that Blum and McHugh likened a social or political decision to an explanation governed by social rules. The constitution of action must be examined through the logical rules employed by the members of the social system trying to make sense of the interactions that surround them.[45]

The point here is to show that a phenomenological assessment of a social situation centers around explanatory concepts coinciding with the basic concerns of evaluative logic in the validation phase. In particular, focus is placed on the phenomenological concepts of "social relevance," the "logic of the situation," and the concept of "systems of social relevance."[46] To be sure, the phenomenological approach to social science is complex and not explored in detail here. My purpose is only to establish that the validation phase captures the key concerns of phenomenological social science.

Social Relevance

Step 1 of validation states that the normative criteria for evaluation must be shown to be relevant (i.e., relevant to the particular normative framework of the evaluator who employs the criteria). This Step 1 probe rests at the foundation of the phenomenologist's inquiry. Concerned with the social actor's cognitive reality constructed on subjective experience, phenomenology's task is to empirically explicate the actor's subjective framework, which provides the rules and standards for his or her actions. In phenomenological terminology, this subjective framework is derived from the actor's "store of experience" and "stock of knowledge." Operating in the social life-world that constitutes the whole of everyday experience, social actors interpret their experiences and observations, define the situations they are in, or make plans for action by consulting their existing store of experience and knowledge.[47] Solidified into a "natural attitude," this store of experience and knowledge becomes the social actor's stance taken in recognition of the hard facts (the conditions for action as encountered in the surrounding objects, the will and intentions of others with whom the actor must cooperate or otherwise deal with, the imposition of customs and prohibitions of law, and so on). It is a stance that is essentially pragmatic and utilitarian.[48]

The concern for relevance sets the phenomenological agenda. Accordingly, the factors that take on social relevance are said to "define the situation." In a discussion of political evaluation, it is important to see the essential relationship between the concept of the "definition of the situation" and the idea of a "political" point of view itself. The connection is shown clearly in the policy literature by Bachrach and Baratz. They identify the critical stage in the policymaking process as the one that defines the nature of the issues to be considered by the relevant political participants. For them, control of the processes that "define the situation," thus establishing what constitutes a feasible set of policy alternatives in the situation, is the primary function of political institutions.[49] Likewise, the communication across an organizational decision structure hinges on the definition of the situation. As Norton Long explained, "to a considerable extent the holders of power in an organization hold their power because they are able to get their definitions of the situation accepted by others."[50] These definitions become fixed in the dominant belief and value systems that constitute a key element in the decision-making structure, determining which factual propositions are admissible and the goals that are acceptable. From this standpoint, political conflict in public communication and debate may be understood in terms of incompatible definitions of the situations.

Where the phenomenologist is concerned with rendering empirical descriptions of the individual's natural attitude and the general distribution of social knowledge across the social structure, the analytic philosopher is interested in the logical relationships between principles, standards, and rules within any stock of knowledge or across the various outlooks distributed in the society. Taylor, for example, has described how social outlooks will vary in terms of stability and coherence, depth, conventionality, and explicitness.[51] In a large society, there will be a general attitude or outlook to which the majority of its citizens will have a commitment. For the phenomenologist, this is the "dominant reality." Most members will be committed to it because they were brought up under its influence. According to Taylor, "they have not committed themselves as a matter of choice, but have been committed by others. If they remain uncritical and conventional in their outlook, they will have a coherent and stable way of life."[52] There will, however, be those for whom the existing way of life becomes a source of doubt. In such cases, the individual may decide to seek a new way of life. With the exception of the choice of the private way of life—such as that of the hermit or the monk—the selection and establishment of an alternative way of life is likely to breed social and political conflict. As individuals band together in the struggle for a new way of life, the discrepancies between the existing system and the establishment of a new way of life sharpen. At this level it is easy to see the relevance of the classical definition of politics as the struggle over competing conceptions of the good way of life.[53]

The Logic of the Situation

Where Step 1 probes the relevance of normative criteria employed to define a situation from a particular normative orientation, Step 2 calls the particular situation itself into question. In phenomenological terms, the natural attitude confronts a specific situation in the life-world. At any given moment in the actor's life-world, there are dominant factors that circumscribe his or her conduct. The specific situation will contain limitations, conditions, and opportunities that bear on the actor's pursuits. It is at this stage, Step 2 for the philosopher, that the social actor must determine the "logic of the situation"—the phenomenologist's primary explanatory concept.

A number of writers have elevated the concept of the "logic of the situation" to a primary status in social science explanation.[54] According to I. C. Jarvie, the basic explanatory model of the social sciences is situational. He has outlined the concept this way:

1. A man, for the purposes of the social sciences, can be viewed as in pursuit of certain goals or aims, within a framework of natural, social, psychological and ethical circumstances.

2. These circumstances constitute both means of achieving his aims and constraints on that achievement.

3. A man's conscious or unconscious appraisal of how he can achieve aims within these circumstances can be called sorting out the logic of the situation he is in (or his situational logic).

4. [It is called] "logic" because he tried to find out the best and most effective means, within the situation, to realize his aims. There is *no* suggestion that there exists some perfect scrutiny of the situation which yields a uniquely effective move: most often several moves may be indicated, although it is unlikely the actor will be emotionally or morally indifferent to them.

5. The actor's ideas are part of his situation in a complicated way. It is assumed that the situation, if objectively appraised, should favor certain means which are more effective than others and that the measure of rationality consists in the success in approaching such an objective appraisal.[55]

The logic of the situation essentially aims at empirical description of the explanatory procedures employed in everyday practical arguments. Phenomenologists offer the logic of the situation as a normative prescription for reform of positivistic behavioral science explanations. It is in essence the *verstehen* methodology for interpreting or understanding what constitutes plausible social explanations.

Karl Popper, well known for his studies of the scientific method, has elevated the concept of situational analysis to major status in the historical and social sciences. Popper stressed the objective character of situational analysis. Unlike those who view the process of *verstehen* as a sympathetic reconstruction of the original experience, he conceived of it as a metatheory about the actor's reasoning. As he described it, "Being on a level different from the [actor's] reasoning, it does not re-enact it, but tries to produce an idealized and reasoned reconstruction of it, omitting inessential elements and perhaps augmenting it."[56] The primary metaproblem thus addresses the decisive or essential aspects of the social actor's problem situation. To the degree that the social scientist is successful in resolving this metaproblem, he or she understands the situation.

Thus, in Popper's words, the historian or social scientist "is not to re-enact the past experiences, but to marshal objective arguments for or against his conjectural situational analysis."[57] The crucial point is that a social science based on a situational logic can proceed independently of psychological intuition. Objective understanding of the situation essentially involves determining whether the social or political action was "objectively appropriate to the situation." The circumstances of the situation are "analyzed far enough for the elements which initially appeared to be psychological (such as wishes, motives, memories and associations) to be transformed into elements of the situation."[58] Social actors are thus people with intentions or motives whose situations can be elucidated by reference to the objective intentions they pursue. Holding specific ideas, information, and goals, an actor must be characterized as attempting to achieve ends or purposes within the particular circumstances of a social situation, which establishes both potentials and limits. Such explanatory characterizations are rational, theoretical constructions. As Popper said "They can possess a considerable truth content and they can, in the strictly logical sense, be good approximations to the truth, and better than certain testable explanations."[59] For the method of situational analysis, the logical approximation is an indispensable explanatory concept. The important point is that such explanatory approximations are capable of improvement through empirical criticism.

For the phenomenologist, the logic of the situation is a shorthand description of what social scientists actually do in explaining social action. For example, in trying to explain black riots in his study *The Negro Family*, Moynihan generated sympathy in the reader by presenting a picture of life under frustrating social conditions that lead to riots, such as high unemployment, wretched housing, crime, and single parent family structures.[60] The argument is structured to reveal to the reader the nature of the life-world experience of a desperate situation. It conveys a sense of how in such a situation one can empathize with the desire to join in the riots and protest. Such data is marshaled to interpret and persuade rather than calculate and prove.

For the analytical philosopher, the idea of a situational logic is the logic of Step 2. Where the principal task of the phenomenological social scientist is to empirically describe the actor's relationship to situational relevances, the philosopher is primarily concerned with the logical relationships between circumstances and relevant norms. The task is to determine what constitutes a "good reason" for validly inferring conclusions entitled by particular circumstances. In practical terms, this involves organizing the objective facts and arguments for and against specific goals and subjecting them to the logical rules of reason. Here the significance of Gunnell's analogy between the critical assessment of social phenomena and the rational justification of normative judgments is clear. It reflects the parallel relationship between social explanation in phenomenology and the logic of evaluation. Phenomenology addresses itself to the rules of assessment employed in the substantive context of social relations while philosophy focuses on the formal explication and logical reconstruction of these rules and procedures.

Step 3 in validation asks whether there is conflict between applicable norms and, if so, whether those applied take precedence. This step coincides with the phenomenologist's empirical interest in the various "systems of social relevance" found in a society at any given time. Phenomenology focuses on the differentiation of subsystems of social relevance that occur in a complex society characterized by a multiplicity of institutional roles. These variations in the general framework of ideas, referred to as the social distribution of knowledge, are derived from the "here and now" of the various roles of the social class system. Members in different parts of the social class structure focus on social situations in different ways, thereby reading (or accounting for) what is ostensibly the same situation differently. Within the establishment of socially distributed subsystems of relevance, a variety of perspectives on the total social system develop, each refracted from the angle of its own subjectively experienced everyday world, each anchored in its own expectations, purposes, and motives.[61] The chiropractor's angle is different from that of the medical school professor; the criminal's different from the criminologist's. The result is what the phenomenologist calls the "multiple realities" of everyday life.

The analytical philosopher's concern at Step 3 is with the logical relationships between the multiplicity of norms subsumed under the general value framework of the way of life. From the ethical point of view, the philosopher asks how these distinctively different norms can be brought together under more general principles that provide a basis for rational justification. This question is founded on the principle of generalization.

Richard Flathman, a political philosopher, has provided an interesting example of the logical-analytic process of bringing competing norms under higher-order principles designed to mediate conflict. He has labored to show how the concept of the "public interest" has emerged in the ordinary language of political argumentation to serve as a basis for justifying public policies.[62] Employed as a higher-order principle, the principle of the public interest is essentially a logical test of a policy's generalizability. In the instance of conflicting norms, the evaluator's task is to logically explicate the norm that fulfills the requirements of the public interest. In philosophical terminology, the norm that takes precedence is the one that has the range or scope of application to include the class of comparisons provided by the higher-order public interest rule or principle. For the policy evaluator presenting a practical argument, the claim that a policy is in the "public interest" is basically an assertion that it ought to be normatively acceptable to the relevant political interests. The policy analyst must ask if a policy is equitably imposed upon all similar citizens in similar situations or circumstances. In short, the public interest principle, reflecting the generalization principle, "requires that political actors consider the impact of their actions and demands on the other members of society, reduce idiosyncratic demands, and seek constantly to find common ground with other men."[63] Citizens must recognize themselves as members of particular groups and social classes with both general and particular goals. Through an appeal to higher (more general) principles in political discourse, they must attempt to "subsume their interests under a larger precept or maxim and thereby begin to transform them into 'claims' which can legitimately be pressed in the public forum."[64] In this fashion, the concept of the public interest serves as an organizing concept in ordinary political language. The question as to whether it can itself serve as a substantive test— i.e., provide specific criteria along with other criteria such as justice or efficiency—is a question that must be resolved in the two higher phases of evaluation: vindication and rational choice.

Phenomenology and Policy Evaluation

While most of the interest in the validation phase of evaluation has come from analytic philosophers and phenomenological sociologists (often themselves philosophically oriented), there are some recent signs of change. Several specialists in evaluation research have begun to turn to phenomenology and the methods of *verstehen* in an attempt to synthesize an alternative paradigm. Recognizing behavioral science's limitations in dealing with value-laden problems of interpretation and meaning, Michael Patton and Patricia Carini have produced important and suggestive monographs that open the way for discussion of phenomenology in evaluation research. For Patton, an alternative methodology must focus on "the *meaning* of human behavior, the context of social interaction . . . and the connection between subjective states and behavior."[65] As the core method of social knowledge, *verstehen* is essential for the understanding of purpose, interest, value, meaning, and point of view. According to Patton, such an alternative paradigm must rely on the field techniques borrowed from anthropology rather than natural science methods—techniques such as participant observation, in-depth interviewing, detailed description, and qualitative field notes. Where scientific method focuses on the generalizable event, Patton's paradigm includes the unique situation or event. Where science stresses objectivity and reliability, he has emphasized subjectivity and validity. In place of scientific analysis of components, phenomenological evaluation stresses the holistic view. Patton's discussion is not designed to replace the scientific model but rather is aimed at showing the legitimacy of the phenomenological alternative in evaluation research. For present purposes, Patton's search for a synthesis can be understood as an attempt to move evaluation research beyond scientific or technical verification to include the phenomenologically based validation phase of the logic of evaluation.

Carini's monograph is particularly useful because it describes methods for doing phenomenological research in evaluation studies, particularly a method of observing, recording, describing, and analyzing human action called documentation. Documentation, which in several respects resembles ethnomethodological techniques, involves a "process of selecting and juxtaposing recorded observations and other records of phenomenal meaning in order to reveal reciprocities and therefore to approach the integrity of the phenomenon."[66] Since the task is not to exhaust the singular meaning of an event but to reveal the multiplicity of meanings, and since it is through the observer's encounter with the event that these meanings emerge, no standard format for collecting observations would be appropriate for different settings and purposes. The process of documenting goes through steps that represent a movement toward a fuller understanding of the multiple realities of the phenomena, realities from which alternative evaluative criteria are derived.

This completes the discussion of verification and validation (the two lower-level phases of the logic of evaluation) and their relationship to evaluation research methodology and phenomenology. The analysis turns now to the two higher-order levels, vindication and rational choice. In the course of the discussion, the study examines their methodological relationships to the behavioral systems approach and political philosophy.

Notes

1. William K. Frankena, *Ethics* (Englewood Cliffs, N.J.: Prentice-Hall, 1973), p. 108.

2. In the social sciences see the work of Abraham Kaplan, *The Conduct of Inquiry: Methodology for Behavioral Science* (Scranton, Pa.: Chandler Publishing Co., 1964); and, especially in political science, Eugene Meehan's *The Foundations of Political Analysis: Empirical and Normative* (Homewood, Ill.: Dorsey Press, 1971).

3. Paul W. Taylor, *Normative Discourse* (Englewood Cliffs, N.J.: Prentice-Hall, 1961).

4. The notion of an "informal logic" was discussed in Chapter 3. Taylor's purpose, although he did not employ the term, was to "reconstruct" the informal logic of normative discourse, that is, to render it in its ideal form.

5. Taylor's work is concerned with the logic of both evaluation and prescription. The discussion in this chapter focuses exclusively on the logic

of evaluation. In important respects, prescription is merely an extension of evaluation. It relies on the same logical procedures and essentially represents the outcome of an evaluation of evaluations, selecting the alternative most appropriate for the action situation that is the object of the decision.

6. Taylor's work represents the first full-scale attempt to apply informal logic to the problem of evaluation. Although he considered his book *Normative Discourse* to be only a "suggestive beginning" in 1961, the work remains a seminal landmark in the literature. Since then there has been a growth of interest in practical reason. Taylor himself has suggested the need for revisions and modifications based on recent writings. The overall framework, however, stands as a contribution containing key insights that in general have not received sufficient recognition in more recent writings. Particularly important in this respect is the elaboration of the phases of evaluation and the questions on which they focus.

7. Although *Normative Discourse* is widely cited in ethics bibliographies and occasionally appears in references on values in the social sciences, no one has attempted to elaborate its practical implications. Only one other writer, Edward Kelly, in a discussion of curriculum evaluation, has drawn on Taylor's study as a method for probing normative questions. Kelly, however, did not explore the larger methodological-theoretical significance of Taylor's informal logic for evaluation. See Edward Frances Kelly, "Curriculum Evaluation and Literary Criticism: The Explication of an Analogy" (Ph.D. diss., University of Illinois, 1971). Early in the development of this study I had an opportunity to discuss the project with Professor Kelly. I am indebted to him for the encouragement he gave me to continue this line of study.

8. The largest portion of Taylor's analysis is devoted to an epistemological explication of evaluative logic. One reason the practical implications of his analysis have remained unrecognized is probably related to its rather high level of abstraction. A second reason may be the slow pace of original work in the very difficult field of metaethics.

9. Brian M. Barry, *Political Argument*, International Library of Philosophy and Scientific Method (Atlantic Highlands, N.J.: Humanities Press, 1976), pp. 66–67.

10. Edward A. Suchman, *Evaluative Research: Principles and Practice in Public Service and Social Action Programs* (New York: Russell Sage Foundation, 1967), pp. 91–114.

11. See, for example, Francis Caro, ed., *Readings in Evaluative Research* (New York: Russell Sage Foundation, 1971); Marcia Guttentag and Elmer L. Struening, eds., *Handbook on Evaluation Research* (Beverly Hills, Calif.: Sage Publications, 1975).

12. F.S.C. Northrop, *The Logic of the Sciences and the Humanities*

(New York: Meridan Books, 1959), pp. 119–131. Northrop refers to operationalization as the problem of "epistemic correlation," an intellectual feat that joins a thing known in one way to what is in some sense the same thing known in another way.

13. Ilene N. Bernstein and Howard E. Freeman, *Academic and Entrepreneurial Research: The Consequences of Diversity in Federal Evaluation Studies* (New York: Russell Sage Foundation, 1975), pp. 1–40.

14. Martin Rein and Robert S. Weiss, "The Evaluation of Broad-Aim Programs: A Cautionary Note and a Moral," *The Annals* 385 (September 1969):139–140.

15. Henry W. Riecken, "Social Experimentation," *Society* 12 (July–August 1975):35.

16. Bruce Gates, "Knowledge Management in the Technological Society: Government by Indicator," *Public Administration Review* 35 (November–December 1975):589–592; see also Norton Long, "Indicators of Change in Political Institutions," *The Annals* 388 (March 1970):35–45.

17. Walter Williams and John W. Evans, "The Politics of Evaluation: The Case of Head Start," in *Evaluating Social Programs: Theory, Practice, and Politics,* ed. Peter H. Rossi and Walter Williams (New York: Seminar Press, 1972), pp. 249–264.

18. *The Impact of Head Start: An Evaluation of the Effects of Head Start on Children's Cognitive and Affective Development,* Study by the Westinghouse Learning Corporation, Ohio University, Athens, Ohio, July 12, 1969.

19. *New York Times,* cited by Williams and Evans, "The Politics of Evaluation," p. 263.

20. Ibid., pp. 257–259.

21. These questions incorporate the Head Start issues into a dialogue paraphrased from Kelly, "Curriculum Evaluation and Literary Criticism," p. 63.

22. Williams and Evans, "The Politics of Evaluation," p. 257.

23. The dialogue is taken from Kelly, "Curriculum Evaluation and Literary Criticism," p. 65. It combines Kelly's line of questioning with the Head Start illustration. The questions that follow in the next paragraph are also borrowed from Kelly.

24. Taylor, *Normative Discourse,* pp. 86–103. These steps are paraphrased to adapt them to the present context.

25. Norms serve as criteria. Two types of criteria may be distinguished: standards and rules. Both standards and rules are justified by the same process, so the distinction is of no immediate importance in the present analysis. For a comparison of standards and rules see ibid., pp. 3–47.

26. Ibid., p. 86. For further explanation of the role of rules and

consequences in ethical argument, see Andrew Oldenquist, "Rules and Consequences," in *Ethics*, ed. Julius R. Weinberg and Kenneth E. Yandell (New York: Holt, Rinehart & Winston, 1971), pp. 133–141.

27. Taylor, *Normative Discourse*, p. 87. Taylor offered the following example: "Consider the relation between the standard of benevolence and the standard of liberality in giving to charity. A person fulfills the standard of benevolence when, in certain circumstances, he is liberal in giving to charity. But he also fulfills the standard of benevolence when, in other circumstances, he helps a person in distress (as in an automobile accident), and when, in a third set of circumstances, he joins a movement for racial equality, and when, in a fourth set of circumstances, he goes out of his way to speak up in behalf of a man being unjustly defamed. This may be put in the form of a simple diagram:

Fulfilling$\quad\Big\{$ In C_1, fulfilling standard S_1 (being liberal)
Standard $S'$$\quad$ In C_2, fulfilling standard S_2 (being helpful)
(being$\quad$ In C_3, fulfilling standard S_3 (participating in political action)
benevolent)$\quad$ In C_4, fulfilling standard S_4 (protecting the innocent)."

28. Taylor's example continues: "If we adopt standard S' as validly applicable to an object X (say, any human being), then the statement 'X fulfills S'' entails the statements 'X fulfills S_1 in C_1'; 'X fulfills S_2 in C_2'; and so on. When this relationship between S' and $S_1, S_2, \ldots S_n$ holds, I shall say that $S_1, S_2, \ldots S_n$ are *deducible* from S'. Of course, if S_1 is deducible from S', then the fact that an object X fails to fulfill S_1 in C_1 entails its failure to fulfill S'. However, the failure of X to fulfill S_1 in circumstances *other than* C_1 does not entail such a failure. In a given set of circumstances to be benevolent requires one to be liberal in giving to charity; in a different set of circumstances (say, when the individual himself is destitute), it does not. In these circumstances, failure to be liberal does not mean failure to be benevolent." Ibid., p. 87.

29. Taylor further stated, "It is to be noted that the deducibility of $S_1, S_2 \ldots S_n$ from S' depends on the adoption of S' as a *valid* standard for judging a class of objects K of which X is an instance. If the validity of S' were brought into question a new process of validation would be necessary. In the given case perhaps the standard of benevolence as applied to all human beings (class K) could itself be deduced from a more general standard, such as the principle of brotherly love. Thus we might have the following logical pattern:

$\qquad\qquad\qquad\qquad\qquad\qquad\Big\{$ In C_1, fulfilling S_1
$\qquad\qquad\qquad\qquad\qquad\qquad$ In C_2, fulfilling S_2

Fulfilling$\quad\Big\{$ Fulfilling S_1' (being benevolent)$\qquad\qquad\;\;\bullet$
$S''$$\qquad$ Fulfilling S_2' (being honest)$\qquad\qquad\qquad\bullet$
(brotherly$\quad$ Fulfilling S_3' (being just)$\qquad\qquad\qquad\;\;\bullet$
love)$\qquad$ Fulfilling S_4' (being conscientious)$\qquad$ In C_n, fulfilling S_n

Here the logical relation between S'' and S_1', S_2', ... S_n' would be the same as that between S_1' and S_1, S_2, ... S_n. The applicability of S'' would have to be assumed, just as the applicability of S' was assumed before. If this assumption were questioned, a still higher stage of validation would have to be carried out, and so on, until we reached the supreme norms of the value system we have adopted. ([A]ny further justification would require that we shift from validation to vindication.) To sum up, if a man is judged to be morally good because he gives liberally to charity, one can justify the relevance of the standard used, by showing that it follows from the more general standard of benevolence as a sign of good character. The claim that benevolence is a standard relevant to a moral judgment of good character is itself in need of justification; *if* it is justified, then it follows that being liberal in giving to charity is also validated as a relevant standard." Ibid., pp. 87–88.

30. Ibid., pp. 88–89.

31. Ibid., p. 92.

32. Ibid.

33. Ibid., p. 93.

34. Ibid., p. 95.

35. Taylor provided the following illustration: "Suppose a new library building is being planned for a city. One of the architectural principles (standards) accepted by the city officials is that of functionalism—the best building is the one that most effectively serves the purposes for which it is to be used. According to this standard, good-making characteristics of a library would include such things as spaciousness of stacks and reading rooms, quietness, efficiently organized offices, easy availability of books, and so on. Let us suppose, furthermore, that the best library building as judged by the standard of functionalism would cost so much to build that the city would have to take funds allotted to another project (say, slum clearance) to pay for it. The choice becomes: fulfill the standard of functionalism and damage the slum clearance project, or fail to fulfill the standard and preserve the project. An evaluation is then made of these two alternatives *according to a standard,* such as the welfare of the people of the city. An evaluation according to this standard might result in ranking the second alternative as better than the first. An exception would then be made to the standard of functionalism in architecture. If an architect were to present two plans for the library building, one of which was clearly better than the other according to the standard of functionalism, the better one would *not* be chosen. It would not be considered really better in the given circumstances. Hence an exception to a standard is justified on the basis of the circumstances in which the evaluatum occurs. The standard of what is 'really better' is the standard of the public welfare. If this standard were itself to be challenged, the process of validating *it* by Methods [A],

146 Evaluation Research and Phenomenology

[B], and [C] would have to take place." Ibid., pp. 96–97.

36. Ibid.

37. Ibid., pp. 98–100.

38. Ibid., p. 103.

39. This illustration is drawn from Kelly's discussion of curriculum evaluation, "Curriculum Evaluation and Literary Criticism," p. 67.

40. Ibid., p. 67–68.

41. Robert M. MacIver, *Social Causation* (Boston: Ginn and Co., 1942).

42. Ibid.

43. Alfred Schutz, *The Phenomenology of the Social World* (Chicago: Northwestern University Press, 1967).

44. John G. Gunnell, "Social Science and Political Reality: The Problem of Explanation," *Social Research* 35 (Spring 1968):187.

45. Cited in David Walsh, "Sociology and the Social World," in Paul Filmer et al., *New Directions in Sociological Theory* (Cambridge, Mass.: M.I.T. Press, 1972), p. 30.

46. The discussion of phenomenology in this section closely follows Alfred Schutz, *On Phenomenology and Social Relations,* ed. Helmut R. Wagner (Chicago: University of Chicago Press, 1970).

47. The "life-world" of everyday experiences includes the orientations and actions through which individuals pursue their interests and affairs by manipulating objects, dealing with people, conceiving plans and carrying them out.

48. This natural attitude or outlook can be structured in various ways. In any particular situation, some of its elements are very relevant, others marginal, while still others irrelevant. On the other hand, certain items in the outlook may be precise and distinct, others vague and obscure. Moreover, an individual's natural attitude is by no means coherent and free from contradictions. As long as incoherent and contradictory elements are not brought to bear on the same situation, the individual may remain blissfully unaware of them. The same pragmatic bent prevents the individuals, as long as they remain in the natural attitude, from seeking systematic and logically clear knowledge about anything beyond the requirements of their practical operations and plans, which frequently assume routine character. See Schutz, *On Phenomenology and Social Relations.*

49. Peter Bachrach and Martin Baratz, "Decisions and Non-Decisions," *American Political Science Review* 58 (September 1963):632–642.

50. Norton Long, "Administrative Communication," in *Concepts and Issues in Administrative Behavior,* ed. Sidney Mailick and Edward H. Van Ness (Englewood Cliffs, N.J.: Prentice-Hall, 1962), p. 141.

51. Taylor, *Normative Discourse,* pp. 156–157.

52. Ibid., p. 156.

53. Ibid. On the classical conception of politics, see Hannah Arendt, *The Human Condition* (Chicago: University of Chicago Press, 1958).

54. I. C. Jarvie, "The Logic of the Situation," *Concepts and Society* (London: Routledge & Kegan Paul, 1972), pp. 3–36; Karl Popper, "The Logic of the Social Sciences," in *The Positivist Dispute in German Sociology,* ed. Theodor W. Adorno et al. (New York: Harper and Row, 1976), pp. 87–104; A. R. Louch, *Explanation and Human Action* (Berkeley: University of California Press, 1969); and Dick Atkinson, *Orthodox Consensus and Radical Alternatives: A Study in Sociological Theory* (New York: Basic Books, 1972).

55. Jarvie, "The Logic of the Situation," p. 4. The present study has taken the liberty of delineating Jarvie's passage in five parts to sharply set off the key points.

56. Karl Popper, *Objective Knowledge: An Evolutionary Approach* (Oxford: Clarendon Press, 1972), p. 188.

57. Karl Popper, "The Logic of the Social Sciences," p. 102.

58. Ibid.

59. Ibid., p. 103.

60. U.S., Department of Labor, Office of Policy Planning and Research, *The Negro Family,* prepared by Daniel Patrick Moynihan (Washington, D.C.: U.S. Government Printing Office, 1965); also known as the "Moynihan Report."

61. These subsystems of relevance must, at least in a smoothly operating social system, relate in some way to a broader, more general domain of relevance that constitutes the society's "form" or "way" of life. The institutional framework of a society is thus seen as a man-made construction held together by a common perspective that is shared—to one degree or another—by a broad spectrum of social members. From this perspective society is organized around certain values that are "taken for granted." These values constitute the actual cultural frame of reference through which a society achieves normative integration and unity of purpose. This "actual" way of life stands in contrast to the "ideal" way of life advanced by the political philosopher (a distinction that becomes especially important in the rational choice phase of evaluative logic). In the literature of phenomenological sociology, see Peter L. Berger and Thomas Luckmann, *The Social Construction of Reality* (New York: Doubleday & Co., 1967). See also Georges Gurvitch, *The Social Frameworks of Knowledge* (New York: Harper & Row, 1971).

62. Richard E. Flathman, *The Public Interest: An Essay Concerning the Normative Discourse of Politics* (New York: John Wiley & Sons, 1966).

63. Ibid., p. 41.

64. Ibid.

65. Michael Quinn Patton, *Alternative Evaluation Research Paradigm* (Grand Forks: University of North Dakota Press, 1975), p. 7.

66. Patricia F. Carini, *Observation and Description: An Alternative Methodology For The Investigation of Human Phenomena* (Grand Forks: University of North Dakota Press, 1975), p. 29.

5

The Logic of Evaluation:
The Systems Perspective and
Political Philosophy

The effective crusader for good causes will in any campaign of persuasion deliberately or by temperament or in ignorance select for emphasis at least in the existent circumstances a single general principle, or a small number of presumptively harmonious general principles, and will leave to those hostile to his cause the search for intellectual or practical flaws in his argument.

—Jacob Viner[1]

When the logic of evaluation turns from the validation phase to vindication, the evaluation process shifts ground in a fundamental way. Validation comes to an end when there are no more normative criteria within the value system to which an appeal can be made. Thus, to vindicate criteria it is necessary to step outside of the value framework. "Instead of assuming the value system has already been adopted and proceeding to justify our judgment on the basis of it," as Taylor explained, "we now attempt to justify our adopting the system in the first place."[2] This fundamental shift in the method of reasoning represents the transition from first-order to second-order normative discourse.

Justifying Fundamental Value Judgments

It is at the level of second-order discourse that the long-standing philosophical debate between ethical absolutism and relativism takes place. Absolutism claims that fundamental values are in the final analysis simply true or false, not just true or false for someone. From this perspective, a value is true when it can be demonstrated or proved to be preferred by every-one to all others. In contrast, the relativist holds that the reso-lution of value conflicts between different subcultures, or across different cultures, can never be decided by objective criteria. Such conflicts must in the final analysis be decided through cultural domination, political pressure, or physical force. In this view, no rational choice can be made between fundamental values. Good reasons can be given for engaging in specific actions only if all parties to the deliberation hold the same basic values. It is here that the debate between scientific naturalists and noncognitivists is encountered. In the social sciences, it is recognized as the debate between the behavioralists who sub-scribe to the fact-value dichotomy and the post-behavioralists who advocate extension of scientific research into fundamental value questions.

The unique advantage of an informal logic of evaluation is that it avoids much of this dilemma. It does this by accepting the inability of philosophy and science to justify ultimate values while at the same time indicating the range of normative ques-tions that can be investigated in the absence of such value cri-teria. The normative logic of the ordinary-language approach brings out this neglected but essential aspect of normative de-liberation. The point is well illustrated by Singer's example about lying. Consider the rule "lying is wrong." To vindicate the rule, Singer has suggested what would happen if people were to lie whenever it suited their purposes—i.e., "if lying became the rule and truth-telling the exception."[3] The impli-cations and consequences of the rule can be amplified in de-tail: "Lying is wrong because it breeds distrust and suspicion, breaks down confidence, frustrates human purposes, wastes resources, and leads to unavoidable injuries." The evaluator might further explore the implications of a breakdown of confidence and trust:

> An important argument against lying is that it has the consequence of breaking down the fabric of confidence and trust in society. To the extent that lying becomes prevalent, one person cannot rely upon the statements, assurances, and representations of others.

This breeds suspicion and distrust and creates the need for constant surveillance and watchfulness, which in turn diverts human and material resources that could otherwise be devoted to more positive and constructive ends.[4]

Information about the limitations of surveillance might also be supplied:

Since such surveillance can never be wholly successful, lying regularly leads to the injury of the person or persons to whom the lie is told. If A commits himself or his resources on the basis of false information received from B, he is likely to suffer injury, and the injury will be in part a consequence of B's lie.

Based on these factual premises, the evaluator concludes that "lying is wrong." As a statement based on informal discourse, the judgment is established by summoning certain facts and applying an evaluative adjective. Most people find such a conclusion fully justified—warranted by reasons, in Toulmin's framework. Shifting from everyday discourse to formal philosophical analysis, however, the statement loses persuasive force. Philosophers can accept the facts behind the judgment but many will raise questions about the justification of the evaluative adjective. It is here that the proponents of the view that moral judgments are arbitrary leap enthusiastically into the debate. How does one *know* that lying is good or bad? Since such a judgment cannot be formally determined from facts or intuition, any agreement that lying is bad would seem to ultimately require some personal preference for which nothing properly called a "reason" can be given. From this position, it might be argued that the reasons given against lying are "really no improvement on the shorter answer that the consequences are disastrous." Such a contention implies that the evaluator simply "recited in greater detail the *facts* concerning what happens when lying becomes a general practice" and has "smuggled in" the evaluative terms—waste, breakdown, injury, and distrust— that appear to support the judgment that "lying is wrong." The noncognitivist might even go a step further and demand justification for believing that "lying is wrong" in the first place. Suppose a hostile, suspicious society is regarded as the best possible system. Lying could then be judged as good. What kind of publicly demonstrable evidence might the evaluator offer against such a conclusion? At this level, evidence based on non-subjective criteria is hard to produce.

The very nature of this question, however, starts to generate some suspicion as to what the interrogator would count as a reasoned justification for such a value judgment. Probably only the most impetuous philosophical antagonist is likely to pursue the issue to this point. For most people, everyday arguments against lying would be regarded as providing good reasons for thinking that lying is wrong. The sentence "lying is wrong because it breeds distrust and suspicion, breaks down confidence, frustrates human purposes, wastes resources, and leads to unavoidable injuries" represents a vast improvement over the simple statement that "lying is wrong," accompanied by a threatening gesture of moral indignation such as shaking one's fist. Clearly, as Flathman argued, policy advice accompanied by such evidence is preferable to merely asserting that something should be done, or arguing that "if you don't carry it out, I won't support your reelection."[5] An approach to public policy that is unable to differentiate among these types of replies is without doubt unsatisfactory.

With the assistance of the ordinary-language approach and informal logic, it is possible to see that practical men and women are capable of reasoning about their commitments in a rational manner. By resting their value judgments on normative rules, accompanied by the evaluation of specific consequences, they can even at times speak of the truth or falsity of a normative judgment.

Some, no doubt, will continue to argue that there is not enough of a value hierarchy to facilitate meaningful deliberation. In this respect, one can take the value of life itself as an example: it is often thought to be a duty to sacrifice one's life to protect a just way of life. In spite of general aversion to human misery, suffering is frequently inflicted with a clear conscience, as in the case of war or the death penalty. Similarly, injustice is at times deliberately sanctioned to secure social stability. How, some ask, can normative deliberation be carried out in a rational manner if there is conflict among even the highest values?

The question, from the view of an informal logic, misses the thrust of the argument. First, there is substantial agreement on the worth of a range of high-level values. The fact that they conflict in certain types of situations should not overshadow the existing consensus on such values. Moreover, such values often provide for their own exceptions, as in the case of promising discussed in the preceding chapter. Second, a distinction can be made between fundamental principles and local rules. Even if it is impossible to discover a geometrylike hierarchy, there is enough of an order to resolve a large number of everyday life disputes. The loss of life is ordinarily thought to be more serious than loss of money; causing suffering is considered to be more heinous than creating inconvenience. Given the hierarchy that does exist, it is possible, with the assistance of the structure and rules of evaluative discourse, to pose the appropriate questions and indicate the kinds of information that might, and sometimes do, resolve such disputes.

The advantage of an informal logic of evaluation is that it shifts attention from final answers (which are unobtainable) to questions and data that mediate practical deliberations. In view of the idiosyncratic or ad hoc character of most normative arguments, evaluative logic introduces an important measure of clarity and consistency seldom found in public discourse. In contrast to the tenets of the fact-value dichotomy, this is a particularly significant conclusion. Even if certain philosophical doubts cannot be eliminated (by combining facts, circumstances, and consequences with the rules and principles of evaluation) it is still possible to judge value questions in a rational manner. The frequent mistake is to confuse objective proof with agreement. As Dorfman stated, "the fact that there is no way to 'prove' that denuding forests is bad is perfectly consistent with universal agreement that it *is* bad."[6] Normative logic opens the possibility of exploring such agreements.

Political philosophers influenced by this approach have extended it to the study of political evaluation. For these writers, one of political philosophy's most important tasks should be to provide standards for judging political proposals. Theorists such as Wolin, Leys, and Smith have maintained that philosophy should serve evaluation by supplying standards and rules that govern the process of giving "sound advice."[7] Such standards and rules can serve as guides for both formulating and asking deliberative questions about policy judgments. As the basis for rational-analytic questions, standards and rules function as pointers or direction finders, turning attention to values and situational circumstances that might not otherwise be seen.

This approach underscores the fact that sound policy advice must also involve more than "correct" arguments. Also, such advice must be about the right questions. Human problems, as James Ward Smith has explained, "are complicated enough to be read in wholly different ways."[8] Sometimes, in fact, it is even difficult to say what one "stands for" in a given set of circumstances. In addition to hard evidence, the advocacy or defense of a normative position must also draw on tutored insight and trained speculation. What is required, as Smith maintained, is the development of standards and principles that help guide such decisions.

Only recently has the conception of policy evaluation as argumentation and sound advice begun to appear here and there in the writings of policy theorists. If political philosophy can help to improve practical argumentation and judgment by systematizing deliberative standards and rules, this perspective should be given more attention in the policy literature. Martin Rein and Charles Anderson are among the few to suggest the methodological potential of such a conceptualization.[9]

So far, the discussion has focused on basic contextual issues: vindication as second-order evaluation, the problem of justifying fundamental or second-order value judgments, and the approach of language-oriented political philosophers. With this background in mind, it is appropriate to turn to the two second-order phases of evaluative logic. The first of the two, vindication, asks if the value system from which the normative criteria under investigation are drawn can be shown to contribute to the accepted way of life of the society. The second, rational choice, examines the way of life itself and asks if it has been chosen by rational methods.

Vindication

Vindication begins when one is no longer able to answer a "why" question in a practical deliberation. When the normative inquiry in the validation phase reaches the uppermost criterion of a value system, questions like "Why do you say or judge that to be the case?" cannot be answered by an appeal to some other criterion. To vindicate is to justify the value system from which the criteria employed in verification and validation are drawn. Essentially this involves a shift from making "local" decisions based on the fundamental criteria given by the dominant value systems to testing the selection of "fundamental" decision criteria. The attempt to justify the criteria or principles of an entire value system involves demonstrating that its adoption leads to consequences that would be judged better than those resulting from the adoption of an alternative value system. In vindication, it is the inherent instrumental or contributive value of the value system toward the adopted way of life that is examined. Philosophers and social scientists will recognize this phase of the logic of evaluation as a form of rule utilitarianism.[10]

Vindication as Method

Vindication requires good empirical evidence for adopting a specific value system as the fundamental source of standards and principles. In this respect, the reasoning shifts from the logical mode of argumentation employed in validation back to the empirical mode of inquiry.

By asking someone to justify the adoption of a value system as a whole, the questioner is asking whether the consequences of doing this furthers certain ideals that the person wants to see realized and whether living in accordance with that system is consistent with the whole way of life he or she wants to live by. As such, vindication is principally a "pragmatic test." A value system is demonstrated to have instrumental value when it is shown to be pragmatically successful in furthering certain ends a person has adopted; it has contributive value if it is an essential part of the whole.[11] The class of comparisons in the pragmatic test consists of acts of adopting (or making commitments to) other actual or possible value systems that have instrumental and contributive value (or disvalue) when judged against the same standards. This raises the two following questions: What is the end with reference to which the members of the class of comparisons are being judged to have instrumental value or disvalue? And what is the whole with reference to which the class can be judged to have contributive value or disvalue? The answer to both questions is a "way of life." Before turning to more concrete illustrations, it is useful to sum up vindication in a series of questions that organize the investigation: (1) From which value system or systems are the norms utilized in validation derived? (2) Which points of view—political, economic, aesthetic, etc.—do these value systems reflect? (3) Does the value system conflict with other value systems that also apply to the adopted way of life? (4) Does the value system possess instrumental or contributive value for the adopted way of life? (5) Are the consequences that follow from the adoption of this value system judged better for the way of life than those that flow from other value systems?

Culture as a Way of Life

Taylor defined a way of life as "a set of value systems each of which belongs to a different point of view and all of which are arranged in an order of relative precedence."[12] These include a moral value system, an aesthetic system, a system of etiquette, an economic and political value system, customs and traditions, and so on. Each system is made up of a hierarchy of standards and rules. Moreover, the systems themselves are ordered hierarchically. In the social sciences, the examination of a way of life is the study of culture. Culture is defined as a "complex whole which includes knowledge, belief, arts, morals, law, custom and many other capabilities and habits acquired by man as a member of society."[13] People adopt a culture or way of life because its value systems are in accordance with specific needs and interests that must be satisfied. In this respect, cultural distinctions are made between a Marxist, bourgeois, or puritan way of life:

> What are these needs and interests but the basic aims and ideals of
> a whole way of life? For the Marxist, they will be the interests and

needs of the class struggle, in furthering the overthrow of capitalism and the establishment of a classless society. . . . For the puritan they will be the ideals of godliness and righteousness on the strait and narrow path to salvation.[14]

In each culture, certain values are dominant. A military junta in Brazil, for example, evaluates actions against the standards of economic growth and development. Communist China, in contrast, places its political value system at the pinnacle of the way of life. In the Chinese Cultural Revolution, all actions were assessed in terms of their contribution to the politics of the "protracted struggle."

Beyond such generalizations it is difficult to talk about cultural values with precision. Although survey researchers have provided a substantial quantity of data about the distribution of opinions, attitudes, and values in American society, there is still little solid consensus about what is meant by cultural values, and no simple, economical methods are available for measuring them. In the case of the United States, Robert Angell has provided a suggestive list that at least helps to illustrate the concept:

Dignity of the person including equality before the law.
Civil and religious liberties.
Responsible democracy—control by the people of their common
   life.
Opportunity for all.
Humanitarianism and friendliness.
A high level of effort.
Competition within fair rules.
Technological progress.
Peaceful orientation toward other nations.
Patriotism.[15]

Political Culture

Culture is a very broad, all-encompassing term that must for specific purposes be narrowed substantially. In the case of political evaluation, relevant criteria are drawn from the political subculture or value system. Writers differ as to precisely how to define the term "political culture," but in its most general sense it refers to politically relevant ideas and social practices.[16] Used in this fashion, political culture calls attention to the fact that habits of action, norms of conduct, symbols of good and evil, and even basic notions about the nature of God and man can influence the ways people behave in political contexts and evaluate the behavior of others. Most important to this discussion, the concept leads to the realization that some social arrangements and ideas are politically important while others are not.

As a point of view, a dominant political value system or subculture generally shares certain patterns and orientations with the other points of view and value systems within the culture as a whole. From Angell's list, for instance, equality before the law, civil liberties, responsible democracy, a peaceful orientation toward other nations, and patriotism fall within the purview of American political culture. Moreover, civil liberties share some common ground with religious liberties and equal opportunity. At the same time, however, it is possible to observe conflict between dominant political subcultures and the general American culture. Civil liberties, for instance, have at times throughout history been in sharp conflict with religious liberties.

The Systems Perspective and Vindication

Vindication is essentially an empirical evaluation. Scientific knowledge and techniques are required for valid predictions of the instrumental or contributive role of a value system in realizing the ideals of a way of life. Contemporary social scientists have shown a growing interest in this kind of research, although it remains more a theoretical possibility than a practical reality. In political science, many post-behavioralists fix their sights on this level of evaluation, as was seen in Chapter 2. The focus on the social and psychological consequences of living a particular way of life; the relevance of value systems to different circumstances; and the physical, social, and psychological conditions that make a way of life possible all involve questions that arise in the post-behavioral conception of scientific value theory.

It is the concept of the "whole" that forms the basis of the link between vindication and the systems perspective. George

Graham has suggested that the transition in political science from behavioralism to post-behavioralism is essentially a shift in the level of analysis.[17] Post-behavioralism, he pointed out, represents a transition from micro- to macroevaluation and the systems perspective. In the logic of evaluation presented here, it is the empirical transition from verification in first-order evaluation to vindication at the higher level.

In the epistemological debate in political science, Dror asserted that policy scientists committed to the improvement of the human condition must adopt a systems perspective.[18] An applied systems perspective in the social sciences, he wrote, can respond to the growing demands of both public and student pressure for "social relevance." One of the first benefits of such an orientation, he maintained, can be witnessed in the development of a framework for social reporting based on social indicators. Social indicators—an outgrowth of interest in the systems approach to program budgeting in the 1960s—are advanced as an effort to transcend the narrower focus and implications of existing economic indicators utilized in government decision making.

The epistemological support for this position in the behavioral sciences evolves from the contributions of naturalist philosophers such as R. B. Perry and John Dewey, who defined value questions in terms of their objective behavioral components. In Perry's theory of ethical naturalism, morality is essentially society's endeavor to harmonize conflicting interests.[19] The chief value of his work for political scientists is the use of the concept of interest. For Perry, anything is a value in the elementary sense of the word if it is the object of someone's interest. Such a conception is closely related to the behavioral scientist's empirical referents of value. Where Perry clarified empirical components of values, Dewey emphasized scientific methodology. For Dewey, value statements are to be treated as empirical hypotheses subject to verification. He stressed the following characteristics of value statements:

1. Value statements can be organized as cognitive propositions.

2. Interests are behavioral phenomena; therefore, the conditions and results of value statements based upon interests can be explored empirically.
3. Value statements of this type exist "whenever things are appraised as to their suitability and serviceability as means"; rather than representing propositions about present or past events, such statements are about phenomena that can be brought into existence.
4. Such propositions can be designated as "ends in view," referring to plans or anticipated outcomes.
5. An anticipation or forecast is justified to the extent that it is derived from conclusions based on accurate observation.
6. The assessment of such ends-in-view is "dependent upon observation of consequences attained when they are compared and contrasted with the content of ends-in-view"; the evaluation of such ends is based on the testable consequences that actually occur.[20]

Dewey advocated his naturalistic position for the study of public policy. Policies, he maintained, represent plans of action selected from alternatives having scientifically observable consequences that provide the basis for valid testing.[21] The systematic study of value-oriented policy questions should follow the experimental method. This approach was adopted by Harold Lasswell, who established it as a foundation for the development of the policy sciences. Lasswell linked Dewey's naturalistic epistemology to the emerging behavioral science orientation.[22]

The shift in behavioral methodology from a narrow means-ends perspective to a systems orientation, reflected in post-behavioral policy analysis, largely mirrors underlying epistemological transitions within naturalism itself. Early policy scientists like Lasswell, attracted to the means-ends naturalism of philosophers like Dewey, advocated the use of decision theory and operations research techniques emphasizing efficiency. As the contemporary social world has over the years become vastly more complex and interdependent, the scope of such efficiency techniques has increasingly been recognized as insufficient.[23] Consequently, policy scientists like Churchman and Dror have drawn on the works of modern scientists and philosophers who advance general systems theories of society, particularly the works of Ludwig von Bertalanffy and Ervin Laszlo.[24] Such theories have assisted policy theorists in transferring policy research from the narrow base of efficiency to a systems foundation stressing multiple objectives. Where traditional decision theory has focused on the efficient maximization of some "payoff" function expressing objectives to be accomplished, systems analysis in the modern policy sciences attempts to explicate and clarify policy alternatives within the social system as a whole. Stimulated by the recognition that what is good for one subsystem may be bad for the system as a whole, the multiplicity of interdependent values and objectives has become a primary focus of investigation.

An Illustration

David McClelland's book *The Achieving Society* is one of the few well-developed examples of empirical inquiry at this level of evaluation. Essentially, McClelland has attempted to examine the instrumental role of achievement motivation for economic growth in industrial systems. The study is enormous in scope, drawing on scientific evidence, historical data, and philosophical speculation in cross-cultural perspective. By isolating basic psychological factors—motives and values—that characterize the value systems of the entrepreneurial classes, McClelland was able to establish empirical connections between these value systems and a specific kind of economic system. Such value systems, which appear to be widely held in advanced industrial systems, are traced to certain beliefs, values, and child-rearing practices of the family. The relationship suggests an important policy implication: A government interested in accelerating economic development should foster achievement motivation through the school system and other institutions involved in socializing children into the cultural system.[25]

These kinds of questions have been central to policy debates about our domestic social crises, especially debates on issues concerning race and poverty. As the problem of black poverty pressed for attention, it became apparent that the solution required more than a program of income redistribution. Also at issue were basic cultural factors related to poverty itself, a point illustrated by Oscar Lewis's "culture of poverty" concept developed in his study of poor Mexican families. According to Lewis, a culture of poverty—or, more precisely, the "subculture of poverty"—refers to a lower-class value system that denigrates hard work, discipline, and ambition and sacrifices future rewards for immediate gratification. The outcome is poverty resulting from slothfulness. Passed from parent to child, this value system perpetuates a generational cycle of culture. Unable to participate in the dominant achievement-oriented cultural system of American society, these social classes are incapable of pulling themselves up out of their predicament.[26]

The debate over this hypothesis triggered the publication of a number of controversial studies, particularly *The Negro Family* (known as the Moynihan Report) and Edward Banfield's *The Unheavenly City*. The studies precipitated a lively and often vitriolic polemic as to whether fundamental cultural differences exist between the poor and the rich. They raised the concept of a culture of poverty to the level of policy debate by examining its implication for income redistribution programs and the amelioration of poverty. The Moynihan Report presented the proposition that the disorganization of the black family, with its disastrous effects on the black personality, must today be explained not only as a response to social conditions such as discrimination, unemployment, or poor housing but also as a consequence of a self-perpetuating subculture of poverty. In short, the value systems of the black poor have little instrumental value toward the American way of life.[27]

Banfield amplified the policy implications of the scenario. Drawing on available empirical research, he constructed a vivid picture of a lower-class culture that locks blacks and other minorities into hopeless poverty. They are unable to help themselves, let alone contribute to the economic system. The severity of the situation is beyond the reach of governmental policy capabilities. A primary source of government policy failures, according to Banfield, is located in the unwillingness or inability of the liberal reform tradition to address these deeper cultural dimensions of urban poverty. If self-perpetuating cultural factors dysfunctional to the overall way of life are at the root of the malaise, effective solutions must confront the cultural barriers that stand between the poor and mainstream society. Such solutions, of course, would have to be massive in scope. Anything short of total intervention would amount to mere situational changes with only temporary ameliorative effects. Massive intervention, Banfield argued, is politically unacceptable to the power structure. Given existing political structures and decision rules, particularly interest group politics and incrementalism, such policy intervention would not only be too costly, it would also rest on values outside the political culture. Government antipoverty programs that genuinely attack the problem, then, have to be rejected because they cannot be vindicated by the dominant political value systems. At this point, Banfield rested his case. In the urban literature, his analysis is identified as a kind of "new realism" based on the hard facts of the political system.[28]

The point here is not whether Banfield is right or wrong but rather to illustrate how such a dispute might be probed at this level of evaluation. Two types of criticisms have been launched at Banfield's thesis. The first involves a challenge to his empirical assumptions about lower-class culture. A number of writers have argued persuasively that lower-class culture cannot be regarded as an organic whole—a contention supported by empirical evidence.[29] Rokeach and Parker, for example, have put the question to a sophisticated test: Surveying a sample of more than 1,400 Americans, they found that rich and poor, both black and white, are much closer in terms of the fundamental values they hold than Banfield's theory suggests. Socioeconomic position seems to better explain ghetto behavior than cultural value systems.[30]

A second type of argument criticizes Banfield's treatment of existing political institutions as somehow "frozen." Hennessey and Feen attributed this to his underlying political philosophy. Banfield, they argued, "rejects out of hand the possibility that the opinion makers' propensity to imagine a future may lead them to a view of the facts decidedly different from Banfield's— namely, an alarming deterioration in the social and political climate in American cities which in turn impels them to use considerable skill to design realistic programs to alleviate the

problem."[31] But the logic of evaluation does not reject the possibility of alternative visions of political culture. Evaluation
halts at vindication only if all parties agree on the answer to
the question, "Do you accept this political way of life?" It is,
in fact, on this point that Banfield's most truculent critics have
launched their objections. This recognition of alternative visions
of a political way of life moves the argument from vindication
to the next and final phase of the evaluation process, rational
choice. At this stage, evaluation shifts attention from the existing or "real" culture to the pursuit of an ideal culture.

Before turning to rational choice, it is important to say a
final word about the implication of the shift for the systems
perspective, the key methodological issue in the discussion of
vindication. The relevance of the systems perspective is established in vindication, but the transition to rational choice illustrates its limitations. In rational choice, the concept of the
system is preserved but the established system itself is no longer
the source of standards and rules. Evaluative inquiry turns to
the question of which system is the best source of standards.
In this respect, the validity of the systems perspective in the
vindication phase depends wholly on the recognition of the established system as a social construction. To treat it as natural or
fixed is to transform the systems perspective from methodological tool to ideological instrument. A suggestion such as Banfield's
that a policy is bad because it doesn't work in the dominant
system may have implications for short-run political prospects but not for long-run evaluation. In the final scheme, it is
necessary to address the last phase of evaluation and its central
question, namely, which system is best. These questions require
a shift from the empirical orientation of the behavioral systems
theorist to the speculative orientation of the political philosopher
engaged in the imaginative reconstruction of alternative systems.

Rational Choice

As the consummate normative exercise, the development of
alternative visions of the good political system is the traditional
task of political philosophy. Concerned principally with what
should be done, political philosophy is interpretive and creative,

interested in existing realities only insofar as they assist in understanding and constructing ideal models.

The methodological activities of political philosophy fall outside the realm of the practical tasks of empirically oriented policy analysis. Some of the products of the philosopher's activities, however, must be included in a policy science theory that confronts contemporary issues. This study has already discussed policy theorists such as MacRae and Anderson who urge greater interaction between political philosophers and policy scientists.[32] Through exploration of the normative foundations of policy research and deliberation, political philosophers can supply policy scientists with decision models based on alternative political and social systems. In fact, reports show that some political philosophers are increasingly engaging in policy-related studies. One sign of this is the growing number of political philosophers employed in academic policy analysis programs.[33] Another sign is found in the policy literature itself, reflected particularly in the interest in the works of John Rawls and other political philosophers concerned with social justice.[34] Much of this work is carried out at the level of rational choice, a point to which the discussion will return.

The purpose of this study is basically to show the relationship of rational choice to the other phases of evaluation. Although policy science, at least as practical technique, will remain fundamentally utilitarian and instrumental in character, it is essential to see its relationship to the methods of political philosophy.

Rational Choice as Method

In rational choice, an attempt is made to establish a basis for the choice of one way of life over another. The purpose is to substitute reason for arbitrary personal preference. Taylor has specified three conditions required for rational choice to take place. Coinciding with Habermas's concept of an ideal rational discourse, Taylor's conditions are: freedom, impartiality, and enlightenment. Each of these conditions sets up an ideal. No actual choice can ever be completely free, fully enlightened, or altogether impartial. Hence, no choice made among alternative ways of life can be fully rational. The concept of a rational choice is a conceptual ideal. In describing the ideal, Taylor tried to state what would be considered by anyone to be a rational choice if such a choice were to occur under ideal conditions—the way a fully rational person would think in the ideal context. To the extent a way of life is chosen in a manner that fulfills the conditions of rationality specified here, the way of life can be employed as a basis for justifying value judgments. The specific requirements of the three conditions are the following:

Conditions of freedom:

a. The choice is not decisively determined by unconscious motives.
b. The choice is not at all determined by internal constraints.
c. The choice is not at all determined by external constraints.
d. The choice is decisively determined by the person's own preference.

Conditions of impartiality:

a. The choice is disinterested.
b. The choice is detached or objective.
c. The choice is unbiased.

Conditions of enlightenment:

a. The nature of each way of life is fully known.
b. The probable effects of living each way of life are fully known.
c. The means necessary to bring about each way of life (i.e., what is required to enable a person to live each way of life) are fully known.[35]

Most important for the present discussion are the conditions of enlightenment. It is here that the role of knowledge is introduced. Taylor indicated four types of knowledge: philosophical, imaginative, experiential, and empirical. He specified them as follows:

Philosophical:

We must know the canons of reasoning that constitute the point of view to which any value system in the way of life belongs. What are the rules of relevance and the rules of valid inference which govern the justification of judgments, standards and rules within the framework of each value system? That is, according to what criteria is a reason a relevant reason or a good reason in such justification?

Imaginative Knowledge:

[A person] must be able to *envisage* what it is like to live each way of life. He must be able, by imagination, to convey himself into each way of life and experience it vicariously. Short of actually having lived a way of life, there are four particularly effective means for developing this imaginative knowledge: through personal contact with people who live the way of life, through reading, history, biography, and to a lesser extent, anthropology and sociology, through the study of religion, and through appreciation of the fine arts.

Experiential Knowledge:[36]

A person has this kind of knowledge of a way of life when he actually has lived it. This means that he has been inspired by the ideals of the way of life and that he has adopted the appropriate value systems relevant to given situations.

Empirical:

[All] the empirical knowledge necessary for a complete and accurate *description* of the way of life itself, of the probable effects of living according to it, and of the necessary means for bringing it about. Such knowledge must provide us with answers to a whole series of questions.

- What is it like for a person (or group, or culture) to live the way of life?
- What are the ideals of the way of life; what vision of the *summmum bonum* does it embody?
- What value systems are relevant to different sorts of situations and what value systems take precedence over others in those situations?

- What would be the psychological and social consequences of a person's (or group's, or culture's) living that way of life?
- What physical, social, and psychological conditions must be realized before a person (or group, or culture) would be able to live the way of life?[37]

The deep-seated reliance on knowledge is clear. The panoply of data that can be brought to bear on normative decisions by the scientific value theorists is called into play: empirical descriptions of the way of life; causal knowledge about means to ends; data on existing individual and group values; and information about fundamental human needs, natural laws, and human nature.[38] At this level the entire array of empirical data must dialectically interact with subjective knowledge drawn from both personal experience and imaginative reconstruction of past and future events.

Political Philosophy

Where behavioral scientists begin with verification, political philosophers typically start with rational choice and work back to verification deductively. In general terms, a political philosopher constructs a model of a rational way of life by identifying a political value or values (such as equality, freedom or community) that are adopted as the ultimate goals of all subsequent political undertakings. Each philosopher attempts to make a case for one set of values over another. One may argue that security is the highest value, while an equally intelligent and perceptive colleague may just as earnestly consider insecurity the thing to strive for.

The final empirical referents in rational choice are human nature and the needs derived from it. As referents, they serve as the basis for the construction of alternative models of the ideal person. Plato's "philosopher-king," situated at the pinnacle of the ideal Republic, provides an excellent illustration of this, as does Marx's concept of a productive, self-fulfilled man or woman. The essence of Marx's analysis is an attempt to show that under a capitalist system human beings are necessarily alienated from their full potentialities.[39]

The traditional approach is to try to show what will happen

if a society adopts a particular value or value system. The question is not unlike the one asked in vindication; the difference is that here it is applied to an ideal society rather than an existing regime. As in vindication, scientific information can be brought to bear directly on the question. In rational choice, however, it can be only a part of a larger exploration that also includes interpretive methods such as imagination, insight, and speculation. Through the imaginative creation of alternative sociopolitical systems, the political philosopher attempts to highlight the effects resulting from a surplus of one value (or value system) or the implications of the decline of another. Such a society is constructed as a logical system designed to demonstrate that, given basic premises, particular political or social values logically follow. Available empirical evidence about the instrumental or contributive value of particular values can be marshaled to support one conception over another, although scientific "proof" is beyond reach. As the ideal model is necessarily speculative, empirical evidence is generally available only through insightful extrapolation and analogy based on existing systems.

As seen in Chapter 2, Strauss and Voegelin have been important modern-day advocates of such exercises in political theory.[40] Voegelin advocated the construction of conceptual or paradigmatic representations of the good society to serve as frameworks for evaluation of existing regimes. Recognizing the role of such constructions in public policy studies, Gideon Sjoberg suggested that policy evaluation should include a form of "countersystem analysis" based on a Marxian approach to dialectical reasoning. "A countersystem is a negation of and logical alternative to the existing social order . . . and is therefore a kind of utopian model [providing] researchers one means of transcending the inherent tension between the advantaged and disadvantaged in a society."[41] During the period of domestic crisis and epistemological debate in the 1960s, this type of paradigmatic construction was an essential part of the radical spirit, especially of the New Left, which relied heavily on such works as Herbert Marcuse's *One-Dimensional Man*, Eric Fromm's *The Sane Society*, and Paul and Percival Goodman's *Communitas: Means of Livelihood and Ways of Life*.

Perhaps the work of Rawls is the best contemporary illustration of the method of evaluation at this level. His work has both revived general interest in the classic problem of political philosophy and generated important practical discussions that have made their way into the policy literature.[42] Essentially Rawls is concerned with determining which type of social order a rational person would choose to adopt and the reasons that would be given for obeying its rules. To uncover the nature of such an order, he established a fundamental situation called the "original position." Free of distracting circumstances, the original position is a methodological device to assist social actors in making rational choices about basic values. Like the "state of nature" advanced by Rousseau or Hobbes, the device permits social actors to hypothetically establish a social contract. Each person agrees to a civil order that guarantees certain basic rights. The participation in the formation of the contractual agreement itself is the source of the actor's motivation to accept the goals and duties of the ideal order and to further them as the legitimate base of a good society.

The controversial character of Rawls's conclusions rests on his logical rejection of the principle of utility—or, the greatest good for the greatest number—as the fundamental basis for the ideal social order. Although Rawls did not reject the utilitarian principle altogether, his logical system was designed to prove it is not the ideal rule that would be chosen as the basic organizing principle under the rational conditions of the original position. His purpose was to show that "utility," the dominant moral rule accepted in contemporary society, provides insufficient basis for reconciling public and private interests in a just manner. In Rawls's conception of the good society, the utilitarian principle must be subordinated to the principles of justice.[43]

Following Rawls, Ronald Dworkin has similarly attempted to show that a goal-oriented theory of utilitarianism is unable to protect certain kinds of political rights that people value. By examining what he called the "hard cases" in legal argumentation, Dworkin contended that decisions about certain kinds of rights require a shift from arguments based on consequences to arguments based on principle. In political theory, a shift from consequentialist arguments, or "policy" arguments in Dworkin's terminology, to arguments based on principle is essentially a shift from vindication to rational choice.[44]

As the policy sciences are largely based on utilitarian theory inherited from economic analysis, the writings of Rawls and Dworkin have had direct impact on the policy sciences. Their influence can be found in both the theoretical discussions in the policy literature and in substantive public policy debates in areas such as affirmative action, economic opportunity, and environmental protection. The implications of Rawls's and Dworkin's axiological analyses for policy issues have graced the pages of the leading journals of political opinion. In the methodologically oriented policy literature, writers concerned with social relevance have cited Rawls's principles of justice as a foundation for a new policy science.[45]

The point here is not that Rawls's theory actually establishes such a foundation but rather that his work moves certain policy questions to this level of evaluation. Indeed, other writers, such as the utilitarians themselves or Marxist theorists, have taken strong exception to Rawls's arguments. Some economists have contended that actors in the original position would in fact adopt the principle of utilitarianism,[46] while Marxists have questioned the rationality of the original position itself.[47]

From a neo-Marxist position, writers such as Grauhan and Strubelt have proposed an evaluative scheme for rational policy choices built on a principle of "self-enhancement." Derived from empirical analysis of basic human needs, such a principle is set in a historical framework designed to elucidate the potential of a social system at any given time. Such knowledge would open options or alternative visions of human self-realization. According to Grauhan and Strubelt, policy scientists must transcend their instrumental relationship to policymakers by assuming the larger role of "policy critic."[48]

Toward an Integrated Methodology

A primary purpose of an exploration of alternative methods is to find or develop a multimethodological approach to evaluation that offsets the limitations of behavioral science methodology.[49] In the exploration, the contributions of behavioral-oriented evaluation research, phenomenology, behavioral systems analysis, and political philosophy have been shown to offer important contributions to an inclusive evaluation methodology. Each offers a significant contribution, but none satisfactorily reveals its relationship to the others. The search for a unified, systematic methodology thus remains a central task on the epistemological agenda.

At the outset, the present study proposed two specific tests that must be met by such a methodology. First, the method must be able to contribute to the methodological debate that centers around the fact-value problem. As such, it must confront the task of integrating empirical and normative perspectives. This test was met in the examination of the phases of evaluation, when it established the interrelations of the key methodological approaches in the fact-value debate as the discussion progressed through the four levels of evaluation. Second, the methodology must relate to questions that arise in policy evaluation. This test was accomplished by offering relevant questions taken from actual policy evaluations. As a result, the logic of evaluation presented here is proposed as an epistemological framework for organizing these basic methodologies. By integrating key contributions, it suggests the possibility of a unified methodological system.

The Levels of Evaluation

Until now, reference has generally been made to the "phases" of evaluation. At this point, it becomes useful to recognize these phases as levels of evaluation, moving from the most concrete empirical level up to the higher levels of abstract exploration of ideals. With the assistance of the logic of each of these levels of evaluation, it is possible to see that each type of knowledge associated with the four methodologies is only one level of a larger process constituting a full or complete evaluation. Evaluation research, phenomenological analysis, the behavioral or naturalistic systems approach, and political philosophy are, in this regard, better understood as alternative perspectives on social phenomena rather than competing approaches to truth per se. Instead of competing methodologies, they can be viewed as coexisting perspectives on the same social reality, each with its own type of data and internal logic. Where methodologies such as systems analysis or phenomenology have been accused of a narrow ideological focus, they are seen here as one component of a larger process.[50] Incorporating the range of normative and empirical perspectives, this larger process approaches the full dimensions of a theory of justification.

By preserving the importance of each of the four methodologies, the logic shifts emphasis away from any one of the approaches to the more complex question of how they relate to each other. The types of data and the logic appropriate to each level of evaluation is presented in the two tables that follow. Table 2 shows the relationships of the four methodologies to the four levels of evaluation and the basic modes of explanation employed in each.

The relationships are not as neat or clean-cut as the table indicates; its purpose is only to portray the essential relationship of each method to the overall evaluation process. In actual practice, the levels of evaluation to some extent blend into one another. This is especially true with behavioral science methods in the transition from verification to validation and with the naturalistic systems approach in the transition from vindication to rational choice. In large part, this is because empirical consequences are present in all four phases. In two phases of evaluation—verification and vindication—empirical information is decisive: the ideal justification is based on causal knowledge. In the other two—validation and rational choice— empirical knowledge is necessary but not sufficient for justification. Empirical data in these two phases are fitted into an interpretive argument based on the rules of logical interpretation rather than causal inference. Tables 2 and 3 portray both first-order and second-order evaluation as an interplay between causal and interpretive modes of explanation. First-order evaluations are essentially the result of dialectical mediation between empirical or causal information about program means-ends relationships and the phenomenologically based situational interpretation that characterizes validation. Second-order evaluations involve interplay between knowledge about the larger causal relations of the system as a whole and the search

TABLE 2

The Levels of Evaluation: Methodological
Emphases and Modes of Explanation

	Methodology	Evaluation Research	Phenomenological Analysis	Behavioral Systems Approach	Political Philosophy
	Modes of Explanation	Empirical Causes	Situational Interpretation	Causal Relations	Speculative Interpretation
L	Rational Choice				Political Philosophy
E	Vindication			Behavioral Systems Approach	
V	Validation		Phenomenological Analysis		
E	Verification	Evaluation Research			
L					
S					

TABLE 3

The Levels of Evaluation as
Social Science Methodology

Levels of Evaluative Logic	Social Science Methodology	The Role of Empirical Science	Mode of Inference
Verification	Evaluation Research	- Emphasis on research design and controlled experimentation - Reliability through statistical analysis - Knowledge of secondary consequences	- Causal explanation - Knowledge of facts sufficient - Formal inference
Validation	Phenomeno-logical Analysis	- Descriptive facts of the situation - Application of causal knowledge about consequences of following a rule	- Interpretive understanding - Knowledge of facts necessary but not sufficient - Inference based on informal logic
Vindication	Behavioral Systems Approach	- Descriptive knowledge of de facto individual and group values - Empirical data about instrumental and contributive consequences	- Causal explanation - Knowledge of facts sufficient - Formal inference
Rational Choice	Political Philosophy	- Experiential knowledge about alternative ways of life - Knowledge of human nature	- Interpretive speculation - Vision, imagination and logical speculation - Knowledge of facts necessary but not sufficient

for the ideal system based on the speculative method of political philosophy.

Critical Methodology

Finally, it is important to point out that the contribution of the logic of evaluation converges with Habermas's epistemological program for a unified methodology of critical theory. Insofar as Habermas's epistemological exploration of contemporary social science is one of the major efforts of our time, it provides a set of standards and criteria against which a critical evaluation methodology can be examined.[51] Moreover, for the present study, these standards potentially have special relevance. The initial impetus of my study was drawn from Habermas's revitalization of practical reason, and the fact that it converges with important aspects of the larger corpus of his work suggests the presence of internal logical connections that supply additional support to this line of investigation.

As a critic of positivistic methodology, Habermas contended that a full understanding of the human condition requires a critical epistemological perspective capable of transcending the limits of modern social science. Such an epistemology is to be located between philosophy and science or interpretation and empirical demonstration. It must, as a method capable of establishing the full justification for validity claims, incorporate the dialectical relationships between the empirical-analytic sciences, phenomenologically based historical hermeneutics, and critical reflection in political philosophy. These three epistemologies are, for Habermas, the methodological "moments" upon which a critical theory of evaluation must be constructed.

Although it is beyond the scope and purpose of the present discussion to examine the details of Habermas's contribution (a task that would itself require a full volume), the basic convergence of perspectives is easy to recognize. The epistemological requirements that ground Habermas's critical theory are basically the same methodological orientations that shape the structure of the logic presented here. In both critical theory and the logic of evaluation, positivistic empiricism (both means-ends evaluation and the larger systems perspective, examined in

Habermas's later works) interact with the two levels of interpretation: the phenomenological level of the situation and the philosophical level of critical reflection.

Much of Habermas's own project remains programmatic. By his own admission he has not established "results" in terms of finished or final products.[52] In large part due to the enormous complexity of the undertaking, his "research program" provides only a skeletal outline of a critical evaluation methodology—a suggestive framework that remains to be filled in. It is in this light that the convergence between the logic of evaluation and critical theory is pointed out. If the relationship is valid, Habermas's work offers a deeper epistemological analysis of the issues dealt with here on a more practical methodological level. It thus provides the source of an agenda for further work on the practical methodological dimensions of critical evaluation. For Habermas's own research program, the logic of evaluation helps to clarify the relationship between the epistemological moments of a critical theory and the logical framework of practical reason.

Having concluded the discussion of the contribution of the logic of evaluation, I have set the stage for the explication of practical procedures for public policy evaluation—a task requiring a shift from the theoretical and philosophical foundations of social science methodology to the more mundane levels of policy analysis. Up to this point, the analysis has primarily focused on theoretical methodological problems that stand in the path of a practical method. The effort has centered around the development of a framework of practical reason capable of bypassing the epistemological problems that have impeded the construction of a political method for policy evaluation. The central task has been the elaboration of an analytical framework capable of incorporating the empirical and normative requirements of a critical evaluation methodology, particularly as such requirements arise in policy evaluation issues. The study now turns to its concluding task of schematically presenting the framework as a procedure for policy analysts. Chapter 6 concludes with a logic of policy questions based on the four interrelated methodologies that constitute the logic of evaluation.

Notes

1. Jacob Viner, "The Intellectual History of Laissez Faire," *Journal of Law and Economics* 3 (October 1960):62-63.

2. Paul W. Taylor, *Normative Discourse* (Englewood Cliffs, N.J.: Prentice-Hall, 1961), p. 132. It is important to understand that the "standards and rules that make up a value system have a double function. They are the norms a person appeals to in validating other (lower) standards and rules, and they guide a person's conduct. When a person adopts a value system, he decides to accept certain standards and rules as the basis for justifying his value judgments. But he also decides to place his conduct under the regulation of all the standards and rules of the value system. He commits himself to trying to fulfill the standards and to acting in accordance with the rules. This in turn involves his attitudes. He comes to have a pro-attitude toward whatever fulfills the standards or complies with the rules, and a con-attitude toward whatever is not in accordance with them. When a person has adopted a value system, then, he is not only disposed to *reason* in a certain way (by appealing to its constituent standards and rules), but he is also disposed to *live* in a certain way (by trying to realize the ideals it proposes)" (p. 129).

3. Marcus George Singer, *Generalization in Ethics* (New York: Alfred A. Knopf, 1960), p. 121.

4. These examples are adapted from Flathman's discussion of Singer. Richard E. Flathman, *The Public Interest: An Essay Concerning the Normative Discourse of Politics* (New York: John Wiley & Sons, 1966), p. 148.

5. Ibid., p. 149.

6. Robert Dorfman, "An Afterword: Human Values and Environmental Decisions," in *When Values Conflict: Essays on Environmental Analysis, Discourse and Decision,* ed. Laurence H. Tribe, Corrinne S. Schelling, and John Voss (Cambridge, Mass.: Ballinger Publishing Co., 1976), p. 168.

7. Sheldon S. Wolin, "Political Theory as a Vocation," *American Political Science Review* 62 (December 1969):1073-1074; Wayne A. R. Leys, *Ethics for Policy Decisions* (Englewood Cliffs, N.J.: Prentice-Hall, 1952); and James Ward Smith, *Theme for Reason* (Princeton, N.J.: Princeton University Press, 1957).

8. Smith, *Theme for Reason,* p. 14.

9. Martin Rein, *Social Science and Public Policy* (New York: Penguin Books, 1976), pp. 261-268; and Charles W. Anderson, "The Logic of Public Problems: Evaluation in Comparative Policy Research," in *Comparing Public Policies: New Concepts and Methods,* ed. Douglas E. Ashford (Beverly Hills, Calif.: Sage Publications, 1978), pp. 19-42.

10. See David Lyons, *The Forms and Limits of Utilitarianism* (Oxford:

Clarendon Press, 1969). According to rule utilitarianism, people have an obligation to follow the rule of social practice that would lead to the best consequences if all others in the situation agreed to follow the rule. Such a rule of social practice must be shown to produce better results than any other rule of conduct that might be employed in the situation and better consequences than those that might result from following no rule whatsoever.

11. A gasoline motor has instrumental value on a cross country trip. A spark plug has contributive value in a gasoline engine. Taylor's approach to vindication draws on Herbert Feigel's essay, "Validation and Vindication: An Analysis of the Nature and the Limits of Ethical Arguments," in *Readings in Ethical Theory,* ed. Wilfred Sellars and John Hospers (New York: Appleton-Century-Crofts, 1952), pp. 667–680.

12. Taylor, *Normative Discourse,* p. 41.

13. Edward B. Tylor, cited in *Modern Dictionary of Sociology,* ed. George A. Theodorson and Achilles G. Theodorson (New York: Macmillan, 1968), p. 95.

14. Taylor, *Normative Discourse,* p. 141.

15. Robert Cooley Angell, *Free Society and Moral Crisis* (Ann Arbor: University of Michigan Press, 1965), p. 22.

16. See, for example, Gabriel A. Almond and Sidney Verba, *The Civic Culture* (Princeton, N.J.: Princeton University Press, 1963).

17. George J. Graham, Jr., "The Concept of 'Political Evaluation' and Levels of Theory," mimeo. (Nashville, Tenn.: Vanderbilt University, 1977); and George J. Graham, Jr., and Scarlett G. Graham, "Evaluating Drift in Policy Systems," in *Problems of Theory in Policy Analysis,* ed. Phillip M. Gregg (Lexington, Mass.: D. C. Heath & Co., 1976), p. 77–87.

18. Yehezkel Dror, "Applied Social Science and Systems Analysis," in *The Use and Abuse of Social Science,* ed. Irving Louis Horowitz (New Brunswick, N.J.: Transaction, 1971), pp. 109–132; see also Dror, "Policy Analysis: A Theoretical Framework and Some Basic Concepts" (Paper presented at the Sixty-fifth Annual Meeting of the American Political Science Association, New York, September 2–6, 1969).

19. See Ralph B. Perry, *The Realms of Value* (Cambridge, Mass.: Harvard University Press, 1954).

20. John Dewey, *The Public and Its Problems* (London: Allen & Unwin, 1946).

21. Ibid.

22. Harold D. Lasswell, "The Policy Orientation," in *The Policy Sciences,* ed. Daniel Lerner and Harold D. Lasswell (Stanford, Calif.: Stanford University Press, 1951), p. 12.

23. C. West Churchman, *The Systems Approach* (New York: Dell Publishing Co., 1968); and John W. Sutherland, *A General Systems Philosophy*

for the Social and Behavioral Sciences (New York: George Braziller, 1973).

24. Ludwig von Bertalanffy, *General System Theory* (New York: George Braziller, 1968); and Ervin Laszlo, *The Systems View of the World: The Natural Philosophy of the New Developments in the Sciences* (New York: George Braziller, 1972).

25. David C. McClelland, *The Achieving Society* (Princeton, N.J.: D. Van Nostrand Co., 1961).

26. Oscar Lewis, *Five Families: Mexican Case Studies in the Culture of Poverty* (New York: Basic Books, 1959).

27. U.S., Department of Labor, Office of Policy Planning and Research, *The Negro Family,* prepared by Daniel Patrick Moynihan (Washington, D.C.: U.S. Government Printing Office, 1965); also known as the "Moynihan Report."

28. Edward C. Banfield, *The Unheavenly City: The Nature and Future of our Urban Crisis* (Boston: Little, Brown and Co., 1970).

29. See, for example, Herbert J. Gans, "Culture and Class in the Study of Poverty: An Approach to Antipoverty Research," in *On Understanding Poverty,* ed. Daniel P. Moynihan (New York: Basic Books, 1968), pp. 201–208; and Lee Rainwater, "The Problem of Lower-Class Culture and Poverty-War Strategy," in ibid., pp. 229–259.

30. Milton Rokeach and Seymour Parker, "Values as Social Indicators of Poverty and Race Relations in America," *The Annals* 388 (March 1970), pp. 97–111.

31. Timothy M. Hennessey and Richard H. Feen, "Social Science as Social Philosophy: Edward C. Banfield and the 'New Realism' in Urban Politics," in *Varieties of Political Conservativism,* ed. Matthew Holden, Jr. (Beverly Hills, Calif.: Sage Publications, 1974), p. 29.

32. Duncan MacRae, Jr., "Policy Analysis as an Applied Social Science," *Administration and Society* 6 (February 1975):380; and Anderson, "The Logic of Public Problems," p. 22.

33. Edward B. Fiske, "Ethics Course Now Attracting Many More U.S. College Students," *New York Times,* February 20, 1978, A1.

34. John Rawls, *A Theory of Justice* (Cambridge, Mass.: Belknap Press, 1971); and Ronald Dworkin, *Taking Rights Seriously* (London: Duckworth, 1977).

35. Taylor, *Normative Discourse,* pp. 165–172.

36. Ibid. Taylor has called this "practical" rather than "experiential" knowledge, but this creates some semantic confusion for the present study. Here the word "practical" is reserved for the everyday processes of reasoning as a whole. Also, the term "empirical" knowledge has been substituted for Taylor's term "intellectual" knowledge to be consistent with usage here.

37. Ibid., pp. 166–169.

38. Kurtz asserted that "most moral and political theories of decision criteria have erred by taking into account one, two or something less than all . . . factual data." He explained that "simple descriptive naturalism considers the particular facts of the situation . . . or the general laws . . . to be central in decision; but this appeal is so far removed from the subject matter of desire and value that it is no wonder that vigorous protests have been offered to it. Extreme pragmatism lays emphasis on our technology . . . as if knowledge of means alone is sufficient for decision. Another form of naturalism attempts to derive decision from a description of existing desires . . . but knowledge of what men do is not enough to determine what they should do in the future. Subjectivism relates decision to individual attitudes or social approval, but it fails to recognize that a decision occurs in a context of behavior, and that a conscious expression has its deeper motivation and effects. Finally, classical natural-law theories refer to 'human nature' as some ideal or hidden essence to be fulfilled . . . but this explanation lacks any relation to the complexity of human behavior and to the existing framework of desires. We need to unify these separate theories. Each indicates one strand that is relevant to choice. Separately they are narrow and partial, but their synthesis may provide some aid in decision." Paul Kurtz, *Decision and the Human Condition* (New York: Dell Publishing Co., 1965), pp. 247–248.

39. For an excellent explication of Marx's method at this level of analysis, see Bertell Ollman, *Alienation: Marx's Conception of Man in Capitalistic Society* (London: Cambridge University Press, 1976).

40. Leo Strauss, *What is Political Philosophy?* (Glencoe, Ill.: Free Press, 1959), pp. 9–55; and Eric Voegelin, *The New Science of Politics* (Chicago: University of Chicago Press, 1952).

41. Gideon Sjoberg, "Politics, Ethics and Evaluation Research," in *Handbook of Evaluation Research,* ed. by Marcia Guttentag and Elmer L. Struening (Beverly Hills, Calif.: Sage Publications, 1975), pp. 29–51.

42. Allan Bloom, "Justice: John Rawls vs. the Tradition of Political Philosophy," *American Political Science Review* 69 (June 1975):648–662.

43. Rawls, *A Theory of Justice.*

44. Ronald Dworkin, *Taking Rights Seriously;* and Dworkin, "The Original Position," *University of Chicago Law Review* 40 (Spring 1973): 500–533.

45. See David K. Hart, "Social Equity, Justice and the Equitable Administrator," *Public Administration Review* 34 (January–February, 1974): 3–17; Nicholas Henry, *Public Administration and Public Affairs* (Englewood Cliffs, N.J.: Prentice-Hall, 1975), pp. 33–51; Raymond D. Gastil, *Social Humanities* (San Francisco: Jossey-Bass, 1977); and Lawrence A.

Tribe, "Policy Science: Analysis of Ideology," *Philosophy and Public Affairs* 2 (January 1972):66–110.

46. See, for example, John Harsanyi, "Can the Maximin Principle Serve as a Basis for Morality," *American Political Science Review* 69 (June 1975):594–606.

47. See Richard Miller, "Rawls and Marxism," in *Reading Rawls,* ed. Norman Daniels (New York: Basic Books, 1976), pp. 206–230.

48. Rolf-Richard Grauhan and Wendelin Strubelt, "Political Rationality Reconsidered: Notes on an Integrated Scheme for Policy Choice," *Policy Sciences* 2 (Summer 1971):270.

49. See Gerard Radnitzky, *Contemporary Schools of Metascience,* 2 vols. (Chicago: Henry Regnery, 1973).

50. See Robert Lilienfeld, *The Rise of Systems Theory: An Ideological Analysis* (New York: John Wiley & Sons, 1976); or, for a critique of phenomenologically based methods, see Robert Lichtman, "Symbolic Interactionism and Social Reality: Some Marxist Queries," *Berkeley Journal of Sociology* 15 (1970–71):76–94.

51. For a discussion, see Trent Schroyer, "The Dialectical Foundations of Critical Theory: Jürgen Habermas's Metatheoretical Investigations," *Telos,* no. 12 (Summer 1972):93–114; and Schroyer, "A Reconceptualization of Critical Theory," in *Radical Sociology,* ed. J. David Colfax and Jack L. Roach (New York: Basic Books, 1971), pp. 132–148.

52. On this point see Thomas McCarthy, *The Critical Theory of Jürgen Habermas* (Cambridge, Mass.: M.I.T. Press, 1978).

6

The Logic as Policy Methodology

If there is a logic of practical judgment, it is a logic of questions. It does not supply factual information, but is a reminder of the kind of facts that may need investigating. . . . [A]s a discipline of questions [it] should unparalyze the mind at the moment of action. It suggests the unremembered or unperceived angles that may need investigation.
—Wayne A. R. Leys[1]

The final task of this study is to translate the logic of evaluation into a political methodology that addresses the objectives of policy analysis. The perspective shifts from political theory and epistemology to practical politics and policy methodology. Specifically, the task is to schematically present a methodological procedure for policy evaluation.

Such an adaptation cannot be accomplished with precision. The logic of political evaluation was defined very generally in Chapter 4 as the logic of evaluation applied to decisions about political action. The generality of this definition is further complicated by the fact that in the study of politics even the most established concepts, such as "interest groups" or "public opinion," are difficult to define precisely. Nonetheless, a discussion of the political character of public policy and the relevant categories of political data that bear on policy evaluation is an appropriate place to start.

Policy as a Political Agreement

Public policy, as the outcome of a political process, is essentially a statement of the general goals to be pursued. Such policy goals serve as the basis for developing specific objectives. In this respect, policies are political agreements on courses of action, whether arrived at through political discussion, vote, or decree. As such, policies contain—both explicitly and implicitly— the standards or criteria adopted by the established governing bodies for the evaluation of public programs. These criteria provide the grounds for deciding whether a program objective (of, say, manpower training) fulfills the policy goal (of reducing unemployment).

It is important to stress the distinction between policy goals and program objectives.[2] Drawing on Kaplan's concept of levels within a value space, discussed in Chapter 3, policies are properly understood to state goals while programs are concerned with objectives. Policies embody the broad attainable goals that are derived from higher level ideals. Goals are the concrete specifications of the political system's ideals—for example, liberal education is an ideal while schooling is a goal. Programs, in turn, are based on the specific operational objectives derived from the general goals. A bachelor's degree in political science at City College is an objective of the goal of schooling. Thus, where policies seek to respond to the widest possible range of the political system, programs are directed at specific situations within the system.

Table 4 shows the complex linkages that operate in policy evaluation. Although it is often quite difficult to analytically separate these variables and relationships, the primary concern of political evaluation in policy analysis is represented by arrows B and F and C and D. Political evaluation, in this respect, is an evaluation of the acceptability of a policy to the relevant political groups whose support or opposition bears on the policy's adoption, focusing attention on the criteria or standards employed by the various political groups. The full assignment in policy evaluation must, therefore, combine judgments about the political acceptability of criteria with evidence on how the program actually measures up to these criteria.

In a political evaluation, the analyst and policymaker are not just looking for the "best" solution in the narrow technical sense of the term. For political evaluators, the best solution must ultimately be the one permitting them to show that bene-

TABLE 4
Linkages in Policy Evaluation

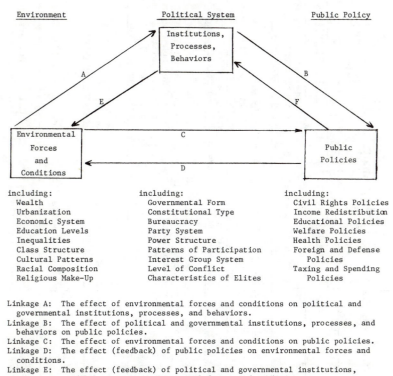

| Environment | Political System | Public Policy |

including:
Wealth
Urbanization
Economic System
Education Levels
Inequalities
Class Structure
Cultural Patterns
Racial Composition
Religious Make-Up

including:
Governmental Form
Constitutional Type
Bureaucracy
Party System
Power Structure
Patterns of Participation
Interest Group System
Level of Conflict
Characteristics of Elites

including:
Civil Rights Policies
Income Redistribution
Educational Policies
Welfare Policies
Health Policies
Foreign and Defense
   Policies
Taxing and Spending
   Policies

Linkage A: The effect of environmental forces and conditions on political and
  governmental institutions, processes, and behaviors.
Linkage B: The effect of political and governmental institutions, processes, and
  behaviors on public policies.
Linkage C: The effect of environmental forces and conditions on public policies.
Linkage D: The effect (feedback) of public policies on environmental forces and
  conditions.
Linkage E: The effect (feedback) of political and governmental institutions,
  processes, and behaviors on environmental forces and conditions.
Linkage F: The effect (feedback) of public policies on political and governmental
  institutions, processes, and behaviors.

Source: Thomas R. Dye, <u>Understanding Public Policy</u>,
1978, p. 9. Reproduced by permission of
Prentice-Hall, Inc., Englewood Cliffs, New Jersey.

fits to recipients are also in some way benefits to those who pay
the costs. As Diesing explained, the question is not only which
proposal offers the most efficient or effective solution but also
who makes and who opposes the proposal.[3] The political
evaluator, in this regard, has a specific orientation and cognitive
style. Table 5 compares the political evaluator's cognitive style
with that of the economist concerned with the technical criteria
governing efficient solutions.

The relationship between political and economic criteria has
generated an extensive body of literature, some of which has

TABLE 5

Cognitive Styles of Hypothetical Policy Analysis

Process of Inquiry	Elements of Analysis	Illustrative Considerations	
		Economist	Political Analyst
Select problem		Allocation of resources	Increase support for and effectiveness of president/party
Define, formulate, and delimit problem	Objective	Explicit Agreement Stable	Confusion Conflict and disagreement Instability
	Criteria	Maximize difference between benefits and costs	Maximize probability of political acceptance
Determine and search for relevant data	Alternatives	Exclude the infeasible Present solution/policy	Exclude the infeasible Present solution/policy
	Costs and Benefits	Program related Quantitative	Program and nonprogram related (political costs and benefits) Mostly qualitative
Calculate and explain	Model	Closed General Parsimonious	Open Idiosyncratic Complex-contextual
Interpret results, test, or start over if unhappy	Communication	Technical A good study sells itself	Advocacy and persuasion Sell the president and other actors

Source: Adapted from Arnold Meltsner, Policy Analysts in the Bureaucracy (Berkeley, Calif.: University of California, 1976), p. 118. Reproduced with permission of the author and the publisher.

been surveyed in this study. The treatment, or lack of treatment, of political criteria has been a central question in the search for a socially relevant methodology. Given the fact that public policymaking is rooted in the political context, political criteria, as often as not, take precedence over technical economic considerations. This has led writers such as Churchman, MacRae, and Lindblom to suggest asking how policy evaluation can be incorporated into the political decision processes, rather than how decision processes can be made to accommodate evaluation (see Chapter 2). The critical character of this question has led in recent years to the development of a newly emerging field of inquiry in policy studies called "knowledge utilization." In the literature of this field, alternative models like Churchman's have come to be described as the "organization of enlightenment."[4] In contrast to the traditional engineering model of applied policy research, which is closely attuned to the technical evaluation of policy, the enlightenment model focuses on the sociology of the knowledge relationship between policy analysts and decision makers. Recognizing that analysts and decision makers operate from different normative perspectives and empirical methodologies, the organization of enlightenment approach attempts to understand policy decisions as a social process involving conflict and interaction between scientific methods and organizational decision criteria.

Political Data for Policy Evaluation

Having discussed the political dimension of public policy, it is appropriate to examine next the types of data that provide the context for a "political" evaluation. Although a definitive set of categories is beyond reach, the political science literature is filled with suggestive studies about such information.[5] To establish the direction, Table 6 offers eight basic political categories.

Such political data—concerned with the participants, available resources, power and influence, rules of the game, and so on—provides the special context that translates a general logic of evaluation into a political evaluation. It establishes both the potentials for and constraints on political decisions and action.

TABLE 6
Categories of Relevant Political Data

Political
Actors

1. Political actors may be individuals, pressure groups, elected leaders, administrators of government agencies, political parties, opinion leaders, business leaders, and so on.

Motivations
and Goals
of Actors

2. Each political actor will possess a number of motives, needs, interests, desires, goals and objectives that shape his or her order of preferences and actions. Even though political actors at times conceal their motives and goals, they serve as a general guide to behavior.

Beliefs and
Values of
Actors

3. The political actor's beliefs, attitudes, and value systems establish his or her orientation to the empirical world. This frame of reference is a generalized statement of goals, specifying what is desirable and which means to utilize in achieving them. It may involve a disjointed set of beliefs and values, or it may be a well-organized political ideology. The intensity with which a political actor holds a belief or value system will at times be a crucial factor.

Political
Resources
(Power and
Influence)

4. The most significant political actors will possess resources that translate into power and influence in the building of political coalitions and support. Such resources may be material or physical possessions, money, symbolic statuses, social position, information, skills, and so on.

Political
Decision
Rules and
Time

5. Political decisions will often be guided by specific decision rules, legislative requirements, and existing laws, which will tend to channel many of the interactions between political actors.

TABLE 6 (Cont.)

Political Decision Sites	6. Political decisions will occur at specific decision sites involving different rules, leverages, disadvantages, and the like that will often have an important bearing on the outcomes. Also, the time period or range over which the decisions extend may have an important influence on the political perceptions of the relevant actors.
Public Opinion and Political Climate	7. The general political temper of the times will influence the outcome to a considerable degree. For example, the more intensely dissatisfied large groups and strong actors become with the present situation, the more support may be available for innovative alternatives.
Relevant Political Culture	8. Different decisions will call different political values into question: equality before the law, civil liberties, representative control of institutions, equal opportunity, peaceful orientation toward other nations, fraternity, patriotism, etc.

For the policy analyst, such information determines the framework of a specific policy space and issue area—that is, the general political environment in which the policy deliberation is set, as well as the specific aspect of the environment that has become an issue.[6]

Political data of this type is mostly qualitative, contextual, and often somewhat idiosyncratic. Utilizing such a framework, the analyst begins the investigation grounded in specific political orientations located in society itself.[7] As characterizations of the cognitive orientations of particular political groups, such frameworks permit the analyst to identify not only the problems to be solved but also the potentialities and limitations to which he or she must appeal in proposing solutions.[8]

Political Evaluation as Policy Methodology

Because of its practical character, set within the context of power, political evaluation in policy analysis is never concerned with the full range of scientific and philosophical analyses included in second-order normative discourse.[9] Insofar as the questions that confront the policy analyst—as policy analyst—do not formally involve problems concerned with the foundations of values, or the justification of a philosophical theory of value, the questions advanced in the highest stage of evaluation do not arise. If conflict arises at the level of rational choice in the logic of evaluation, the inquiry has stepped beyond the bounds of policy analysis.

The purpose of this point is not to underplay the importance of second-order evaluation; rather, it is to recognize a realistic division of labor, dictated by both the purposes and capabilities inherent in the policy analyst's assignment. To paraphrase Toulmin, the analysis or evaluation of these second-order philosophical questions may be considered outside the "game" of policy analysis.[10]

Policy analysis, then, operates within the boundaries of verification, validation, and vindication. It is important to examine each of these phases in the context of policy analysis objectives. In the case of vindication, the logic is based on two principal tasks. The first is an attempt to determine if the value system (which provides the rules of political precedence) is in fact instrumental or contributive to a system of social order constructed around the ideals or ideology of which the value system is a part. The second task involves an effort to determine the generalizability of this value system and its rules across the value systems and interests held by other relevant participants. It is an attempt to determine if the relevant participants judge the system consequences to be fair and equitable in terms of the system's accepted rules and standards. These tasks are derived from the two basic procedural tests of normative analysis: the principle of consequences and the principle of generalizability.[11] The first can be explored with the assistance of an empirical systems perspective, the second through the methods of logical interpretation. Empirical evaluation at this level can be illustrated by the following example, shown in Table 7.

Table 7 could be developed by a political analyst on an economic advisory staff. The value hierarchy shown in the table is an outline of the logical connections between the levels of values that constitute the standard interpretation of classical liberalism. The vindication of a value system under liberalism must ask whether this particular value system (which is employed to adjudicate between goals) actually contributed to the fulfillment of the higher-level ideals of the system of which it is

TABLE 7
A Value Hierarchy for Economic Policy Decisions

	DECISION CRITERION	GOALS OR OBJECTIVES
	4. The Individual	Individual Welfare
		Self-realization
		Rationality of the individual
		Liberty
		Human dignity
L E V E L S O F	3. Society	Social Welfare
		The common good
		Culture
		Justice
		Order
O F		Plan
V A L U E S	2. Economy	Consumer Welfare
		Efficient allocation of resources
		Maximum production and distribution of goods and services
	1. Business	Ownership Welfare
		Profits
		Survival
		Growth

Adapted from Wilmar F. Bernthal, "Value Perspectives in Management Decisions," *Academy of Management Journal*, 5 (December 1962), 196. Reproduced with the permission of the author and the publisher.

a component part. In the table, for example, the vindication of
a businessman's profit-oriented value system depends upon the
ability to show its contribution to consumer welfare, which,
in turn, must be demonstrated to advance social and individual
welfare. In economics, Adam Smith's theory of "consumer
sovereignty" in *The Wealth of Nations* remains the classical attempt to vindicate the value systems of liberal capitalism.

Marxism's persistent attack on liberalism provides an excellent
illustration of this level of evaluation. Like liberalism, Marxism
basically accepts the ideals that have evolved since the French
Revolution.[12] But Marxist analyses (both the scientific and
philosophical schools) are in essence endeavors designed to
show that such ideals cannot be achieved through the value systems of capitalism. Liberal capitalism, in short, is not in reality
instrumental to the achievement of individual self-realization or
enhancement. For the Marxist, the political-economic system
of liberal capitalism realizes the ideals in almost complete
reverse order of their presentation in the table. In the Marxist
description of the actual operation of the system, ownership
welfare and business profits are at the top of the list, followed
by economy and society, with the individual at the bottom.
Where the classical liberal, or liberal capitalist, argues that private enterprise promotes the highest level of individual freedom
and self-realization, the Marxist contends that such a system
operates to thwart these ideals. Thus, while liberals and Marxists
can agree on the essential ideals, they disagree over whether a
social order based on capitalistic value systems fulfills them.
Positing socialism as the alternative political-economic order,
the Marxist must in turn submit the value systems of a socialist
society to the test of vindication. Even a cursory examination
of the efforts to vindicate the value systems of liberal capitalism
or socialism reveals the profound scientific and philosophical
complexity of the task at this phase of evaluation.[13] Although
policy analysts, at least as policy analysts, seldom carry out investigations at this level, the available scientific and empirical
evidence on the question at any one time is an important de-
terminant of the political context within which analysts operate.

In the absence of adequate knowledge, decision makers necessarily fall back on political ideologies to bridge the empirical

gaps. Based on a combination of logical interpretation and empirical extrapolation, ideologies present pictures of how different socioeconomic systems and their political orders are believed to operate, why they work the ways they do, whether or not they are good, and what strategies to take if they are not. Essentially, ideologies are images that both describe and interpret political action in the everyday world of affairs. As descriptions, ideologies are mental maps, telling decision makers where observed facts fit into the full picture. As interpretive schemes, they show how to understand the significance of the particular factual elements. In this respect, they provide the basis for evaluation. As evaluative frameworks, political ideologies simplify the task of choice by offering decision rules that indicate which criteria take precedence in political judgments. These rules of precedence—whether implicit or explicit—evolve from emotional commitments to specific needs and interests and the experiences gained in attempts to satisfy them. Such rules generally reflect enough reality to serve those needs and interests but stop far short of truth validity.

For policy analysis to be successfully employed in a particular political situation, there must first exist some fundamental political agreements.[14] Such agreements serve as mediating principles under which conflicting elements of belief systems, ideologies, or value hierarchies can, at least potentially, be organized. The possibility of systematically organizing conflicting elements under a higher principle establishes a potential basis for normative consensus in policy deliberation. Without such a possibility, the introduction of policy analysis is inappropriate.

In addition to making policy analysis feasible, the presence of fundamental ideological agreements serves an important role as a specialized aid that greatly simplifies the evaluation process. As a loosely organized set of intersecting substantive generalizations and formal principles, an ideology permits the analyst to remove certain beliefs or alternatives from the realm of consideration (say, corporate profit margins under a socialist system). It allows the assumptions of its arguments to be treated as facts, permitting the analyst to evade the overwhelming empirical task that verification of these assumptions often requires (say, the demonstration of the primacy of labor over capital).

Writers such as Lindblom have argued that even when such assumptions are mistaken, they can still be useful in guiding the evaluation toward policy decisions. For instance, even though a commitment to a market system may be based on false assumptions about the structure of the economy, it can be still employed successfully as a standard in analyzing and formulating policies designed to combat the growth of monopolies. Lindblom contended that in such cases all that need be asked of policy evaluation is that it leads from the unquestioned assumption to a policy that secures agreement. On other occasions, however, political ideology is too far removed from the facts to be helpful in policy evaluations. In these instances, it may produce policies that are politically acceptable but fail to work. For example, the budget-balancing policies of the 1930s, based on appropriate ideological standards, lengthened rather than shortened the depression.[15] Policy scientists, therefore, must include the analysis of ideological systems within the purview of their activities. Even though they are not directly concerned with the development of ideological systems, they are necessarily consumers of such products. Ideological belief systems provide basic data for policy analysis, especially the political evaluation of policy.

As practical tools employed in the everyday world, ideologies shift the emphasis from the philosopher's search for primary ideals to a more practical focus on the mixture or patterns of ideals that govern the decision-making processes. Such a shift offers the analyst a more manageable realm of workable consensus and agreement, permitting avoidance of some of the more sticky epistemological questions that confront the justification of a primary ideal. In this respect, it is important to recognize that fundamental conflicts do not arise in every practical situation. Moreover, there is much greater consensus on the general configuration of ideals than there is on the relative merits of one particular ideal over another. For instance, widespread agreement exists on the general primacy of ideals such as economic progress, the reduction of human suffering, the protection of human life, political freedom, and social reciprocity.

Such values emerge as fundamental agreements that command more respect than lesser values such as money making or winning political elections. It is, of course, possible to identify policy-makers in dictatorial regimes who do not respect human life or decision makers in pluralistic countries who accept the value of social reciprocity but make exceptions in the case of blacks and other minorities. In fact, at times the violation of an ideal may be sanctioned by official policy, such as the taking of human life during war. Nonetheless, there is enough agreement for Wayne Leys to expound a framework of ideals to serve as a guide for probing policy decisions (and to argue convincingly that his guide leaves out very little of human value that bears on policy decisions). In modified form, Leys's six basic value clusters are presented in Table 8.[16] Such a value framework is not a tight logical system but rather a loose-jointed one in the sense that sound policy decisions will result from successive reviews from the standpoint of each of these six value clusters. By employing all six value clusters, few values or normative assumptions escape the policy decision-making process. The framework is to be viewed as a set of standards, tests, or criteria that are always relevant but none of which is controlling. As Leys has stated, "In the making of a decision, it is possible to consider these values in a somewhat orderly fashion"; . . . [those policy makers] "who learn to review these criteria in an orderly manner are the ones who have acquired the art of 'asking the right questions,' and that by practicing this art they improve the quality of their judgment."[17]

Kaplan has offered a similar set of values in the form of policy principles. Advanced as formal or procedural evaluative criteria, such principles do not determine the ends of policy per se but rather set limits to such ends and the programs by which they can be realized. They function in policy evaluations as necessary conditions to be satisfied, permitting the analyst to reject programs that do not provide sufficiently for all relevant criteria. Kaplan likened them to fundamental principles of science, such as the law of conservation of matter in physics: "Hypotheses whose consequences are inconsistent with such principles are (ordinarily) rejected; but the whole of physics is not deducible from such principles alone."[18] Kaplan suggested the

TABLE 8
Basic Value Clusters

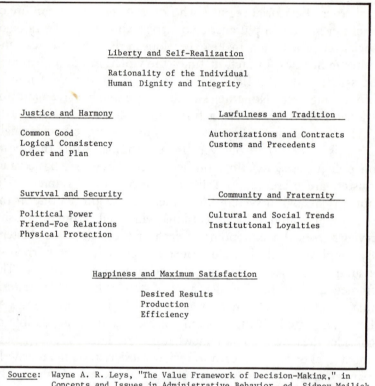

Liberty and Self-Realization

Rationality of the Individual
Human Dignity and Integrity

Justice and Harmony   Lawfulness and Tradition

Common Good   Authorizations and Contracts
Logical Consistency   Customs and Precedents
Order and Plan

Survival and Security   Community and Fraternity

Political Power   Cultural and Social Trends
Friend-Foe Relations   Institutional Loyalties
Physical Protection

Happiness and Maximum Satisfaction

Desired Results
Production
Efficiency

Source: Wayne A. R. Leys, "The Value Framework of Decision-Making," in
          Concepts and Issues in Administrative Behavior, ed. Sidney Mailick
          and Edward H. Van Ness (Englewood Cliffs, N.J.: Prentice-Hall,
          1962), p. 88. Reproduced by permission.

following policy planning principles, which are presented as a
tentative beginning:

1. *The Principle of Impartiality*
   There is no prior specification of persons or groups who are
   to benefit or suffer from governmental policy. There is no place
   for love and hate in policy, i.e., discriminatory treatment of
   some sectors of the population only because they are the
   people that they are, without regard to acts or traits that others
   might conceivably share. Examples of violations of this principle
   are the Nazi policies against the Jews, or colonial exploitation
   of a native population on behalf of the master-class.

2. *The Principle of Individuality*

Values are finally to be assessed as having their locus in the individual. No groups or abstract aggregates, like the State, provide proper substantives for value adjectives—save indirectly, and with ultimate reference to individuals. A "strong State" or "wealthy State" is not a value save insofar as it implies, sooner or later, individuals who enjoy security or a high standard of living. The State is made for man, not man for the State.

3. *The Maximin Principle*

Improvements in a value distribution consist in cutting off the bottom of the distribution, not extending the top. The achievement of a policy or program is appraised by its minima, not its peaks. We assess a technology, from the standpoint of social planning, by the price of shoes rather than the achievement of a Sputnik. Equivalently, the principle dictates that those with least of a particular value should have the first priority for more of it.

4. *The Distributive Principle*

The more people that have a good thing, the better. This is the principle that declares against elite formation, part of that aspect of democratic thought that gives weight to sheer number. It implies the use of the method of summation in assessing the values for a set of individuals. However attractive a particular configuration to a philosopher of aristocracy of Plato's stamp, we can never have too many enjoying a particular good.

5. *The Principle of Continuity*

Changes in patterns and practices are of no value for their own sake, and are subject to established procedures of change. No merit attaches to a break with tradition merely because it is a break. However revolutionary the changes made, their value lies in the substance of the changes, not in the fact of their having been made. It is this principle, in effect, that distinguishes immature rebelliousness from the achievement of mature independence.

6. *The Principle of Autonomy*

Government is to do for people what people cannot do for themselves. This is another basic component of democratic theory, repudiating paternalism, dictatorships of whatever benevolence, and the like. It is not necessarily a distrust of government but rather a faith in the governed.

7. *The Principle of Urgency*

"If not now, when?" The rate of progress toward social goals
is to be maximized. The presumption is in favor of dealing with
present needs; postponement on behalf of future goods requires
explicit justification.[19]

Like substantive ideals, such procedural principles are his-
torically conditioned rules rather than fixed and immutable
truths. The value of such principles rests on their dialectical
potential. On the one hand, they are products of particular
world views and social systems and operate to maintain them.
On the other hand, they serve as agents of change by illuminating social contradictions that emerge in the process of historical struggle. Through political struggle and historical change, the
substantive application of such procedural principles undergoes a
process of evolution and change. The principles find justification
in the value of their products, which Kaplan defined in terms of
"the experienced good of the way of life they help to shape."[20]

As normative standards, such principles can be related to the
two abstract procedural principles of ethics—the principle of
consequences and the principle of generalization. As more concrete expressions of these rules, there is a considerable amount
of overlapping between them. When stated more precisely, it
may be that the distributive principle can be derived from
impartiality, or the principle of autonomy from individuality.

However, more important than the similarity that may be
found between some principles is the conflict generated by
others. It is the conflict between procedural principles that gives
them a critical edge in policy evaluation. For instance, the
principle of continuity expresses a kind of conservatism that
may resist pull from the principle of urgency. Frequently, there
are no overriding principles that can mediate such conflicts,
which is problematic for policy analysts and decision makers,
at least in the immediate situation. In the longer view, it is the
possibility of just such conflicts that makes the principles comprehensive and viable. As a dialectical product of forces, society
is the expression of the forces of both stability and conflict.
Decision makers, as Kaplan suggested, "must inevitably look
now in one direction, now in the other."[21] The purpose is to

probe the situation for conflict and stability—to test the circumstances to see which goal is relevant in a specific context.

There is a logical similarity between this successive review of competing criteria and the attempt in theoretical welfare economics to maximize one variable subject to the constraints of others. Barry elaborated on this similarity through the economist's concept of an indifference curve and the idea of substitutability. If, for example, the concern is with the relative importance of efficiency to equity in an evaluation, a trade-off between the two might be represented by an indifference map. Stressing the logical (rather than empirical) character of the analogy, Barry argued that a political evaluation can be likened to an attempt at deciding the trade-offs between alternative value configurations examined from competing points of view.[22]

Conceptually, the comparison is quite helpful. The notion of successive reviews resembles the intuitionist approach to practical reason promoted by philosophers such as W. D. Ross, Nicholas Rescher, and Barry himself.[23] As a metanormative theory, intuitionism offers a plurality of values or first principles that apply to normative decisions. There is no exact method for determining the relative precedence of these principles when they conflict in specific circumstances or situations. Such conflicts are decided intuitively, that is, by choosing the value or principle that seems most right in the situation. Like the methods of *verstehen* or interpretation in general, intuitionism is anathema for rational cognitivists. As a recognizable account of how decisions are actually rendered, however, it does offer solace to policymakers.[24]

Substantively, the approach offers two primary advantages. First, it bypasses the operational barriers presented by the rational-comprehensive approach to policy, even if it falls short of the requirements of the more demanding metanormative theories. By presenting the plurality of values as an ordinary-language checklist, rather than as a mathematical calculus or technically derived algorism, the possibility of technical advances is held open while permitting the evaluation to proceed on the policymaker's own cognitive terms.

This methodological consideration is related to a second political advantage. In a democratic system, where the final decision is to rest with the citizenry, it is essential that issues be presented in both the language and cognitive style of that body. Rather than present findings in mystifying technocratic language, in a democracy it is incumbent upon policy scientists to translate theoretical conclusions into the citizen's practical-world language. Baier captured this point with a medical analogy: Doctors, he explained, scientifically describe hay fever symptoms in terms of the histamine fluctuations measured in the bloodstream. But this precise scientific language is inadequate unless it can be translated into the patient's own terms for describing and explaining his or her symptoms, i.e., excessive sneezing, irritation in the nose and eyes, headaches, and so on. Similarly, policy science findings must be translated into "terms belonging to the everyday conceptual framework, for the troubles to be diagnosed and cured arise in everyday life."[25] Based on everyday language, the approach to political policy evaluation presented here is uniquely suited to facilitate such translation.

At this point, the discussion can leave the policy methodology problem posed by the vindication of basic political choices and turn to verification and validation, the two principal phases of concern in policy analysis. As first-order levels of evaluation, the technical verification of program objectives and the validation of policy goals focus on four primary questions determining: whether a program fulfills its objectives, whether the objectives are properly derived from the relevant policy goals, whether the goals are appropriate to the situation, and whether they are logically deduced from the principles offered in their support. In empirical terms, the first-order level of evaluation is the focus of behavioral policy analysis and evaluation research. At least within the initial phase of first-order discourse, behavioral science cannot be charged with a fundamental epistemological error. Rather, it can be criticized only for failing to deal with the larger implications of evaluation, discussed in Chapter 5.

First-order evaluation is closely geared to the key empirical questions that arise in the policy evaluation process. Operating under the general umbrella of ideals established by the adoption of a political ideology, first-order policy evaluation is lodged in the lower regions of a value area. It deals with concrete goals such as elimination of crime, educational opportunities, trade with China, full employment, and so on. At this level, the character of practical discourse differs sharply from that of more abstract second-order evaluation. Unlike the evaluation of principles and ideals, most evaluative statements about goals and objectives can be constructed as empirical propositions subject to testing and measurement. (The question of verifying whether a particular program actually fulfills its goal objectives has been discussed in detail.) After the verification of program objectives has been determined, the consequences of following the goal itself (which may take the form of a rule) can be empirically measured.

For example, if the evaluation confronts the rule "everyone should have a good job," it could be supported by an appeal to the consequences that eventuate from adopting it. In this case, it might be argued that everyone should have a good job because everyone ought to be well fed and housed. If so, the rule can be interpreted to mean that good jobs are instruments in achieving the goals of nutrition and sanitary conditions, which also can be empirically tested. A naturalist, attempting to carry out the entire evaluation process by reference to empirical consequences, might try to further test the proposition that everyone ought to be well fed and housed. This proposition might be defended by empirically verifying the proposition that being well fed and housed leads to happiness. As the probe reaches this linkage, however, abstractions such as happiness increasingly take on the fuzziness of ideals, making it impossible to verify them in practice if not theory.[26]

Insofar as empirical science is incapable of providing sufficient data to mediate higher-level value disputes, it is necessary in practice to rely on the alternative method of logical inference to complete the project. This involves the justification of a policy goal or rule through a logical appeal to other higher goals or rules.

Higher goals or rules owe their existence to some relationship to empirical consequences but are not generally supported by science in the strict sense of the term. Derived from a mix of ideological commitment and experience, they provide general orientation and guidelines in practical discourse. At any point in time, they may be subjected to empirical investigation if technical capabilities and resources permit. But most practical reason is carried out in the absence of such evidence and involves the logical application of rules and standards, with empirical data fitted in where available or appropriate.[27]

The complexity of policy judgments is reduced by the fact that all issues or problems do not come up in every social context. Policy evaluation, unlike philosophical inquiry, is greatly simplified (even made possible) by the fact that it doesn't have to deal with all conflicts at once. All values in the social and political world are usually not problematic at the same time, even though social systems undergo constant change and transformation that create value conflicts. Only rarely is there wholesale chaos.

Even though lower-level goals and objectives are often very much in conflict (or potential conflict), writers on organizational decision making such as Richard Cyert and James March have emphasized that multiple, conflicting goals need not be pursued at the same time.[28] Many organizational goals will not be in conflict in the short run. In fact, goals are generally pursued in sequence: growth, for example, may take precedence over profit for a period, and then profit over growth; or both may be pursued and met at the same time. In mental hospitals the goals of custody and treatment are usually in some conflict, but if the organization is large and complex enough, some units may be providing mostly treatment for their clients and others mostly custody. In business organizations, increased market shares or sales volume may (or may not) conflict with profit goals. This does not suggest that all goals can at some point be fulfilled; some goals are never acceptable to particular value orientations. It does, however, underscore a crucial dimension of practical deliberation that has not received sufficient attention in the policy literature.[29]

Grasping the nature of goal conflict provides an important clue for understanding how consensus building is possible. The goals upon which general agreements are established tend to be at least somewhat ambiguous and, as such, do not lend themselves easily to operationalization. Consider the goals "reforming delinquents" or making "satisfactory profits." Such goals do not indicate the specific operations or steps that must be taken for their achievement; thus, there can be many routes to them. Further, one cannot even be sure when they are achieved adequately. Satisfactory profits this year may be at the expense of satisfactory profits three years later. The fact that conflicting interpretations can be attached to goals underlines the normative character of the deliberative process. Any "preference ordering" of goals that exists must be recognized as the product of bargaining—explicit or implicit—among groups with competing values. Such bargaining is subject to a learning process that facilitates mutual adjustment. The aspirations and goals of competing groups rise and fall in accord with the successes and failures of their strategies.

This ambiguity or looseness of goal preferences, operating within a bargaining context, establishes the possibility of consensus building. It presents analysts with a certain leeway in which competing views can be brought together in new ways, leading to insights that generate group learning and consensus. In this respect, social actors are not to be understood as "given" but rather as changeable. Etzioni has stated it this way: "The capacity of two or more actors to realize their values is significantly affected not only by the congruence of their commitments but also by their ability to establish the degree to which their goals are complementary or shared and the extent to which their paths toward goal-realization are affected by the degree to which, in the process of such interaction, the goals of the actors are re-specified in the direction of reciprocal or shared projects."[30] Frequently the initial positions of the various competing groups are relatively vague and fluid; then, if consensus building is effective, they become specified in a congruent direction. Political actors are frequently willing to change their positions in the consensus process for a number of reasons, including the realizations that they cannot always succeed by pursuing their original positions and that they generally prefer change over deadlock or being "left out." Given the possibility of developing new shared goals (beyond bargaining to split the differences between existing perspectives) there is enough flexibility to make political consensus building feasible in a wide variety of situations.

The possibility of consensus building establishes the necessary groundwork for the use of policy evaluation as a tool for rational persuasion. Persuasion, of course, often involves nonrational appeals and outright deceit, especially when directed at the mass public. However, when policymakers are engaged in a mutual inquiry, such manipulative techniques prove ineffective. In such situations, analysts and policymakers generally consent only after convincing evidence is brought to bear. Employed as a rational technique, policy evaluation can be used by decision makers to discover and explore alternatives that bring a particular policy in line with the ideals and goals of the other policymakers whose agreements must be secured. Lindblom offered the example of a president worried that Congress will reduce his foreign aid budget: "His most effective means of inducing Congress not to cut may be to find a value that he believes stirs Congressmen—like restraining the spread of Communism in Latin America—and show them how aid achieves that value."[31] To the degree that policy evaluation can demonstrate a connection between his desired policy and their fundamental disposition or values, the president can use it to influence legislative thinking on the matter.

Congressmen might be persuaded by this approach for a number of reasons. Perhaps the most important one is that policy decision makers cannot feel wholly secure in any policy position given the complex nature of the policy process. Even though they may be deeply attached to a particular value system or ideology, they must not only confront the uncertainty that their policy may not be the best for their objectives but also must remain open to the fact that a policy that is good for the moment is not necessarily good in the future. Under these circumstances, decision makers are vulnerable to the kinds of new data and information that policy evaluation can bring to bear on decision making. Politicians and policymakers whose fortunes often ride on the success or failure of their policies generally recognize the necessity of listening to new evidence as well as countering with policy studies of their own.[32]

It was to generate this kind of policy deliberation that Churchman and others introduced the forensic communications model of policy argumentation to bring rational organization and procedures to the process of partisan analysis and consensus building. The communications approach is designed to facilitate a dialectical exchange between normative policy perspectives.

A Logic of Policy Questions

Having examined the phases of evaluation in the policy context, the last step is to gather them into a table of policy questions. Table 9 presents the framework; Table 10 provides the specific questions. The questions are a framework of component parts designed to constitute a complete policy argument. The components serve as a set of test questions that can be systematically applied in practical argumentation to probe for empirical accuracy, logical clarity, and contradictions. Rather than supply empirical information per se, such questions indicate the types of data that require examination and direct attention to unperceived angles and forgotten dimensions that require exploration. As such, they are constructed to aid the analyst in determining the kinds of evidence needed to support, reject, or modify a policy proposal.

The answers to the questions are "reasons" given for supporting a policy. "Good" reasons are those providing facts or circumstances that satisfy the logical and empirical requirements of the twelve components. As a tool for policy criticism, the logic provides an informal guide for the development of warranted policy conclusions. As a political tool, it is designed to stimulate the open and free communication that is impeded by authoritative decision structures.

It is important to remember that the validity of the answers obtained from such questions do not hinge on proof per se, but rather on the persuasive force of the arguments advanced. Like Toulmin's jurisprudential analogy, the persuasive argument aims first at establishing a way of viewing the problem. The policy analyst's job is to marshal the facts and values (objectives, goals, and ideals) in such a way as to stress or emphasize those dimensions of the situation that favor a particular view.[33] Instead of an attempt at proof in the scientific sense, the task is to defend, convince, or persuade. As Habermas, Baier, and Taylor have made clear, statistical validity or causal reliability

TABLE 9
A Framework of Policy Components

	Probe	Inference	Reasons	Criticism
Technical Verification of Program Objectives				
Program Objectives				
Empirical Consequences				
Unanticipated Effects				
Alternative Means				
Validation of Policy Goals				
Relevance				
Situational Context				
Multiple Goals				
Precedence				
Vindication of Political Choice				
System Consequences				
Equity				
Ideological Conflict				
Alternative Social Orders				

of data can produce only a provisional judgment (see Chapters 3 and 4). Such data must be placed in a larger interpretive context that specifies the relevant goals and values pursued as well as the circumstances of the situation. The validity of a policy argument is determined by its ability to withstand the widest possible range of objections and criticisms in an open, clear, and candid exchange between the relevant participants. The valid claim is the one that generates consensus under regulated rules. Following J.F.M. Hunter, a persuasive policy claim

TABLE 10
The Components as Policy Questions

TECHNICAL VERIFICATION OF PROGRAM OBJECTIVES

1. Program
   Objectives

   Is the program objective logically
   derived from the relevant policy goals?

   - Does the program have several
     objectives?

   - Is the objective(s) compatible with
     more than one policy goal?

2. Empirical
   Consequences

   Does the program empirically fulfill
   its stated objective(s)?

   - Is there general agreement
     about the appropriateness of
     the methodology employed to
     establish the empirical evi-
     dence?

   - Are there disagreements over
     the interpretation of the
     results?

3. Unanticipated
   Effects

   Does the empirical analysis uncover
   secondary effects that offset the
   program objective(s)?

   - What are the factors in the
     situation that cause these
     consequences?

   - Do the secondary effects impede
     the long-run effectiveness of
     program objectives?

   - Do they affect other objectives
     that take priority over these
     program objectives?

4. Alternative
   Means

   Does the program fulfill the object-
   ive(s) more efficiently than alternative means available?

   - Is there empirical evidence
     (measured as benefits and costs)
     to support the use of alterna-
     tive approaches?

   - Would the alternative avoid the
     secondary effects that result
     from the program under investi-
     gation? Does the alternative
     introduce other unanticipated
     consequences?

VALIDATION OF POLICY GOALS

5. Relevance

Is the policy goal(s) relevant? Can it be justified or grounded by an appeal to a higher principle(s) or established causal knowledge?

- Is it possible to secure agreement on the relevance of the goal(s) by an appeal to a higher criterion -- goal, rule, or principle?

- Are there any empirically established consequences or causal relationships associated with the use of this criterion that can be offered in its support?

6. Situational Context

Are there any circumstances in the situation which require that an exception be made to the policy goal or criterion?

- Is there anything about the political situation or policy context that raises questions about the relevance of the criterion?

- Are there economic and social facts and norms which suggest that the situation has not been defined properly?

7. Multiple Goals

Are two or more goals equally relevant to the situation?

- Is there an urgency or exigency in this particular policy situation which suggests that one of the criteria is of more immediate importance?

- Can it be shown that one of these criteria has already been provided for through some other variable in the policy situation? Or, can the conflicting criteria be fulfilled sequentially through interrelated policy contexts or continuity over time?

- Are there any policy principles that assist in determining the appropriate criterion in this particular situation?

8. Precedence

Does the decision-maker's value system place higher precedence on one of the conflicting criteria? Or does it lead to contradictory prescriptions in this situation?

- Is the decision rule or ideal which takes precedence in the value system in conflict with the rules or ideals of the other value systems that bear on the judgment?

- Which ideal(s) does each decision rule emphasize and which does it minimize: maximum satisfaction, liberty, community, etc.?

- Is there fundamental disagreement here, which brings further inquiry to a halt?

VINDICATION OF POLITICAL CHOICE

9. System Consequences

Do the practical consequences resulting from a basic commitment to the decision-maker's value system facilitate the realization of the ideals of the accepted social order?

- Applying the principle of consequences, what kinds of empirical evidence can be produced to demonstrate the instrumental or contributive utility of the value system for the realization of the ideals?

- What are the implications of the consequences for the social system as a whole?

---

10. Equity

Do other value systems, which reflect interests and needs in the social system as a whole, judge the consequences (as benefits and costs) to be distributed equitably?

- To what extent can a conflicting judgment be based on an appeal to the principle of generalization?

- Do the relevant participants judge the system consequences to be fair and equitable in terms of the system's accepted rules and standards?

11.	Ideological Conflict	Do the fundamental ideals that organize the accepted social order provide a basis for an equitable resolution of conflicting judgments?
		– Are the operating ideals of the ideology explicit or implicit? Does the organization of these ideals provide a logical basis for a judgment?
		– To what extent can an unequal distribution of benefits be shown to be advantageous to all needs and interests?
		– What are the implications for political acceptability? Does the possibility of resolution, either in general or in this specific situation, establish the basis for potential political consensus or compromise?
12.	Alternative Social Orders	If the social order is unable to resolve value system conflicts, do other social orders equitably prescribe for the relevant interests and needs that the conflicts reflect?
		– Is there empirical evidence to support an alternative social order?
		– Are there alternatives (based on logical or critical speculation) that move the probe to the highest level of evaluation, rational choice?

may be said to have "traction." It can be "likened to a magnetic force: it exerts a real tug, but whether anything actually yields depends on whether countervailing forces exist or can be set up."[34]

With the assistance of the questions presented here, it is possible to begin giving some shape to the characteristically general discussions that typify much of the social science literature on normative methodology. In the case of the policy sciences, the logic of questions represents an approach built upon an integration of emerging themes in the policy literature, which can be epistemologically grounded by contemporary contributions in ethics and the philosophy of science. In this respect, key aspects of the contributions of a diverse collection of policy writers, such as March and Simon, Dror, Churchman, and Hambrick, are shown to bear on central themes advanced by philosophers such as Habermas, Toulmin, Baier, and Taylor.

For policy science, the most important methodological test of the scheme must rest upon its ability to plug facts into normative policy deliberations. As an empirically oriented discipline, alternative normative perspectives function in policy science as interpretive backgrounds or contexts that organize empirical data into meaningful units. An important metanormative test of such an interpretive framework must be its success at incorporating the array of empirical data that can be brought to bear on policy deliberations. One way to examine this is by relating the metanormative framework to the naturalistic conception of ethical theory, which emphasizes the factual dimensions of normative discourse.[35] Naturalists list six types of factual knowledge that can influence value judgments: (1) knowledge of the consequences that flow from alternative actions, (2) knowledge of alternative means available, (3) knowledge of the established norms and values that bear on the decision, (4) the particular facts of the situation, (5) general causal conditions and laws relevant to the situation, and (6) knowledge about the fundamental needs of humankind. Table 11 presents the outcome of such a test applied to the logic of policy questions developed here. It shows that these six types of facts (numbered in the table) can be located across the twelve component questions representing the full range of normative enquiry. (For comparison, Hambrick's empirically oriented policy questions of Table 1 can be fitted to specific points provided by the framework.)

The ability to logically analyze policies advanced by others also provides insight into the construction of acceptable alternative policies. After organizing the policy argument into its component parts, the analyst may choose to try his or her hand at political consensus formation. Essentially, this involves an attempt to convert a static conception of a policy argument into a dynamic one that has persuasive power. After identifying the possible areas of policy consensus and conflict, the analyst designs an alternative policy proposal that addresses the key issues of conflict. The test of the alternative proposal is how well it can stand up to the criticisms and objections of the

TABLE 11
Policy Questions: The Role of Empirical
and Normative Analysis

POLICY QUESTIONS: PRACTICAL REASON	ROLE OF EMPIRICAL AND NORMATIVE ANALYSIS	HAMBRICK'S POLICY QUESTIONS
Program Objectives	Logical Rules of Normative Analysis	
Empirical Consequences	Empirical Knowledge of Consequences (1)	Causal Proposition Instrumental Proposition
Unanticipated Effects	Knowledge of Consequences (1)	External Impact Proposition Constraint Proposition
Alternative Means	Knowledge of Alternative Means (2)	Comparative Proposition
Relevance	Knowledge of Established Norms (3) Causal Conditions and Laws (5)	Normative Proposition Grounding Proposition
Situational Context	Particular Facts of the Situation (4)	Time-Place Proposition
Multiple Goals	Normative Logic	
Precedence	Normative Logic	
System Consequences	Causal Conditions and Laws (5)	
Equity	Normative Logic	
Ideological Conflict	Normative Logic	
Alternative Social Orders	Knowledge of Fundamental Needs (6) Normative Logic	

political audiences it must convince or persuade, the breadth of its appeal, the number of views it can synthesize, and so on. In many cases, this means the political analyst must attempt dialectically to move the proposal beyond the narrow defense of a particular argument in order to present a more comprehensive picture of the political situation. Since a narrow argument can be defended only within a limited context of belief, the policy analyst must at times try to offer a new or reformulated view to replace or revise the belief or value system that impedes the construction of consensus.

The development of such policy proposals must remain as much an art as a science. The process is a paper-and-pencil exercise involving conjecture and speculation, analogy and metaphor, and logical extrapolation from established causal relationships and facts. Unlike the scientist's analysis based on a closed, generalized model, the political analyst's proposal will be open and contextual. Where the former model follows the formal principles of inference, the latter is based on informal rules and methods. The important point is that they are alternative modes of inquiry, each with its own logic and purpose. The mistake is to subject political evaluation as a whole to the scientific rules appropriate only to phases of the evaluation process.

In the recent policy literature, there are some encouraging signs that point to greater recognition of these methodological implications of political evaluation. Barry and Rae, for example, suggested that analysts interested in political evaluation should place greater emphasis on the study of "political rhetoric"— the way in which arguments are marshaled in politics to reconcile people pursuing different goals and objectives.[36] Anderson correctly pursued the problem to a more fundamental level, calling for the study of the "metapolitical" languages of policy evaluation.[37] Johnson alluded to instructive parallels that can be drawn between literary criticism and public policy evaluation viewed as policy criticism.[38] Outside of mainstream social science, the study and investigation of the rules and principles of criticism are widely endorsed as a serious, systematic endeavor. Through the further exploration of policy languages and argumentation, normative political theorists can make an important contribution to public policy studies.

Concluding Remarks

Methodologists, as Meehan wrote, are "parasites on the substantive inquirer, though they can repay their hosts many times over by supplying criteria of adequate criticism and identifying the goals that inquirers should pursue."[39] As a methodological analysis, this study has attempted to supply criteria and goals for political evaluation. It has done this by developing a political methodology around a logic of evaluation that integrates empirical and normative questions arising in policy evaluation. To the extent that it has succeeded in this endeavor, it can be advanced as a foundation for the elaboration of a critical policy methodology.

Even if this scheme proves unable to satisfy a number of metaethical requirements at the philosophical level, its value for policy evaluation is not necessarily diminished. There are many reasons for engaging in normative deliberation, all of which do not have to fulfill precisely the same requirements. In fact, it may be that some of the study's limitations in ethics are strengths in policy evaluation. The final proof must rest on the outcomes that political and policy scientists can obtain with the method in policy evaluations. It is my hope that they will put it through the necessary tests.

The test of this approach, however, is not the most important issue here. In a study that explores relatively uncharted territories, the primary purpose must be to indicate new directions and establish openings. If the effort succeeds in focusing evaluative inquiry in policy deliberation on the normative political questions that tend to remain unexplored, it will serve its intended purpose. At this stage, it is not so much specific methodology as dialogue that must be nurtured. If this study contributes to furthering the underdeveloped but emerging dialogue about political evaluation in the social and policy sciences, the effort behind it will have been worthwhile.

Notes

1. Wayne A. R. Leys, *Ethics for Policy Decisions: The Art of Asking Deliberate Questions* (Englewood Cliffs, N.J.: Prentice-Hall, 1968), p. 11.

2. For some examples see Daniel P. Moynihan, "Policy vs. Program in the 1970s," *The Public Interest*, no. 20 (Summer 1970):90–100.

3. Paul Diesing, *Reason in Society: Five Types of Decisions in Their Social Contexts* (Urbana: University of Illinois Press, 1962).

4. For illustrations of work in this field, see Douglas R. Bunker, "Organizing to Link Social Science with Public Policy Making," *Public Administration Review* 38 (May–June 1978):223–232; Nathan Caplan, "The Two-Communities Theory and Knowledge Utilization," *American Behavioral Scientist* 22 (January–February 1979):459–470; and Charles E.

Lindblom and David K. Cohen, *Usable Knowledge: Social Science and Social Problem Solving* (New Haven, Conn.: Yale University Press, 1979). For an introduction to the field of "knowledge utilization," see Robert F. Rich, "The Pursuit of Knowledge," *Knowledge* 1 (September 1979):6-30.

5. For a useful review of this literature, see Austin Ranney, ed., *Political Science and Public Policy* (Chicago: Markham, 1968); and Ira Sharkansky, ed., *Policy Analysis in Political Science* (Chicago: Markham, 1970). For a discussion of how policy analysts might organize such data, see Arnold J. Meltsner, "Political Feasibility and Policy Analysis," *Public Administration Review* 32 (November-December 1972); and Yehezkel Dror, "The Prediction of Political Feasibility," *Futures* 1 (June 1969). Table 6 draws heavily on these resources, especially on Meltsner's essay.

6. The distinction between a policy space and an issue area was developed by Meltsner, "Political Feasibility and Policy Analysis," p. 860. Meltsner stated: "A policy space is more inclusive than a policy issue area and contains those political ingredients that help us understand a broad area such as health or education. Every political system contains a number of overlapping policy spaces. There is a health policy space, an education policy space, and a transportation policy space. The space is characterized by a stable set of actors whose specific policy preferences are ambiguous. Because of their continuing concern, certain actors and certain attentive publics dominate the policy space. No one can doubt that the American Medical Association, the Department of Health, Education, and Welfare, and the House Ways and Means Committee have something to say in the health policy space. Whether these actors will exercise their potential is a matter that leads to defining the policy issue areas. . . . While the policy space provides a beginning clue to the political environment, the policy issue area is that part of the environment which is tied to a particular policy analysis. Health insurance, biomedical research, hospital construction, and group delivery of medical services are all policy issue areas within the more inclusive policy space, health."

7. In epistemological terms, these categories anchor political evaluation to the pragmatic world of phenomenology where attention is drawn to that which is problematic. The political information culled from the policy space and issue area thus funnels directly into the validation phase, which emphasizes political relevance and situational context. As both phenomenologists and pragmatist philosophers point out, questions are seldom raised for their own sake, especially in the inherently pragmatic evaluation of public policy. Inevitably, they arise from some interest or problem fixed in the "natural attitude" of the political world in which the policy analyst operates. As such, the analyst in practice generally addresses the validation phase before verification.

8. See, for example, M. Shapiro and G. M. Bonham, "Cognitive Processes and Foreign Policy Decision Making," *International Studies Quarterly* 17 (June 1973):147–174; and Eric S. Moskowitz, "Neighborhood Preservation: An Analysis of Policy Maps and Policy Options," in *The Policy Cycle*, ed. Judith V. May and Aaron B. Wildavsky (Beverly Hills, Calif.: Sage Publications, 1978), pp. 65–87.

9. For a discussion of this point, see Abraham Kaplan, "On the Strategy of Social Planning," *Policy Sciences* 4 (March 1973):41–61; Raymond Gastil, *Social Humanities* (San Francisco: Jossey-Bass, 1977); and Gastil, "Social Humanities," *Policy Sciences* 5 (March 1974):1–14.

10. Stephen Toulmin, *An Examination of the Place of Reason in Ethics* (Cambridge: Cambridge University Press, 1970), pp. 130–143.

11. For an excellent discussion of the application of these two principles to public policy, see Flathman, *The Public Interest*, pp. 68–84.

12. On this point, see Brian Barry and Douglas W. Rae, "Political Evaluation," in *The Handbook of Political Science*, ed. Nelson W. Polsby and Fred D. Greenstein (Reading, Mass.: Addison-Wesley Publishing Co., 1975), 1:380. Actually, the validity of the point may be dependent upon a neo-Kantian or rationalistic conception of ideals rather than a dialectical, historical Marxist conception. In fact, Barry and Rae may themselves provide a suggestive clue. They concede that it is difficult to formulate an adequate account of Marx's concept of alienation in terms of the traditional understandings of such ideals as fraternity, equality, or liberty. Nonetheless, for present purposes, the general point here helps to illuminate the nature of the vindication process.

13. For an example of a Marxist analysis that addresses the kinds of questions arising in the vindication phase, see Michael Harrington, *Socialism* (New York: Bantam Books, 1970); for an attempt to vindicate political liberalism, see Robert A. Dahl, *A Preface to Democratic Theory* (Chicago: University of Chicago Press, 1956).

14. Kaplan, "On the Strategy of Social Planning," pp. 48–53; and Charles E. Lindblom *The Policy-Making Process* (Englewood Cliffs, N.J.: Prentice-Hall, 1968), p. 23.

15. Lindblom, *The Policy-Making Process*, p. 23.

16. Wayne A. R. Leys, "The Value Framework of Decision-Making," in *Concepts and Issues in Administrative Behavior*, ed. Sidney Mailick and Edward H. Van Ness (Englewood Cliffs, N.J.: Prentice-Hall, 1962), pp. 81–93.

17. Ibid., p. 81.

18. Kaplan, "On the Strategy of Social Planning," p. 54.

19. Ibid., pp. 54–55. The relationship of these principles to ideals is close. The principle of impartiality is clearly related to the ideal of justice,

the principle of autonomy to self-realization of the individual, and so on.

20. Ibid.

21. Ibid.

22. Brian M. Barry, *Political Argument,* International Library of Philosophy and Scientific Method (Atlantic Highlands, N.J.: Humanities Press, 1976).

23. See W. D. Ross, *The Right and the Good* (Oxford: Clarendon Press, 1930); Nicholas Rescher, *Distributive Justice* (Cambridge, Mass.: Belknap Press, 1971); and Barry, *Political Argument.*

24. Nicholas Henry, *Public Administration and Public Affairs* (Englewood Cliffs, N.J.: Prentice-Hall, 1975), p. 41.

25. Kurt Baier, "The Concept of Value," *Journal of Value Inquiry* 1 (Spring 1967):1–2.

26. This example is taken from Lindblom, *The Policy-Making Process,* p. 16.

27. If, for instance, a normative rule states, "no political campaigning within 500 feet of a voting booth," it is customary to appeal to the higher rule of impartiality or freedom of choice to justify the norm. It is, of course, possible to test the rule empirically to determine if it does indeed lead to freedom of choice, but it is not an operation normally carried out. In this case, it is more likely that another kind of empirical evidence will press for attention. At this point it may become necessary to explore the specific circumstances to which the rule has been applied. In doing so, it might be discovered that the voting booth has not yet opened, in which case an exception can be made to the rule. Or, maybe it is determined by measurement that the campaigner is 501 feet from the booth, in which case the rule does not apply.

28. Richard Cyert and James G. March, *A Behavioral Theory of the Firm* (Englewood Cliffs, N.J.: Prentice-Hall, 1963); also see Amitai Etzioni, "Two Approaches to Organizational Analysis: A Critique and a Suggestion," *Administrative Science Quarterly* 5 (September 1960):257–278.

29. One important exception is Paul Diesing's essay, "Non-economic Decision-Making," in *Organizational Decision-Making,* ed. Marcus Alexis and Charles Z. Wilson (Englewood Cliffs, N.J.: Prentice-Hall, 1967), pp. 185–200. Diesing has delineated a number of principles of decision making designed to reduce the process to manageable proportions.

30. Amitai Etzioni, *The Active Society* (New York: Free Press, 1968), p. 468.

31. Lindblom, *The Policy-Making Process,* p. 33.

32. Ibid., pp. 33–34. Lindblom suggested six advantages that accrue to the policymaker who avails himself of such "partisan analysis": "(1) For the policymaker who practices it, it serves to clarify his own policy prefer-

ences. . . . If an interest-group leader . . . searches for features of his desired policy that suit the general value position of others whom he wishes to persuade, it will occur to him that his policy may not be the only one that could attain his own values or goals. . . . (2) This kind of analysis is not frustrated . . . by lack of agreement on policy goals, for it does not challenge the values of the policymaker to whom it is addressed. . . . (3) But partisan analysis is not simply a method of rationalizing. . . . [I]t is not an effective tool of persuasion unless it discovers a connection between a given set of goals or attitudes and a policy to serve them. And, secondly, because it is practiced on others and self simultaneously, it serves as much to find a new position as to prove the merits of one already taken. (4) It does not need to be conclusive . . . ; it need only go so far as to persuade a voter, legislator, prime minister, or administrator with respect to what he should do about the decision task he faces. . . . (5) Hence this kind of analysis is clearly a kind subordinated to the play of power. . . . It does not avoid fighting over policy; it is a method of fighting; (6) Finally, this kind of analysis makes use of all the devices for extending analytical capacity."

33. On the relationship between a logical structure of questions and persuasion, see Erwin P. Bettinghaus, "Structure and Argument," in *Perspectives on Argumentation,* ed. Gerald R. Miller and Thomas R. Nilsen (Chicago: Scott, Foresman and Co., 1966), pp. 130-155.

34. J.F.M. Hunter, "The Possibility of a Rational Strategy of Moral Persuasion," *Ethics* 84 (April 1974):185-186.

35. Naturalism is discussed in Chapter 3.

36. Barry and Rae, "Political Evaluation," p. 378. On the uses of rhetoric in social science, see Richard Weaver, *The Ethics of Rhetoric* (South Bend, Ind.: Gateway Editions, 1953).

37. Charles W. Anderson, "The Logic of Public Problems: Evaluation in Comparative Policy Research," in *Comparing Public Policies: New Concepts and Methods,* ed. Douglas E. Ashford (Beverly Hills, Calif.: Sage Publications, 1978), p. 23; and Anderson, "The Place of Principles in Policy Analysis," *American Political Science Review* 73 (September 1979): 711-723.

38. Ronald W. Johnson, "Research Objectives for Policy Analysis," in *Public Policy Evaluation,* ed. Kenneth M. Dolbeare (Beverly Hills, Calif.: Sage Publications, 1975), p. 82.

39. Eugene J. Meehan, "Science, Values, and Policies," *American Behavioral Scientist* 17 (September-October 1973):75.

Appendix

A discussion of policy models designed to infer cause-and-effect relationships is beyond the scope and purposes of the present study. However,
it may be helpful to provide a few brief illustrations that direct attention to
the literature on the subject.

As an abstraction of some part of reality, a policy model is a representation of the real world; the model is designed to adequately specify a
research problem. "Models," as Nachmias explained, "are made up of variables that are relevant to the problem of concern and the relations among
these variables." These relationships are ideally specified in mathematical
form for the purpose of empirical analysis. The following diagram provides
an introductory illustration of a policy impact model specifying the expected relationships between a compensatory educational program such as
Head Start and educational achievement.

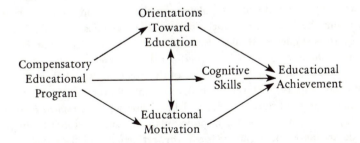

As Nachmias explained, "Further elaborations of impact models consist
of attempts to delineate the concrete variables involved: to outline the
boundaries within which the variables operate (the target population); to
specify the time lag between implementation of the policy and manifesta-

tions of its effects; and to formulate the theoretically expected relationships among the variables—direct versus indirect causal variables, and recursive or nonrecursive relationships." See David Nachmias, *Public Policy Evaluation* (New York: St. Martin's Press, 1979).

The construction of a model of a policy's political acceptability involves integrating the empirical variables of a policy model (such as magnitudes of educational motivation or cognitive skills) and social or political judgments about the relative importance or desirability of each variable. Hammond and Adelman provide an illustration of the integration of social scientific data about policy variables and normative judgments about the variables elicited from the political environment. The general framework of their model is represented by the following algebraic equation:

$$Y = W_1 X_1 + W_2 X_2 + W_3 X_3 \ldots W_n X_n$$

where Y (the dependent variable) is a statistical statement of the overall acceptability of a policy; W_1 represents the statistical mean of an analysis of each participant's value judgments concerning the relative desirability of hypothetical magnitudes of the variables; and X_1 designates the predicted magnitudes of a particular independent variable (e.g., educational motivation) in the policy impact model. Hammond and Adelman provide an empirical illustration of the application of their model to a handgun ammunition dispute involving the Denver Police Department. See Kenneth R. Hammond and Leonard Adelman, "Science, Values and Human Judgment," in *Judgment and Decision in Public Policy Formation,* ed. Kenneth R. Hammond (Boulder, Colo.: Westview Press, 1978), pp. 119–141.

There is a large body of comparative policy output research aimed at establishing causal linkages between dependent and independent variables of policy models. Many of these efforts search for causal connections between the determinants of policymaker behavior and policy outputs, including the influence of specific normative variables and decision rules. For an example see Douglas Rae and Michael Taylor, "Decision Rules and Policy Outcomes," *British Journal of Political Science,* 1 (January 1971), pp. 71–90; and for a critical review of the literature, see Herbert Jacob and Michael Lipsky, "Outputs, Structure, and Power: An Assessment of Changes in the Study of State and Local Politics," *Journal of Politics,* 30 (May 1968), pp. 510–538. In policy mapping, such research findings provide an important beginning for further refinements of the social scientific approach. This, however, does not affirm the operational potential of the scientific approach for policy decision making. It only points to the theoretical or logical possibility of the project. Even if theoretically valid, the scientific approach to integrating empirical and normative judgments suffers important operational limitations. Given both the state-of-the-art of quantification and the enormous complexity of the linkages between values expressed in the phenomenological world of policymaking and their statistical designations in an abstract mathematical policy model, the scientific approach is far removed from the realm of practical decision-making techniques, especially when it comes to the normatively complex social problems that press for policy solutions. For documentation of these operational limitations in the context of specific projects in policy evaluation research, see Robert A. Scott and Arnold R. Shore, *Why Sociology Does Not Apply: A Study of the Use of Sociology in Public Policy* (New York: Elsevier, 1979).

Index